OECD PROCEEDINGS

Foreign Direct Investment and Recovery in Southeast Asia

ORGANISATION FOR ECONOMIC CO-OPERATION AND DEVELOPMENT

ORGANISATION FOR ECONOMIC CO-OPERATION AND DEVELOPMENT

Pursuant to Article 1 of the Convention signed in Paris on 14th December 1960, and which came into force on 30th September 1961, the Organisation for Economic Co-operation and Development (OECD) shall promote policies designed:

- to achieve the highest sustainable economic growth and employment and a rising standard of living in Member countries, while maintaining financial stability, and thus to contribute to the development of the world economy;
- to contribute to sound economic expansion in Member as well as non-member countries in the process of economic development; and
- to contribute to the expansion of world trade on a multilateral, non-discriminatory basis in accordance with international obligations.

The original Member countries of the OECD are Austria, Belgium, Canada, Denmark, France, Germany, Greece, Iceland, Ireland, Italy, Luxembourg, the Netherlands, Norway, Portugal, Spain, Sweden, Switzerland, Turkey, the United Kingdom and the United States. The following countries became Members subsequently through accession at the dates indicated hereafter: Japan (28th April 1964), Finland (28th January 1969), Australia (7th June 1971), New Zealand (29th May 1973), Mexico (18th May 1994), the Czech Republic (21st December 1995), Hungary (7th May 1996), Poland (22nd November 1996) and Korea (12th December 1996). The Commission of the European Communities takes part in the work of the OECD (Article 13 of the OECD Convention).

OECD CENTRE FOR CO-OPERATION WITH NON-MEMBERS

The OECD Centre for Co-operation with Non-Members (CCNM) was established in January 1998 when the OECD's Centre for Co-operation with the Economies in Transition (CCET) was merged with the Liaison and Co-ordination Unit (LCU). The CCNM, in combining the functions of these two entities, serves as the focal point for the development and pursuit of co-operation between the OECD and non-member economies.

The CCNM manages thematic and country programmes. The thematic programmes, which are multi-country in focus, are linked to the core generic work areas of the Organisation (such as trade and investment, taxation, labour market and social policies, environment). The Emerging Market Economy Forum (EMEF) and the Transition Economy Programme (TEP) provide the framework for activities under the thematic programmes. The EMEF is a flexible forum in which non-members are invited to participate depending on the theme under discussion. The TEP is focused exclusively on transition economies. Regional/Country programmes, providing more focused dialogue and assistance, are now in place for the Baltic countries, Brazil, Bulgaria, China, Romania, Russia, the Slovak Republic (a candidate for accession to the OECD), and Slovenia.

FOREWORD

The financial crisis in Asia has prompted searching questions concerning appropriate policies for sustainable economic recovery and development. One area of particular importance is the set of policies regarding foreign investment. Foreign direct investment (FDI) has played a leading role in the economic development of many Southeast Asian economies and has been an important source of foreign capital during the crisis.

The Organisation for Economic Co-operation and Development (OECD) sponsored a workshop in Bangkok in November 1998. Participants from OECD and non-OECD countries discussed the role of FDI in development. They explored how further liberalisation of policies in Southeast Asia could attenuate the present crisis and avert future ones.

This publication presents comprehensive case studies of Indonesia, Malaysia, the Philippines and Thailand. The studies bring into sharp focus the role of FDI in the development strategies of the four countries and the response of foreign investors to the changes in each country's economic and political environment. The studies are particularly timely representing the situation through April 1999.

Stephen Thomsen (DAFFE) prepared the overview chapter and, together with Françoise Nicolas (consultant), the country studies. Maiko Miyake (DAFFE) provided research assistance and Edward Smiley (DAFFE) technical support.

The workshop and this publication were prepared as part of the programme of work of the OECD Centre for Co-operation with Non-Members with the Directorate for Financial, Fiscal and Enterprise Affairs (DAFFE). It is published on the responsibility of the Secretary-General of the OECD.

Eric Burgeat
Director
Centre for Co-operation with Non-Members

TABLE OF CONTENTS

OVERVIEW

Introduction and summary

The financial crisis in Asia has brought to the fore the question of the appropriate policies for recovery and for future sustainable development. One area of particular importance is the treatment of foreign investors. Foreign ' direct investment (FDI) has played a leading role in many of the economies of the region, particularly in export sectors, and has been a vital source of foreign capital during the crisis. The four countries reviewed in this study[1] -- Indonesia, Malaysia, the Philippines and Thailand (referred to hereinafter as the ASEAN4) -- have all to varying degrees welcomed inward investment for its contribution to exports. As a result, although only a small share of total investment or employment in each economy, FDI has been a key factor driving export-led growth in Southeast Asia. Foreign firms have by no means been the only actors, but they have played a leading role in those sectors with the fastest export growth such as electronics. Through such investment, host economies have rapidly been transformed from agriculture and the exploitation of raw materials into major producers and exporters of manufactured goods.

For many years, Malaysia and Thailand were among the most open in the developing world to foreign investment. They were quick to recognise the powerful role that foreign investors could play in fuelling export-led growth, and they were well-placed to attract such investment during the years of regional structural adjustment in the late 1980s. Partly as a result of FDI inflows, the two countries were among the world's fastest growing economies before the crisis. At the same time, however, the years leading up to the crisis revealed a growing disquiet in some ASEAN countries about their continuing ability to attract FDI in the face of competition from countries such as China. Related to the issue of possible investment diversion, questions were also raised about whether FDI inflows were contributing sufficiently to technology transfer and industrial upgrading.

In the wake of the financial crisis which has swept through the region, it is useful to look once again at the experience of various ASEAN countries and the role of foreign investors in their economic development. In all four countries, development strategies include a selective approach to investment promotion with a clearly circumscribed role for foreign direct investors. Such partial openness allows foreign firms to contribute to rapid economic growth driven by exports, but it has been less adept at delivering sustainable development. In many cases, indigenous capabilities have not been developed sufficiently in those export sectors dominated by foreign multinational enterprises (MNEs), leaving the host country vulnerable to changes in investor sentiment and to growing competition for such investment from other countries. This study draws on the experience of the ASEAN4 countries to suggest that a more balanced treatment of foreign investors which allows foreign MNEs to play a greater role in the domestic economy could yield substantial benefits in terms of restoring investor confidence and placing economic development in the ASEAN4 on a more sustainable basis in the future.

FDI trends in the ASEAN4

With the exception of the Philippines, which until the 1990s had not generally welcomed foreign investors, the ASEAN4 have all been major recipients of foreign direct investment (FDI). The period of most intense foreign investment activity occurred in the late 1980s when firms from Japan and the Newly Industrialising Economies (NIEs) were looking for production bases abroad to escape appreciating home currencies and the loss of preferential access to many OECD markets (for the NIEs). In all cases except Indonesia, FDI flows have held up remarkably well during the crisis, as foreign firms have responded to new opportunities to acquire local companies and to gain access to the local market.

At the same time, however, the continued success of the ASEAN4 countries in attracting foreign investment could not be taken for granted, even before the crisis. Japanese firms have been the most active investors in the region, and recent surveys suggest that they will be investing significantly less in the near future. Furthermore, other countries such as China and Vietnam now compete actively for labour-intensive investment. Annual foreign investments in China have recently been three times as high as those in the ASEAN4 combined. Even within ASEAN, Malaysia and Thailand may have been losing some export-oriented investments to Indonesia and the Philippines before the crisis, as these latter countries adopted more aggressive investment promotion policies.

The policy environment for FDI in the ASEAN4

FDI policies throughout much of ASEAN have formed an integral part of overall development strategies. Whether for import substitution or export promotion, foreign investors have been welcomed in certain cases, subject to strict criteria. Those firms wishing to export most of their output are often treated as favourably as investors in OECD countries. In contrast, foreign investors interested in providing goods and services to the local market face numerous restrictions on their activities, including an outright prohibition in some sectors. In many cases, these latter foreign firms may not acquire a majority stake in a local company or own the land on which the factory is built. They also often face various performance requirements related to the transfer of technology or the employment of local personnel, including directors.

The perceived threat of investment diversion away from ASEAN and towards China had begun to push ASEAN4 policies towards FDI in a more liberal direction even before the crisis. It was also at the heart of the decision to accelerate the process of regional integration through the ASEAN Free Trade Area and the ASEAN Investment Area. The crisis has added impetus to this liberalisation by allowing greater access to the domestic market for foreign investors, including through the acquisition of local firms. Although this openness is limited to two years, those investors which take advantage will continue to enjoy the benefits after that time.

Such liberalisation is to be welcomed, but it is unlikely by itself to foster greater foreign investor confidence or to put future development on a more sustainable basis. Sustainable development depends on the quality of investment received more than on the quantity. The experience of countless developing countries over the past few decades suggests that the benefits from inward direct investment are not automatic; they depend crucially on the overall policy environment in which the firm invests. Policies towards foreign investment in the ASEAN4 can be seen with hindsight to have created distortions which hamper the traditional mechanisms through which foreign investors transfer technology and other know-how to the local economy.

The limits to selective export promotion

Foreign investors have not been the only exporters from the ASEAN4, but they have been well-represented in those sectors with the fastest export growth. Through export-oriented FDI, ASEAN4 countries were able to shift quickly towards a manufacturing-based economy in which economic growth was driven by rapidly expanding exports. The record from this export performance speaks for itself, but so too does the manifest failure in many cases to translate this export success based on FDI into something more durable. Not only have exports been limited to a small number of products (usually intermediate ones) and sectors, but to varying degrees these export sectors have been virtual foreign enclaves within host countries. Investments in these enclaves have often been characterised by low value-added (principally from labour-intensive assembly operations) and a poor record of technology transfer. These shortcomings represented one of the growing structural problems leading up to the crisis.

This dualist policy of aggressively promoting export-oriented investment while protecting the local economy from both imports and market-seeking inward investment has ultimately undermined the very benefits it was intended to achieve. To export successfully to world markets, foreign investors have had to purchase inputs principally from abroad or from other foreign investors in the host country. Many of the most successful export sectors in the ASEAN4 are highly import dependent, and this has limited the impact of massive devaluations in these economies on exports. The primary interest of these exporters in the host economy is as a source of low cost labour.

Foreign investors oriented towards the domestic market frequently have closer links with local companies, and, as the world's most competitive firms in these sectors, they can provide useful know-how and other basic technology for local firms. Because these foreign firms produce goods and services for the local market which meet world standards, they can indirectly help domestic firms to become more competitive in world markets, thereby enhancing the export potential of indigenous entrepreneurs.

The intention here is not argue for one form of foreign investment over another. In an enabling environment in which private sector activity can flourish, each type of foreign investment can make a valuable and in many ways unique contribution to economic growth and to sustainable development more generally. A recent study of 69 developing countries found not only that FDI stimulates economic growth but that it has a larger impact than investment by domestic firms.[2]

Outward orientation through foreign investment promotion remains a viable development strategy which will continue to yield rapid economic growth in the future. Indeed, the potential role of foreign firms may have increased since the crisis. But at the same time, selectivity in incentives based on the degree of export orientation has been shown in light of the crisis to have created a dual economy in which technological spillovers were few. These spillovers, rather than exports per se, should be the focus of investment policies. It is argued here that such spillovers are enhanced in a policy environment in which foreign investors are permitted to establish and produce for both the domestic and export markets under similar conditions.

I.   FDI trends in the ASEAN4

The ASEAN4 countries have collectively been among the most important destinations for FDI outside of the OECD area. As a group, they have been the fifth most popular host to FDI world-wide in the 1990s, though a long way behind China (Table 1). The external environment has strongly influenced the overall level of inflows over time, but policies in each country have largely determined the distribution of inflows within ASEAN.

Table 1. **Total FDI inflows by country, 1990-97** ($ million)

1	US	414 074	21	Denmark	18 177
2	China	200 578	22	**Thailand**	17 177
3	UK	176 889	23	New Zealand	17 083
4	France	149 587	24	Poland	15 882
5	BLEU	84 008	25	Colombia	15 798
6	Netherlands	70 743	26	Hungary	14 945
7	Spain	68 068	27	Norway	14 412
8	Mexico	58 850	28	Hong Kong, China	14 239
9	Canada	53 818	29	Portugal	12 909
10	Australia	52 212	30	Russia	12 774
11	Singapore	49 173	31	Venezuela	11 890
12	Sweden	47 546	32	Chinese Taipei	11 443
13	Brazil	44 228	33	Peru	11 215
14	Germany	40 358	34	Korea	10 534
15	**Malaysia**	35 177	35	Austria	10 438
16	Italy	30 394	36	Japan	10 310
17	Argentina	30 120	37	Nigeria	10 093
18	**Indonesia**	23 684	38	India	9 957
19	Switzerland	20 188	39	Israel	8 398
20	Chile	19 085	40	**Philippines**	8 379
				ASEAN4	84 417

Source: OECD, IMF

Malaysia has translated its early move to export promotion within the ASEAN4 into a sustained ability to attract inward investment by export-oriented firms. Indonesia owes its success principally to the oil and gas sector, while Thailand has attracted both market-seeking and export-oriented investors. The conversion of the Philippines to investment promotion is more recent and is only now beginning to affect its relative ranking.[3]

Figure 1 shows FDI inflows into the ASEAN4 over the past two decades. Inflows are divided by GDP in each case in order to remove the effect of market size, inflation and currency movements. The early and leading role of Malaysia in attracting inward investment is immediately apparent. With the smallest economy of the four countries, Malaysia was the first to reach the limits of import substitution policies as the market became saturated and economies of scale were limited. Malaysia also benefited from its proximity to Singapore, as the substantial foreign presence in the latter offered opportunities for Malaysia to attract labour-intensive manufacturing in which Singapore was rapidly losing its competitiveness.

Figure 1. **FDI inflows as a percentage of GDP**

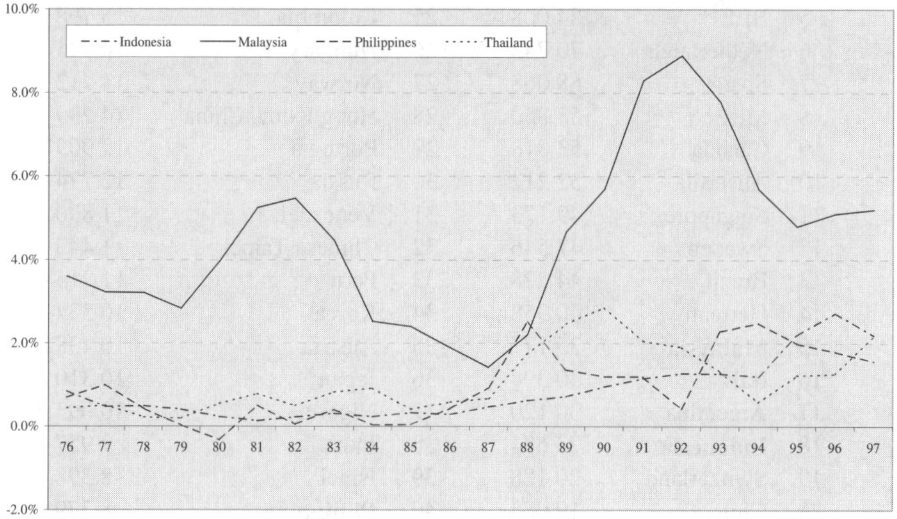

Source: IMF

14

FDI since the crisis

Figure 2 shows the most recent quarterly trends for inflows into each country in dollar terms. Inflows into Thailand grew rapidly after the onset of the crisis, in spite of the sharp depreciation against the dollar. They have fallen somewhat in the past two quarters, however. It remains to be seen whether this is a delayed reaction to the crisis or a temporary downturn. FDI in the Philippines has remained steady, if unspectacular, throughout the crisis. In Malaysia, the sharp drop in inflows in the third quarter of 1998 can probably be attributed to the immediate reaction of foreign investors to the imposition of capital controls on 1 September 1998, even if these controls were not intended to affect direct investment. Investments in Indonesia have been discouraged by the unstable political environment and were negative in three of the last four quarters for which data are available.

Figure 2. **FDI inflows by quarter, 1995 – 1998** ($ billion)

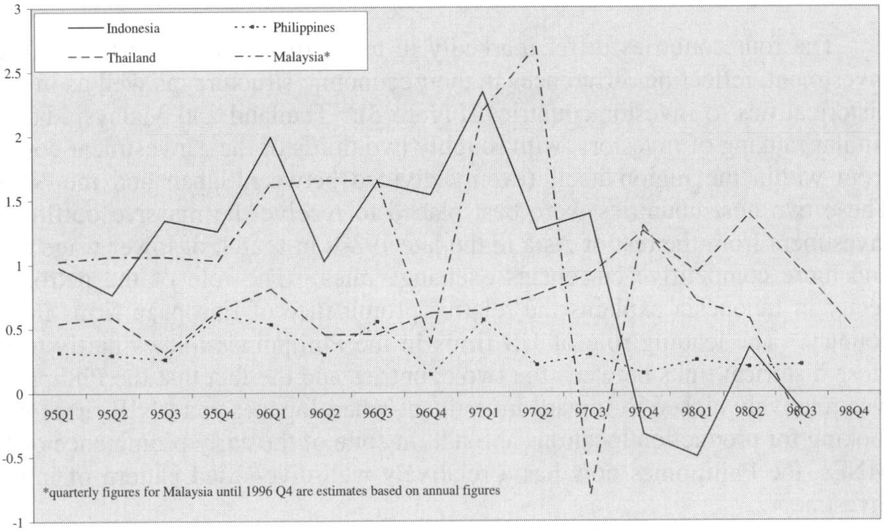

*quarterly figures for Malaysia until 1996 Q4 are estimates based on annual figures

Source: IMF and Central Banks

15

Figures for applications and approvals by various investment agencies also show continued foreign interest in investing in the ASEAN4, in contrast to the severe contraction of domestic investment. In Malaysia, applications by foreign firms fell 12 per cent in local currency terms in 1998, after declining 18 per cent in 1997. Given the depth of the economic slump in Malaysia, these declines can be considered moderate and contrast forcefully with the 68 per cent drop in investment applications by domestic firms. In Thailand, foreign applications to the BOI fell 29 per cent in the first half of 1998 compared with the same period in the previous year, while domestic applications dropped by 87 per cent. In Indonesia, foreign investment approvals in local currency grew in the first eight months of 1998 compared to 1997, although the implementation rate for such projects has been low in recent years. In the Philippines, total approved foreign investments in the first quarter of 1998 were significantly higher than in the same period of 1997, in contrast to the sharp drop in approved domestic investment projects. This growth is especially significant when one considers that total approvals by the Board of Investment were already at record levels in 1997. Investments in export processing zones also continued to expand in the first half of 1998.

FDI inflows by country of origin

The four countries differ markedly in terms of the origin of their inward investment, reflecting differences in their economic structure, as well as in their historical ties to investor countries (Figure 3). Thailand and Malaysia have a similar ranking of investors, with roughly two thirds of their investment coming from within the region itself (evenly divided between Japan and the NIEs). These two host countries were best placed to receive the massive outflow of investment from the rest of Asia in the late 1980s in search of lower wage costs and more competitive currencies exchange rates. The role of the petroleum sector in Indonesia explains the relative prominence of European firms in that country. The leading role of US firms in the Philippines relates partly to the close historical links between the two countries and the fact that the Philippines was relatively closed to inward investment when Japanese and NIE firms were looking for production locations abroad. In spite of the early prominence of US MNEs, the Philippines now has a relatively well-diversified pattern of inward investment.

Figure 3. Inward investment in ASEAN4 countries by investor country
(share of total inward investment stock)

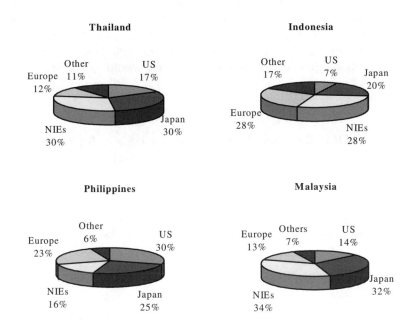

Source: National governments

FDI inflows by sector

The four countries also differ in terms of the sectors favoured by foreign investors. Once again, Thailand and Malaysia are the most similar: in both countries, FDI in the manufacturing sector is dominated by projects in electronics, with significantly more investment in that sector than in any other manufacturing activity. In Thailand, however, manufacturing as a whole represents only one third of total inflows. A large share of the total goes into distribution and finance, as well as construction and real estate. In Indonesia, manufacturing investments have tended to be in resource-based activities such as chemicals and paper. Investment in the Philippines is more diversified, albeit involving a much lower total stock of investment. In both Indonesia and the Philippines, the electronics sector has been growing.

Because the sectoral coverage and the way in which FDI is recorded in each country differs greatly, it is instructive to make comparisons of the ASEAN4 based on source country data. Table 2 looks at investment in the ASEAN4 and China by US and Japanese firms. These firms are not always the largest investors in each country, but they are probably fairly representative of OECD investors as a whole. In addition, unlike many investors from the NIEs, they are often among the world's largest MNEs and possess much of the proprietary technologies from which host countries would like to benefit.

Table 2. **FDI in the ASEAN4 and China by US and Japanese firms**
(Total stock, end 1997; $ million)

	China	Indo.	Mal.	Phil.	Thai.	Total 5
Japan						
Manufacturing	10 822	12 380	7 104	3 176	8 914	**42 396**
Non-manufacturing	5 917	20 662	2 695	2 328	3 420	**35 023**
Total	16 739	33 042	9 800	5 504	12 334	**77 418**
United States						
Manufacturing	2 696	358	3 222	1 616	1 090	**8 982**
Non-manufacturing	2 317	7 037	2 401	1 787	2 447	**15 989**
Total	5 013	7 395	5 623	3 403	3 537	**24 971**
Total (US, Japan)						
Manufacturing	13 518	12 738	10 326	4 792	10 004	**51 378**
Non-manufacturing	8 234	27 699	5 096	4 115	5 867	**51 012**
Total	**21 752**	**40 437**	**15 423**	**8 907**	**15 871**	**102 389**

Source: US Department of Commerce; Japanese Ministry of Finance

As seen in Table 2, the stock of Japanese investment in the five countries is three times higher than that of American firms (although the two countries do not record investments in the same way). For both investor countries, Indonesia is at the top of the list and the Philippines at the bottom. In manufacturing, Indonesia is still first for Japanese firms while American manufacturing firms have invested very little so far in the country. Much of the Japanese investment in Indonesia is intended to serve the large and protected domestic market. US investment in the five countries is greater in non-manufacturing than in manufacturing. Taking US and Japanese investments together, Thailand and

Malaysia are most similar once again, with roughly equal inward investments in both manufacturing and non-manufacturing. China has slightly more manufacturing investment than any of the ASEAN4, but much less than the four ASEAN countries combined. Indonesia, with its abundant natural resources such as oil, takes in more investment in the non-manufacturing sector than the rest of the ASEAN4 taken together. This may change if the service sectors in the other ASEAN countries are opened up as a result of the crisis.

External influences on the trend in FDI in the ASEAN4

Trends in FDI in the ASEAN4 have been strongly influenced by external events over which each country has had little control, notably currency appreciation in major source countries and the emergence of China as a competing location for investment. Those ASEAN4 countries with the most welcoming and stable environment have received a larger share of inflows, but any influence of policies in individual countries on FDI inflows has been circumscribed by these external influences. This explains certain similarities in the trend of FDI inflows into each ASEAN country over time, albeit at vastly different levels. In almost all cases, inflows accelerated rapidly in the late 1980s, fell sharply in the early 1990s and were rising again before the crisis. Indonesia is an exception within ASEAN. With a large internal market and abundant natural resources, it has been able to attract a more steady stream of investors than other ASEAN members.

Faced with these external influences, individual host countries have had to adjust their FDI policies in order to benefit from opportunities offered by a copious supply of investment applications and to confront threats to that supply at other times. For this reason, it is sometimes difficult to establish a direct link between changes in FDI policies and subsequent inflows of investment. To some extent because of the influence of external events, trends in FDI inflows into the ASEAN4 have driven policy changes in host countries and not the other way round. Policies towards FDI have tended to react to events rather than shaping them.

Japanese investment

To understand some of the external factors at play, Figure 4 compares Japanese direct investment in manufacturing in ASEAN4 with movements in the yen/dollar exchange rate. Japanese firms are the largest investors in Asia outside of China, so their decisions have a strong impact of inflows into individual Asian economies. The appreciation of the yen after 1985 pushed many Japanese firms to establish lower cost production bases within the region.

19

Figure 4. **Japanese investment in ASEAN4**

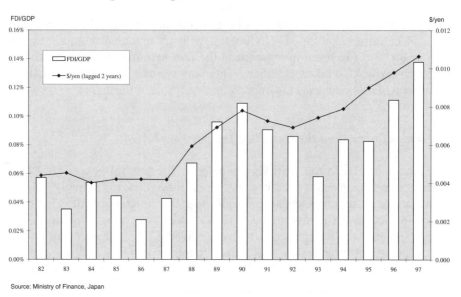

Source: Ministry of Finance, Japan

Firms adjust to exchange rate movements with a lag which varies by sector and according to the extent of exchange rate changes. By lagging the exchange rate by two years in Figure 4, it can be seen immediately that the two trends follow each other very closely. Japanese investors were quick to respond to the initial yen appreciation following the Plaza accord in 1985 when the dollar went from 250 yen at the beginning of the year to 201 at the end. The yen continued to appreciate sharply until 1988, at which point one dollar was worth half as many yen as at the beginning of 1985. Japanese investments continued to expand in Asia for another two years, with outflows over ten times higher as a percentage of GDP than five years earlier.

This surge in manufacturing investment into Asia by Japanese firms resulted in an unprecedented shift in productive capacity within the region. Some countries such as Malaysia and Thailand benefited handsomely in terms of a rapidly expanding manufacturing sector. Industrial restructuring by Japanese firms was mirrored to a lesser extent by investments from Chinese Taipei and other NIEs, faced with currency appreciation of their own and the loss of their preferential access to OECD markets as developing countries.

By 1988, the yen had begun to depreciate slightly, while the structural adjustment of the Japanese and Asian economies as a result of the yen appreciation continued for another two years. Japanese outflows to Asia began

20

to fall rapidly and by 1993 were only one half the level of 1990 (as a percentage of GDP). Once again, the lagged response to further yen appreciation encouraged a further resurgence in outflows to the region after that date.

On the basis of this past relationship between Japanese investment in Asia and exchange rate movements, one might expect to see a decline in such investment in the ASEAN4 over the next few years as a result of the sharp depreciation of the yen against the dollar beginning in 1997. This was borne out in an Eximbank survey of Japanese investor intentions from mid-1997 which found a declining Japanese interest in ASEAN4 countries offset by continued or rising interest in China, India and Vietnam. Paradoxically, the Asian financial crisis beginning in 1997 may actually have temporarily sustained Japanese investments in the region because of the difficulties experienced by affiliates in raising local capital and the need for parent firms to inject liquidity.

Several recent surveys of Japanese firms' investment intentions in Southeast Asia suggest that flows will decline in both 1998 and 1999, not only because of the crisis in host countries but also because of problems at home in Japan. Investments from Japan into each of the ASEAN4 fell in the first half of 1998, particularly in the transport equipment sector because of the sharp contraction in domestic demand. In China, in contrast, another survey finds that the crisis has not yet dampened Japanese interest.

Investment in China

A second external factor which might have impinged on FDI inflows into ASEAN is the prominence of China as a host for foreign investment. For the most part, the notion that countries compete for FDI is a misconception. Foreign direct investment is not a zero sum game with investors choosing one country at the expense of all others. Indeed, it is more likely that investment into one country in Asia will spur further investments throughout the region over time. Singapore, for example, may have acted as a magnet for foreign investment into the whole of Southeast Asia, often involving vertically-integrated activities. Nevertheless, the spectacular rise of China as a host to FDI in the 1990s has been perceived within parts of ASEAN as a threat to its own continuing success in attracting FDI. Beyond China, other potential rivals such as India loom on the horizon. Because of this perceived threat and the impact it has had on ASEAN policies, notably towards regional integration, it is worth exploring in more detail what the rise of China implies for ASEAN and in what ways it might have affected the prospects of the ASEAN4 in attracting investment in the future.

21

Figure 5 shows FDI into ASEAN4 and China in the 1990s. The rapid growth in inflows into China between 1991 and 1994 is immediately apparent, as is the relative stagnation in inflows into the ASEAN4 as a whole. Actual inflows continue to expand into China, but when measured as a percentage of GDP, inflows peaked in 1994. Contracted investment in China is declining, with continued inflows sustained by the steady stream of realised investments as already approved projects come into operation. As a result, the Chinese share of FDI inflows into the developing countries of the region has stabilised following a rapid rise in 1992-93.

Figure 5. **FDI in China and the ASEAN4, 1990-1997** ($ million)

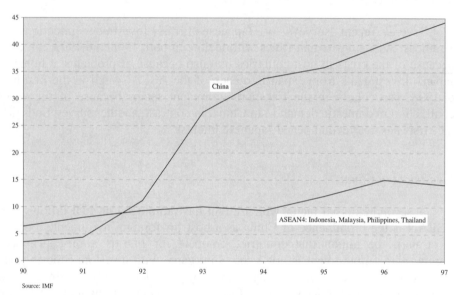

Source: IMF

The question of investment diversion hinges on whether investment in China and in the ASEAN4 are substitutes. In terms of both the country of origin of the investor and the sector involved, FDI in the two areas has tended to be very different. Over one half of investment in China comes from Hong Kong, China, with Japan, Chinese Taipei and the United States contributing another one quarter. Although firms from these four economies also invest in ASEAN countries, the ranking is very different, with Hong Kong Chinese firms much less prominent.

22

Many of the investors in China from Hong Kong, China and Chinese Taipei are small and medium-sized enterprises. Such firms often have limited financial or administrative resources with which to invest abroad, except where, as with China, geographical proximity and cultural affinity are sufficient to minimise transactions costs. The same may not be true to the same extent for investments in ASEAN4 countries, although the overseas Chinese communities in these countries sometimes serve as a useful conduit for such investment. In contrast, investment in ASEAN4 countries is relatively more likely to be from large MNEs, often originating in OECD countries.

To understand more clearly the effect that the opening of China has had on FDI in ASEAN requires a discussion of the motives for investing and the strategies of investing firms. Surveys of both American and Japanese firms suggest that they invest in both China and the ASEAN4 primarily to supply goods or services to the local market. Almost two thirds of the output of Japanese firms in China, for example, is sold within China. Hence, the principal way in which China competes with ASEAN is as a market for investors. Although its lower level of development makes it a relatively smaller market, China is generally ranked as the most important market in the medium and long term by Japanese investors. An OECD study has predicted that China will have the world's largest economy by 2015.[4]

Some investments into both China and the ASEAN4 are for export platforms, with final sales destined for the home market or third countries. Such investments are particularly prominent in the electronics sector and often account for a significant share of total manufactured exports from host countries. Anecdotal evidence suggests that some firms have shifted such activities to China to take advantage of lower labour costs. Figure 6 puts this shift in labour intensive production to China in the perspective of long-standing patterns of regional structural adjustment brought about partly through FDI.

The late 1980s saw a shift in the relative share of OECD investment going to the ASEAN4 as the share in the NIEs fell by almost one half. In 1991, the ASEAN4 took in more OECD investment than the NIEs for the first time, but after that, the ASEAN4 share fell as OECD investors became increasingly interested in China. Since 1995, the NIEs have recovered somewhat at the expense of both the ASEAN4 and China which provides a useful reminder that the causes of FDI are complex and cannot simply be characterised as a gradual shift towards more labour abundant locations. Looking at shares provides interesting evidence of structural adjustment in Asia, but it should not give the impression that total investment is fixed in supply: OECD investment into all three groups has risen over time.

Figure 6. **OECD outflows to major Asian destinations**
(percentage of total OECD outflows to all eight locations)

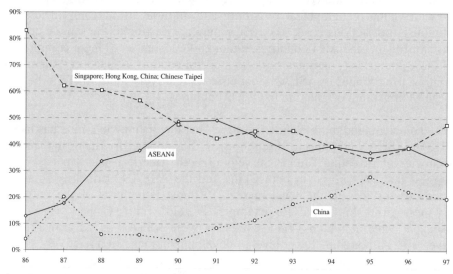

Source: *International Direct Investment Statistics Yearbook* , OECD

Much as the ASEAN4 benefited from the declining competitiveness of the NIEs and Japan in labour-intensive activities in the late 1980s, so too has China benefited from similar circumstances in the ASEAN economies. But while the NIEs and Japan moved successfully to higher value-added activities, certain ASEAN countries have encountered difficulties in effecting this transformation. The focus on investment diversion to China should not deflect attention from the domestic causes of this adjustment problem. As more and more countries compete for export-oriented investments, the period of time during which adjustment must be undertaken has shortened. At the same time, the speed with which countries can transform their economies into manufacturing powerhouses has also increased. Globalisation offers substantial opportunities for participating countries, but it also requires an ability for rapid adjustment to benefit the most from these opportunities.

Summary

To explain the record of individual countries in attracting FDI inflows requires an understanding not only of policies and events in each host country but also of factors influencing the potential supply of such investment in home countries and of changes in other major host countries. The ebb and flow of

24

Japanese FDI and the rise of China have had a significant impact both on inflows into ASEAN4 and on perceptions concerning future inflows. But at the same time, these external events have not operated within a vacuum. The ASEAN4 countries would never have attracted Japanese investment in the first place if they had not had a competitive workforce and relatively accommodating policies towards foreign investors. Countries such as Malaysia and Thailand were in the right place at the right time in the late 1980s, but they also had the regulatory environment to attract export-oriented investors.

Will existing policies be enough to sustain inflows in the future? The financial crisis has made this question even more pertinent given the sharp drop in other forms of capital inflows. The answer depends partly on whether European and American investors will take up the slack left from declining growth in Japanese investment in the region and on whether the gold rush into China has abated. But the answer will also depend on whether the ASEAN4 countries have the appropriate policies in place in the new, more competitive environment for global FDI flows. Policies towards inward investors in each of the ASEAN4 are discussed below.

II.   The policy environment for FDI in the ASEAN4

The role of FDI policies in overall development strategies

Import substitution policies were pursued in all four countries in earlier decades, in keeping with the prevailing development view that government intervention was necessary to promote industrialisation. Strategic sectors were protected from foreign competition through high tariffs. In some sectors foreign investment was proscribed, and in most it was heavily circumscribed. Foreign investors were limited to minority shares of companies, could not own the land on which their factories were built, were required to transfer technology and sometimes to divest after a number of years. Many foreign MNEs nevertheless invested during this period to participate in the economic rents resulting from import protection.

The switch to export promotion began at different times in different countries, with the timing dictated partly by the size of the local market and the availability of natural resources. Small markets limit the scope for economies of scale and hence raise the cost of protection, while natural resources provide export earnings to alleviate balance of payments difficulties. External factors were also important: the example of successful, outward-oriented NIEs, the prolonged commodity slump in the 1980s, and opportunities offered by exchange rate realignments after 1985. Currency realignments, the switch to export promotion, including FDI liberalisation, and the rapid inflow of FDI from Japan and the NIEs all combine to account for the dramatic export-led recovery of the ASEAN4 economies after 1985 following a decade of secular decline (Figure 7).

Because investment incentives and restrictions have often co-existed over several decades in these economies, the move towards export promotion usually reflects more a change of emphasis than a substantially new legislative agenda. Malaysia started to promote exports as early as the 1970s, although for both Malaysia and Thailand, the real export push began only in the mid-1980s. Indonesia and the Philippines are more recent converts to the export-oriented approach to development, but their policies in this area have now converged substantially on those in the other two countries.

Figure 7. **Average real GDP growth in the ASEAN4, 1968-96**

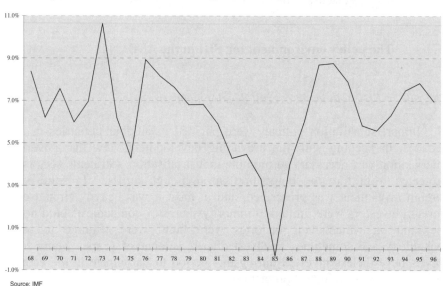

Source: IMF

Rather than replacing import substitution, export promotion was super-imposed on the pre-established structure. The restrictions on FDI for the domestic market remained largely intact; indeed, some of them are enshrined in national constitutions. There has nevertheless been some relaxation in the implementation of these policies over time. Local content requirements have been curtailed as a result of the TRIMs agreement, except in the automobile sector, and divestiture requirements — where they exist — are not rigorously enforced. There has been some further relaxation of policies, often on a temporary basis, as a result of the crisis, but the basic regulatory structure for domestic-oriented investment remains in place.

Restrictions on FDI in the ASEAN4

Not all ASEAN4 countries regulate inward investment in the same way or with the same degree of efficiency, but there are nevertheless many similarities: all four countries routinely screen inward investment, often linked to the granting of incentives; some sectors are proscribed for foreign investors, usually contained in a negative list; equity limits often apply in other sectors and for acquisitions of local companies; and land ownership is sometimes restricted. The most important obstacles to inward investment are presented below.

Screening

A foreign investor wishing to invest in one of the ASEAN4 must usually go through a screening agency or Board of Investment (BOI). Although domestic investors must also usually apply to the same agency, the conditions applied to their investments are not necessarily the same. The screening agency serves a political purpose as well as an economic one. It demonstrates to a local population which may be hostile to, or suspicious of, foreign investment that such investments are actively monitored by the government. The principal aim of such an agency, however, is to further the development strategies of the host government. The agency will favour certain sectors on a priority list or those investors which fulfil pre-established criteria, usually related to exports.

In many cases, screening agencies are evolving from authorising bodies to investment promotion agencies. The criteria for approval have generally been simplified, and approval is now usually only necessary for those investors seeking incentives. The practical implications of this shift have not yet been great: because of distortions in the rest of the economy such as high trade barriers, most investors require some form of incentives if they are going to be able to produce profitably. Important incentives are the exemption from tariffs on imported components and the right to own the land under the factory. These types of "incentives" are likely to be important for both import-substituting and exporting firms.[5]

As part of the transition to investment promotion, Boards of Investment have attempted to set up a one-stop shop to facilitate the approval process.

Success in this area has been hampered by other ministries keen to retain regulatory responsibility. Foreign investors sometimes exploit these rivalries by playing one ministry off against the other, and, in an attempt to avoid this, the BOI is often placed directly under the President or Prime Minister, rather than in a specific ministry. Malaysia is an exception in that its Industrial Development Authority is placed under the Ministry for International Trade and Industry. While the direct link to the President provides some assurance against ministerial in-fighting, it also reduces transparency by making the ultimate decision partly a political one. In addition to inter-ministerial rivalries, the Board of Investment may have internal difficulties evolving towards a more user-friendly approach. A study of screening agencies found that "the initiative for change rarely originates in the screening units themselves".[6] Sometimes a political commitment to speed up the time in which a decision must be made can force the BOI to limit the requirements for investors. In some cases, a new agency is created alongside the BOI to handle export processing zones or other incentive programmes.

Because of its dual developmental and political function, the screening agency is not likely to disappear in the ASEAN4. As long as decisions are based on a clearly defined set of criteria, transparent, free from political interference and rendered within a limited time period, a screening agency can be compared with an investment promotion agency which is responsible for monitoring compliance with the granting of incentives. In this way, the presence of such an agency need not be construed as an obstacle to FDI *per se*. In some cases such as Thailand investors may actually prefer to go through the agency, not least because it offers certain guarantees concerning expropriation.

In practice, however, it is the nature of many Boards of Investment which have evolved from an earlier, more protective era that decision making is still slow and lacks transparency. Both foreign and domestic investors in Indonesia have complained about cumbersome and time-consuming licensing procedures and high facilitation costs, and Japanese investors have ranked the complexity of administrative procedures as the principal problem encountered in their operations in Indonesia.[7] These complaints are in spite of the considerable effort which the Board of Investment (BKPM) has already undertaken to streamline procedures.

Not all Boards of Investment face similar complaints. The Malaysian Industrial Development Authority, for example, is generally recognised to be one of the more effective agencies in the region. Even those which are slow and non-transparent are moving in the direction of greater efficiency. In Indonesia, a recent Presidential decree allows for approvals to be signed by the Chairman of the Board of Investment rather than the President for all joint ventures below $100 million. As this process of streamlining continues, impediments to investment will become exclusively a function of legislation which lists sectors off-limits to foreigners or which prescribes certain equity limits by sector. These are discussed below.

Foreign equity limits

Screening agencies are concerned with new investment projects or the expansion of existing ones. Acquisitions of local companies by a foreign investor are a different matter. In most cases, until recently, foreign investors were limited to minority stakes in local companies, regardless of the specific sector. The foreign equity share ranged from 30 per cent in Malaysia to 49 per cent in Indonesia and Thailand. Some sectors, such as banking, had even lower limits. In some cases, these restrictions are enshrined in the Constitution.

Acquisitions of local companies are often the preferred mode of entry into a foreign market in both OECD and non-OECD countries. Foreign investors will sometimes not require complete control of a joint venture, but in many of the most technologically-sophisticated sectors and those where brand names are important, full foreign ownership is preferred. A minority ownership requirement can thus act as a significant barrier to investment in these sectors, particularly for those investors wishing to sell principally in the local market.

In addition, the authorisation process in these cases is often different from the usual Board of Investment procedure. In Malaysia, for example, the investor must have the approval of either MIDA or the Foreign Investment Committee or both, depending on how the acquisition is financed. Among other requirements, the investor must demonstrate that the merger will lead directly or indirectly to net economic benefits in relation to such matters as the extent of indigenous Malay (or *bumiputera*) participation, ownership and management, as well as income distribution, growth, employment, exports, quality, range of products and services, economic diversification, processing and upgrading of local raw materials, training, efficiency and research and development. Economic needs tests are not uncommon for acquisitions in some sectors within the ASEAN4.

Since the onset of the crisis, Indonesia has relaxed its horizontal equity limits for acquisitions, except in the financial sector. Malaysia has, at various times, allowed firms to exceed legal foreign equity limits. The Thai government has proposed amendments to the Alien Business Law, but efforts have been stalled in Parliament. Foreign investors have nevertheless been allowed to acquire ailing local companies. In the Philippines, equity limits remain as part of the "Filipino First" clause of the Constitution.

Negative lists

A complement to horizontal equity limits for acquisitions is the use of negative lists of those sectors in which foreign investment is not permitted or in which there are specific sectoral foreign equity limits, including for greenfield investments. Negative lists add to transparency in FDI regulations by permitting foreign investors to ascertain quickly whether their sector of activity faces any restrictions. At the same time, a negative list is not necessarily exhaustive. Some sectors may still face the horizontal limits mentioned above, while others may not appear on the list because they involve a sector which is not under the responsibility of the agency compiling the list. Nevertheless, negative lists provide a useful benchmark of the degree of openness of each economy, as well as of the extent of liberalisation over time. Only Malaysia does not have a negative list, although there are some sectors in which foreign investment is not permitted. The absence of such a list may stem from the special nature of Malaysia equity restrictions which are intended to promote *bumiputera* ownership of domestic assets and which cover all sectors not promoted by MIDA.

Indonesia moved from a positive to a negative list as part of its liberalisation of its investment regime. The positive list mentions only those sectors which are open to foreign investment, as in the bottom-up approach of the GATS. Negative lists have been considerably shortened over time in Indonesia, the Philippines and Thailand. As a result of the crisis, the number of sectors with foreign equity limits has been drastically reduced in order to recapitalise industries. A proposed revision to the Alien Business Law in Thailand aims to reduce the number of sectors on the negative list from 63 to 34. The degree of foreign ownership allowed in the remaining sectors is also to be raised in some cases. Indonesia also shortened its negative list by means of a Presidential decree issued in 1998. The Philippines has also opened up several sectors to greater foreign participation.

Restrictions on land ownership

Another restriction which impedes foreign investment concerns the right of foreign-owned corporations to own land. Without the ownership of the land on which the factory is built, the foreign investor faces considerable potential insecurity about the future policies of the host government and is also unable to use the land as collateral for local borrowing. Malaysia requires approval from state authorities before an investor may acquire title to land, except for investments in export processing zones. The three other countries have some form of general restriction on foreign land ownership, except for some promoted companies. In these three countries, investors may generally only lease land for a specific period of time, with only one opportunity for renewal. The period of the lease has been extended in some of these countries as a result of the crisis.

Summary

The restrictions mentioned above are not exhaustive. Other measures relate to the right of foreign investors to bring in expatriate staff or the number of foreigners permitted on the Board of Directors, among others. There are also restrictions are specific to particular sectors which may or may not be included in a negative list. Taken together, these restrictions suggest that foreign investment outside of promoted sectors has been heavily circumscribed in the ASEAN4 — a finding at odds with the conventional view that these countries have built their development strategies largely on the backs of foreign firms.

These policies reflect a lingering suspicion of foreign MNEs in the four host countries. Although a number of liberalisation measures have been undertaken as a result of the crisis, it is sometimes surprising given the urgent need to bring in capital and to recapitalise local firms how difficult it has been to pass legislation through parliaments. Local business interests sometimes represent a powerful lobby against change.

The counterpoint to these restrictions has been an aggressive attempt to promote export-oriented investments. These incentives are described below. The implications of this dualist policy towards inward investment are discussed in a later section.

Investment promotion in the ASEAN4

Export-oriented firms, particularly those locating in export processing zones (EPZs), are given numerous incentives in all four countries, including automatic approvals, land ownership, full control of the affiliate, tax holidays and duty free imports of components. From a regulatory point of view, investors wishing to export most of what they produce will find the ASEAN4 countries almost as open as OECD countries.

All four countries have a priority list of activities for which both domestic and foreign investors receive special promotional privileges. Sometimes this list includes specific sectors which the government would like to promote, but in many cases the priorities relate to particular attributes of the investment rather than the sector itself. Thus, investors wishing to export most of their output or likely to transfer technology will generally be favoured. Incentives by the BOI in Thailand have evolved towards a regional development strategy in which projects are encouraged to locate in the most disadvantaged regions — a policy found in many OECD countries as well. Other ASEAN4 governments also include some regional incentives as well as part of the overall package of measures.

Incentives can take two forms. The first are tax incentives for a defined period. Malaysia, Thailand and the Philippines all offer such fiscal incentives. Indonesia has been more reticent in this area, although certain industrial sectors might benefit from incentives. The criteria for granting incentives are currently under consideration. Unlike the wealthier OECD economies, the ASEAN4 are less in a position to offer grants to potential investors. The second type of incentive represents exemptions from various restrictions on inward investment described above, as well as from import duties on capital goods and raw materials and other trade barriers. There is generally no analogue to such policies within OECD countries, and indeed the idea that these policies constitute incentives in the sense of the term in OECD countries is misleading. They are instead selective removals of distortions.

Policy reform during the crisis

Short-term measures have been undertaken in each country and formalised in an ASEAN initiative to enhance the investment climate in member countries, known as the Hanoi Plan of Action. The measures are only for investment applications submitted between 1 January 1999 and 31 December 2000 but will still apply to those investments after that period. They include fiscal incentives for industries on the priority list, domestic market access and full foreign ownership, except in sectors on the negative list, and a minimum leasehold of industrial land of 30 years. Fiscal incentives include a minimum three-year tax exemption or a minimum 30 percent corporate income tax allowance and exemption of duty on imported capital goods. Restrictions on the employment of foreign personnel are also relaxed. Foreign firms that inject equity into existing companies during the same period are also entitled to the same benefits except corporate tax incentives and land use privileges.

In some cases, these incentives do not go beyond existing measures, but in other cases, they offer unparalleled access to the domestic market, including through the acquisition of local firms. These temporary changes represent a significant shift away from the traditional emphasis on export promotion and industrial or regional targeting and offer far greater access to the domestic market. Negative lists still remain in those countries adopting such an approach, but in many cases full foreign ownership is now possible to a much greater extent, albeit only during a limited period.

ASEAN Investment Area

The ASEAN Investment Area (AIA) is a binding agreement to foster investment liberalisation within the region. Under the Agreement signed in October 1998, several programmes for co-operation, promotion and liberalisation will be implemented in order to realise the AIA by January 2010. Investment barriers will be eliminated and national treatment granted for ASEAN investors by 2010 and for all investors by 2020. The Agreement also paves the way for members to provide transparent investment policies and administrative processes. The programme will initially focus on opening up the manufacturing sector but will later cover other sectors. Signatory countries expected the measures expressed in the Agreement to increase FDI inflows. Like the ASEAN Free Trade Area (AFTA), the AIA is seen as a way of countering the economic weight of China.

III.   The impact of FDI on ASEAN4 development

The role of FDI in development is as multi-faceted as FDI itself. At one level, FDI makes a similar potential contribution to development and to global economic welfare as any other form of capital flow by channelling resources from countries where they are abundant to those where they are scarce. Thus, inflows of capital in the form of FDI allow host economies to invest in productive activities beyond what could be achieved by domestic savings alone. Unlike other forms of capital flows, FDI has proved remarkably resilient during the crisis.

At another level, the benefits of FDI resemble those from trade, especially in sectors producing goods and services which tend not to be traded internationally. Thus, foreign firms can potentially enhance the level of competition in an economy and bring in ideas, innovations, expertise and other forms of technology which the host economy could not necessarily have created on its own. Multinational enterprises (MNEs), with their global network of affiliates, can also channel exports from the host country to affiliates elsewhere in the form of intra-firm trade. Through this mechanism, FDI permits an international division of labour within the MNE which might not have occurred otherwise owing to high transactions costs.

These various channels through which foreign investment can potentially contribute to development are discussed below. With hindsight, it can be seen in those countries which have relied on FDI that the benefits are not necessarily automatic. Host countries may become prodigious exporters, but indigenous exporting capabilities sometimes remain poor. The reasons for this are complex and hinge on more than just investor strategies or FDI regulations. For this reason, it is often necessary to go beyond FDI regulations to look at a range of policies which might impinge on investor behaviour.

FDI as a form of development finance

The crisis has brought into relief the importance of FDI as a stable source of finance for development compared to other forms of international capital flows. Foreign direct investment in Asia has so far held up very well, in spite of the crisis, while other capital flows have reversed themselves (Figure 8). Indeed, in some ASEAN4 countries, inflows have actually increased. It remains to be seen whether this represents simply a lagged response of foreign investors to changing circumstances — which would suggest that inflows would fall dramatically in the future. The Mexican experience following the late-1994 peso crisis suggests that FDI inflows often hold up much better than other forms of capital flows in both the short and medium term.

Figure 8. **Net private capital flows to Asia, 1991-97** ($ billion)

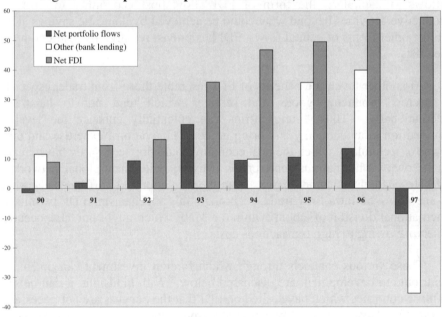

Source: IMF

34

Figure 8 divides net private capital flows to Asia into FDI, portfolio investment and other flows, principally bank lending. The divergence in trends among different types of capital is immediately apparent. Total net private flows to Asia fell from $110 billion in 1996 to only $14 billion in 1997, while FDI flows to the region remained unchanged. One can only imagine the shock to the regional economy if such FDI flows had not been sustained in these circumstances.

Although sustained high levels of inflows are important in order to finance continued investment and as a source of foreign capital, a more significant development may be that the type of inflow is changing. Investments are originating in a far broader range of countries, with greater European and other OECD participation, and the sectors involved are also expanding. For almost the first time, the crisis has provided a window of opportunity for investors wishing to sell in the domestic market. Not only have FDI regulations been eased, but local firms are also more prepared to part with control in return for capital injections.

FDI and exports

The experience of successful ASEAN countries amply demonstrates how FDI can play a leading role in bringing about rapid, export-led growth. Rapidly rising exports have fuelled the world's fastest growth rates in some of these economies which, until recently, had made them the envy of the developing world. But economic development is more than growth, as the crisis has made abundantly clear. The ASEAN countries have not always managed to translate economic growth through FDI into something more durable which builds on existing indigenous capabilities. This section describes the contribution of foreign investors to export-led growth in these economies and points out the weaknesses which were exposed in the recent crisis.

Exports have doubled as a percentage of GDP in all four countries since 1982, with very little annual variation along the long-term trend (Figure 9). Exports have nevertheless grown more at some times and in certain sectors than in others. At a sufficient level of disaggregation, the correlation between export growth and FDI inflows is often strong. The fastest growth in Figure 9 is in the late 1980s when exports grew from 30.5 per cent on GDP to 39.7 in three years. Between 1989 and 1992, the comparable growth was only 2.6 percentage points. These variations correspond roughly to the rapid growth in FDI inflows in the late 1980s and relative stagnation of such inflows in the early 1990s.

Exports would have increased even without FDI, as can be seen in those sectors in which foreign investors are not important, but the ASEAN4 would probably not have experienced the rapid acceleration of exports in the past decade without the presence of foreign investors. In Thailand, exports have been the main engine of economic growth, particularly since the mid-1980s. Historically one of the world's leading rice exporters, it has become a major exporter of manufactured goods, rising from only one third of total exports in 1980 to over 80 per cent by 1997. This shift in exports is mirrored in the structural transformation of the Thai economy, from agriculture and to industry. While agriculture's contribution to GDP was three times that of manufacturing in 1960, by the early 1990s it was less than half as important as manufacturing.

Figure 9. **ASEAN4 exports as a percentage of GDP**

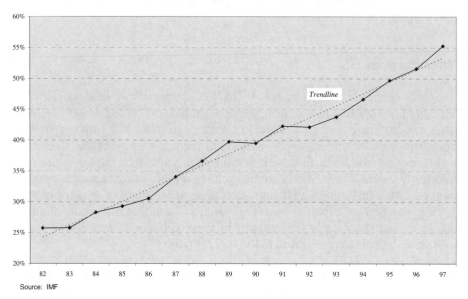

Source: IMF

Foreign investors have played a key role in this process. Electronic products, particularly computer parts and integrated circuits, make up almost one third of total Thai exports. These sectors are dominated by foreign MNEs. Through inward investment, Thailand has become the ninth largest exporter of computers during the 1990s, with computer exports growing fourfold in the past five years. Significantly, however, Thai export success is not wholly contingent on inward investors: the export boom began as early as 1984, while inward investment surged only after 1987. Much of this export growth occurred initially in food products and other sectors in which Thailand has a comparative advantage.

The Malaysian experience is similar to that of Thailand, with exports growing quickly after the mid-1980s. Although the substantial depreciation of the ringgit at the time was a major catalyst, investment liberalisation was an important complementary factor. The role of foreign investors can be seen by distinguishing between exports of electronic goods — a sector dominated by foreign MNEs — and other manufactured goods (Figure 10). Although all Malaysian exports have both increased over time, the driving force behind the rapid growth has clearly been the foreign-dominated export sector.

Figure 10. **Exports of manufactured goods from Malaysia, 1970-97**
(percentage of GDP)

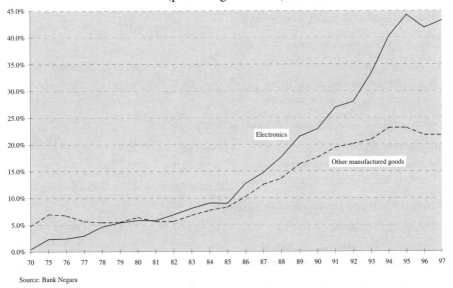

Source: Bank Negara

Through export-oriented FDI, ASEAN4 countries were able to shift quickly towards a manufacturing-based economy in which economic growth was driven by rapidly expanding exports. The record from this export performance speaks for itself, but so too does the manifest failure in many cases to translate this export success based partly on FDI into something more durable. Not only have exports been limited to a small number of products (usually intermediate ones) and sectors, but to varying degrees these export sectors have been virtual foreign enclaves within host countries. They have often been characterised by low value-added (principally from labour-intensive assembly operations) and a poor record of technology transfer. These shortcomings represented one of the growing structural problems leading up to the crisis.

Table 3. **Imports and exports of electronics in four Asian countries, 1994**

	Singapore	Indonesia	Malaysia	Thailand
Exports of electronics products ($ million)				
All electronics products	34 262	1 665	14 768	6 387
Automatic data processing equipment	21 878	193	4 726	3 680
Communication equipment, semiconductors	12 385	1 473	10 042	2 707
Share of finished goods in exports (per cent)				
All electronics products	67.1	80.2	65.3	64.8
Automatic data processing equipment	66.6	49.9	30.9	57.5
Communication equipment, semiconductors	76.4	84.1	81.5	74.8
Imports of parts as a percentage of exports of finished goods				
All electronics products	32.7	26.7	38.5	60.1
Automatic data processing equipment	28.9	33.2	95.4	79.4
Communication equipment, semiconductors	39.3	26.2	28.4	40.0
Imports of parts as a percentage of total exports				
All electronics products	21.9	21.4	25.2	39.0
Automatic data processing equipment	19.4	16.6	29.5	45.7
Communication equipment, semiconductors	26.5	22.0	23.1	29.9

Source: UNCTAD, *Trade and Development Report*, 1996

The import dependence of MNE-related exports can be seen in Table 3. Many of the most successful export sectors in the ASEAN4 are highly import dependent, and this has limited the impact of massive devaluations in these economies on exports. In some sectors, imports represent 80-90 per cent of the value of exports. The high import dependence ratio for MNE-related exports is symptomatic of the poor linkages between foreign affiliates and the local economy more generally. Poor linkages reduce the scope for technology transfers through FDI which could assist in local industrial upgrading. Arguably, the failure to upgrade production in light of greater competition in labour-intensive activities from China and Vietnam is one of the underlying structural problems which served to undermine confidence in the years preceding the crisis.

Technology transfers

The most enduring potential benefit to developing countries from inward direct investment is the transfer of technology. Exports can drive rapid economic growth over long period, but technology transfers can do much more to promote sustainable development by enhancing indigenous capabilities. In this area, the record from decades of FDI in the ASEAN4 is not encouraging. Possible remedies for this situation will be discussed later.

Studies attempting to measure technology transfers to the ASEAN4 resulting from FDI have tended to find that such transfers have generally been limited. In Indonesia, a number of studies find that technology transfer has taken place mainly through on-the-job training and has been limited to basic technological capabilities.[8] Otherwise, FDI and its related technology transfer have not generally been effective at developing indigenous industrial technological capabilities.[9] In Thailand, technology transfers from FDI have been moderate, according to several studies.[10] One finds some evidence of transfer through foreign firms' training of high level staff, while another finds little evidence of transfer through the training of local suppliers. These studies generally cover the period of the 1980s when FDI was relatively recent and when certain sectors were still heavily protected. A more recent analysis suggests that technology transfer has arisen to some extent through relations between foreign companies and local suppliers.[11]

IV.   FDI policies and investor performance

The evidence from several decades of FDI in ASEAN4 countries presented above suggests clearly that foreign firms have played a leading role in successful export-oriented development strategies. At the same time, however, there is general consensus that the presence of foreign investors has not always contributed greatly to indigenous capabilities. While few would disagree strongly with this assessment, the question still remains of what host countries could have done differently and what should be done now. Because attracting foreign investors has now become more important than ever as a policy priority, it may be an opportune moment to reassess policy approaches to inward investment in order to improve the linkages with the local economy in the future. This section sets out a general policy agenda in this area.

One reason for the poor performance in technology transfer is that the capacity of local workers to absorb foreign technologies is weak. Because much of the technology and know-how which has been transferred has tended to come through on-the-job training, policy initiatives in this area could have a significant impact. Local capabilities are fostered in the long run by educational policies which enhance the capacity of local workers to assimilate foreign technology and know-how. Reforms in ASEAN4 are occurring in this area, but any improvement will take a long time to filter through the economy.

A second and more important mechanism for technology transfer arises through the linkages between firms, as local firms co-operate with foreign investors either as joint venture partners or as suppliers. An analogy can be made with the need to enhance the skills and absorptive capacity of local workers. One way to enhance the ability of local firms to absorb technology is to improve the level of training of the workers themselves. But government policies can also influence this exchange more directly by increasing the scope for collaboration between foreign and domestic firms. As will be seen, many policies in this area may well have had the opposite effect to that intended.

FDI policies to enhance technology transfer

Many of the policies adopted in the ASEAN4 towards foreign investors are designed, implicitly or explicitly, to develop indigenous capabilities. These include any or all of the following requirements: local joint venture partners; divestiture of foreign control after a certain period of time; local content levels which force investors to purchase a high share of inputs locally; expatriate personnel limits, including on the board of directors; and compulsory licensing and other forms of mandatory technology transfers. The ASEAN4 countries have adopted most of these strategies at different points in time. Some remain in place, particularly for domestic market oriented investment.

Such policies may have several unintended consequences. First, they might discourage potential inward investors not willing to abide by such conditionality. Proprietary technologies and other intangible assets are the backbone of most firms, and they are understandably reluctant to share them with others who might one day become potential rivals. Thus, the more technology required to produce an item, the less likely the investor will be to locate in a country which imposes the types of restrictions mentioned above. This is implicitly recognised by the ASEAN4 countries in their efforts to attract export-oriented firms. Such investors typically face few restrictions on their activities. Local content requirements sometimes encourage FDI by components producers, but the fundamental problem of linkages with local firms remains.

These policies might also actually limit the eagerness of those firms which do decide to invest because of the risk of leakages to potential rivals. The most common policy in the ASEAN4 countries concerns joint venture requirements. A large body of research has found that such requirements do not achieve the objective of enhancing technology transfers. According to FIAS (1995, p. 30), "Limits on foreign investor ownership have also had the perverse effect of reducing the investor's incentive to make a success of the project." Such limits have only served to weaken the quality of FDI. In a recent survey of the literature, Moran (1998, p. 121) reaches the same conclusion: "Direct evidence is not promising on the use of joint ventures to try to enhance technology transfer, penetrate international markets, or even expand and strengthen backward linkage to the domestic economy". Mansfield and Romero (1980) find that parent firms transfer technology to wholly-owned subsidiaries in developing countries one-third faster, on average, than to joint ventures or licensees.[12]

Similar conclusions have been reached for other policies designed to increase technology transfers. Kokko and Blomström (1995) observe a negative relationship between technology inflows and the host-country technology transfer requirements. In Indonesia and the Philippines, divestiture requirements reportedly have reduced investment and product- and process-technology flows and have done little to enhance domestic capabilities.[13] These broad studies corroborate the description earlier of the poor performance of technology transfers into the ASEAN4.

The limits to selective export promotion

Technology transfer requirements and other regulations concerning FDI are just the first layer of policies impinging on technology transfers. At a much broader level, the emphasis of host countries on export promotion may also have presented an obstacle. Export-oriented investors are often less willing to establish links with local companies because the need for high quality inputs at competitive prices in order to compete in world markets. Most of these inputs come from other foreign firms, either through imports or from home-country suppliers which have also invested in the host country. This tendency is exacerbated by the fact that host governments often promote sectors such as electronics in which there are no pre-existing indigenous capabilities and hence no potential local suppliers.

Local firms are more likely to benefit from interactions with foreign investors if they are already active in that sector or if the competencies developed by local firms in other areas can be applied to the new type of activity. In concrete terms, this means that host governments should promote those activities which build on existing comparative advantage. Attempts to develop wholly new sectors through FDI which are unrelated to the existing industrial structure of the host economy reduce possible linkages between foreign and domestic firms because local firms do not have the relevant expertise. In the absence of industrial targeting, foreign firms would naturally seek out those sectors in which the host economy already possessed the specialised skills.

Links between local firms and exporters are also sometimes hampered by the special treatment accorded to foreign exporters. Because of heavy government regulation and import protection which still prevail in many sectors in ASEAN4 countries, export promotion can only succeed if investors are offered ways of overcoming these distortions. Hence, special operating conditions have been created for exporters, such as duty free imports, which allow exporters to employ host country labour without having to face the otherwise high costs of doing business in the economy owing but which also have the effect of divorcing the export sector from the rest of the economy. The creation of export processing zones may have exacerbated this tendency because they usually constitute separate customs areas from the local economy. As argued in an OECD study of FDI in Malaysia, "if a customs barrier must be crossed [by a foreign affiliate operating in a Malaysian EPZ] to reach suppliers, it might as well be an international barrier to reach already developed suppliers in Singapore".[14]

Local market orientation and technology transfer

Evidence from a wide range of developing countries suggests that domestic market-oriented investments might sometimes be better placed to transfer relevant technologies to the host economy. An early but comprehensive study by Reuber et al. (1973) found that export-oriented projects purchased only one half as large a share of their inputs locally than other projects. In addition, technology adaptation was much less in the former than the latter, in large part because local market-oriented firms had to adapt their products to the specific demands of local consumers.

Even for foreign affiliates selling in the domestic market, however, technology transfers are not automatic. Much of the FDI in the automobile sector in the ASEAN4, for example, has not provided abundant evidence of extensive local linkages. Foreign investors in this sector are more likely to be interested in rent-seeking behind high import barriers than in competing aggressively in the local market. Kokko and Blomström (1995) find that foreign affiliates in their study were most likely to transfer technology if they felt competitive pressures in the host economy. The intuition behind this outcome is clear: when foreign investors face stiff competition within a market, either from imports or from other investors, they are compelled to transfer more technology to their affiliate in that market in order to be able to compete more effectively.

Regional integration, with its commitment to removing barriers to trade (AFTA) and investment (AIA) within ASEAN, will help to stimulate competition within each economy. But it should not occur at the expense of FDI from OECD countries. Most of the world's largest MNEs are headquartered in OECD countries, and these firms are repositories of the lion's share of the most advanced technologies. In addition, an UNCTAD (1993) study found that smaller firms are less prone to transfer technology from the parent company: foreign affiliates of smaller firms in developing countries obtained frontier, state-of-the-art technology in fewer than half the cases surveyed, while around two thirds of the foreign affiliates of larger MNEs received such technology.

A neutral approach to FDI regulation

The arguments presented above suggest that technology transfers are enhanced in a neutral policy environment which permits equal access for foreign investors to both domestic and export markets. The gradual elimination of barriers to imports will, by itself, help to alleviate the most adverse effects of the existing dualist FDI policy by removing one of the principal distortions within the ASEAN4 economies. But this would still not eliminate the differential treatment between types of foreign investors found in FDI regulations in most ASEAN countries. The reassessment of development strategies in light of the crisis provides an opportune time to switch to a more open and balanced regulatory framework for FDI.

NOTES

1. The four case studies will be published shortly by the OECD as Recovery in Asia: Enhancing the Role of Foreign Firms.

2. Borensztein et al. (1995)

3. Definitions of FDI and reporting methodologies differ greatly from one country to another so the exact ranking of countries cannot always be assessed with certainty given the number of countries clustered around the same level of inflows.

4. Maddison (1998).

5. FIAS (1991), p. 18.

6. FIAS (1991), p. 15.

7. Thee (1998), p. 5.

8. Saad (1995), p. 212.

9. Thee (1998), p. 14

10 See TDRI (1994) for a survey.

11 TDRI (1994).

12. Cited in Moran (1998), p. 122

13. Conklin and Lecraw (1997)

14. OECD (1991), p. 100.

REFERENCES

Borensztein, E., J. de Gregorio and J. Lee, "How does foreign direct investment affect economic growth?", NBER Working Paper 5057, 1995.

Conklin, David and Donald Lecraw, "Restrictions on ownership during 1984-94: developments and alternative policies", *Transnational Corporations*, vol. 6, no. 1, April 1997.

Foreign Investment Advisory Service (FIAS), *Foreign Direct Investment: Lessons of Experience*, World Bank, 1997.

Kokko, A. and M. Blomström, "Policies to encourage inflows of technology through foreign multinationals", *World Development* 23(3), 1995.

Maddison, Angus, *Chinese Economic Performance in the Long Run*, OECD Development Centre Studies, 1998.

Mansfield, Edwin, and Anthony Romero, "Technology transfer to overseas subsidiaries by US-based firms", *Quarterly Journal of Economics* 95, no. 4, December 1980.

Moran, Theodore, *Foreign Direct Investment and Development: The New Policy Agenda for Developing Countries and Economies in Transition*, Institute for International Economics, Washington, December 1998

Reuber, G.L. et al. (1973), *Private Foreign Investment in Development*, Oxford: Clarendon Press.

Saad, Ilyas, "Foreign direct investment, structural change, and deregulation in Indonesia", in *The New Wave of Foreign Direct Investment in Asia*, Nomura Research Institute and ISEAS, 1995.

Thee, Kian Wie, "Foreign Direct Investment and Technological Development in Indonesia", paper presented at an International Symposium on Foreign Direct Investment in Asia, Tokyo, 22-23 October 1998.

Thailand Development Research Institute (1998), "Forecast of the twenty most important Thai exported items in the world market". Paper prepared for the Department of Business Economics, Thai Ministry of Commerce.

UNCTAD (1993), Small and Medium-Sized Transnational Corporations: Role, Impact and Policy Implications, United Nations Conference on Trade and Development, New York.

Chapter 1

INDONESIA

Introduction and summary

Indonesia has been the seventeenth greatest recipient of inward direct investment in the 1990s, or sixth among non-OECD countries. Japanese firms have traditionally been the most active foreign investors, and Indonesia is the first destination for Japanese firms in developing countries. Chinese Taipei, Singapore and Hong Kong, China account for another one third of total investment in Indonesia, focused mostly on the primary and tertiary sectors and on light manufacturing. Non-Japanese investors from OECD countries are most prevalent in mining, oil refining and petro-chemicals, and certain services.

Much of this investment has been by firms interested in selling products in the protected local market or in exploiting Indonesia's abundant natural resources. As a result, foreign firms have traditionally played a relatively minor role in Indonesian manufactured exports. For manufacturing production, Indonesia ranks on a par with India and well behind all other major Asian countries for US investors with a stock of only $358 million in 1997. Even Japanese firms have invested far more in China than in Indonesia since 1993.

Indonesia's role as an export platform is nevertheless growing, albeit slowly. Although much FDI is still directed to the oil and gas sector (both in upstream and downstream activities), foreign investors tend increasingly to perceive Indonesia as a location for exports. The majority of very recent investors, in particular from developing Asia, have come to Indonesia to supply third country export markets previously served from their home base. Progressive liberalisation of the FDI regime beginning in the mid-1980s has influenced investor perceptions, but Indonesia has also benefited from the confluence of several push factors in Asian source countries which accelerated the process of outward investment by firms from those countries. These include currency revaluations, rising wage and land costs at home, liberalisation of home country rules on outgoing capital movements, and the loss of preferential

47

access to major markets through GSP[1]. Indonesia was an obvious choice, in particular once Thailand grew more crowded with investors, and after Malaysia started experiencing problems of labour shortages leading to rising wages. Moreover, an increasing share of FDI is also directed to the services sector, partly owing to the opportunities offered by infrastructure development.

Foreign firms also participate indirectly in the manufacturing sector in ways which are not recorded as FDI. Even when foreigners do not take equity stakes in a local company, they are indirectly important as providers of capital and in promoting exports and technological development. These benefits accrue through various forms of foreign linkages such as trading houses, buyer-supplier relations, licensing, sub-contracting and so on. They are particularly important in the oil and gas sectors and in exports of clothing and shoes, with foreign firms providing technology, marketing skills and a distribution network. Through production sharing, for example, foreign oil companies account for 95 per cent of crude oil production.

The role of policy reform in recent patterns of inward direct investment

The policy stance towards inward investment has been conditioned, at least in part, on developments in the oil sector, with a close correlation between fluctuating oil revenues and the attitude towards foreign investors. While a high priority was not attached to attracting FDI in the late 1960s, FDI policy was nevertheless relatively liberal at the time. Under the Foreign Capital Investment Act 1967, foreign investors were granted tax holidays, were allowed full foreign ownership and were not obliged eventually to transfer a given share of the company's equity to Indonesian interests. In the course of the 1970s, because oil provided foreign exchange and capital, as well as opportunities to borrow from international banks, and because of student riots against foreign investment, increasingly severe conditions were placed on inward investment. The rules governing the employment of expatriates and the importing of machinery and materials were gradually tightened, the range of activities closed to foreign investment was increased and rigid requirements were imposed with regard to local partnerships and equity divestment. The tax holiday was also scrapped.

With declining oil revenues in the late 1980s, Indonesia came to appreciate to a greater extent the potential role of FDI in economic development. Starting in 1986, the Indonesian authorities launched a new investment promotion drive by relaxing limits on foreign ownership for export-oriented investments and by facilitating investment licensing procedures. Further liberalisation in May 1994 allowed full foreign ownership throughout Indonesia, reduced the minimum equity holding for Indonesian partners in joint ventures to five per cent, removed all divestiture requirements, and reduced the number of sectors closed to foreign investors (listed in a negative list). The policy relied very little on incentives, except for the regulations applying to export processing zones.

This liberalisation has been part of a broader – though incomplete – process of economic reform, encompassing trade policies, the State-owned sector, the financial sector and other areas. Successive trade reforms have significantly reduced average tariff levels and simplified export procedures. In the financial sector, the relaxation of barriers to entry in banking and insurance also apply to foreign institutions although they remain subject to strict requirements. Among other things, foreign banks which have established through joint ventures with local partners do not have the freedom to locate anywhere in the country and face a minimum paid-in capital twice as high as domestic banks, while foreign insurers are only allowed in life insurance business and are subject to higher initial equity investment requirement than their domestic competitors.

The scope for further reform

In spite of policy reform over the past decade towards a less opportunistic approach to FDI, there remain a number of areas where both foreign investment and the potential for the Indonesian economy to benefit fully from those inflows are greatly impeded. In terms of trade policy, the temptation to resort to protectionist measures has not fully disappeared and certain trade restrictions remain, in particular in the form of import licences. Moreover, some specific industries, such as the chemical and the automobile sectors (with the now-abandoned national car programme), have sometimes been given preferential treatment on a discretionary basis, in order to protect them from foreign competition.

In addition, State-owned firms continue to play a dominant role in important parts of the economy, and the natural resource sector remains off limits to private investment (except through production-sharing agreements). In the banking sector, State-owned banks represented almost one half of banking assets in the mid-1990s. Public enterprises dominate industries designated as strategic by the Government, and the State still occupies a prominent role in the production of petroleum, cement, steel, aircraft, ships, chemicals, fertilisers, paper, rubber, palm oil, and tea and other cash crop estates. Public enterprises are generally sheltered from competition by investment licensing, tariffs and non-tariff barriers.

Privatisation in Indonesia has lagged behind that in other emerging markets and has had a rather limited impact on the degree of competition prevailing in the economy. Nevertheless, in those areas where privatisation has gone ahead, foreign investors have played a large role. As of March 1997, about a third of the available listed shares of Indosat, Semen Gresik and Tambang Timah were in the hands of foreign investors. The share owned by foreigners hovers around 16 per cent in the case of both PT Telkom and Bank BNI. Total privatisation proceeds amounted to around $4 billion in the seven years prior to the crisis. In July 1996 a new inter-ministerial team was set up to formulate and implement a coherent privatisation strategy.

Concerning FDI policy, the Government still retains substantial discretion to reject a foreign investment, in spite of liberalisation of the investment regime over the past decade. Approving an investment application remains a matter of discretion since all approvals for foreign investments had, until recently, to be personally signed by the President, thus encouraging discriminatory behaviour against some foreign candidates when vested national interests were involved. The approval process is symptomatic of a general lack of transparency in the implementation of Indonesian economic policies. Moreover, while some sectors were being deregulated, restrictions on market access were tightened in others such as the automobile sector and some chemical sub-sectors. This lack of consistency sends confusing signals to potential investors.

The absence of a truly competitive economic environment in the private sector because of remaining restrictions and because of a lack of an effective competition policy may deter foreign investors while, at the same time, limiting significantly the potential benefit to be derived from the presence of foreign firms in the country. De facto obstacles remain in the form of cartels (in particular in the agri-business and food sectors), price regulation, entry and exit controls, exclusive licensing and the like. In the wake of the currency and stock-market crisis that hit Indonesia in the second half of 1997, multilateral institutions made the provision of a financial assistance package conditional upon the implementation of measures to increase transparency and promote competition.

The ultimate effect of the currency crisis on the degree of openness of the Indonesian economy cannot yet be determined. It is nevertheless encouraging that the Government has committed itself to certain steps in a more open direction. Imports of some important commodities have been liberalised and some prominent cartels have been dissolved. Some of the most significant liberalisation has occurred in the area of FDI. Restrictions on foreign investment have been removed or are being dismantled in a number of areas, such as palm oil plantations and wholesale and retail trades. The negative list of sectors closed to foreigners has been revised for a period of three years. By decree, all restrictions on the foreign ownership of shares in companies listed on Indonesian stock exchanges were removed in November 1997, except those

50

involved in banking and financial services. Formerly, a 49 per cent foreign share limit was applied in all sectors for acquisitions of local companies. The Government has also pledged to end restrictions on foreign bank ownership as part of the rationalisation of the sector.

These changes, along with the significant devaluation of the rupiah which has occurred, should eventually encourage foreign firms to return to Indonesia and to adopt a more export-oriented approach. For the moment, however, the crisis is likely to imply a significant curtailment of investment projects, particularly in terms of the rate of project realisation. Sectors most affected are likely to be those involving capital-intensive projects such as oil refineries, petro-chemical plants, and power stations. A number of important infrastructure projects have been postponed and in some cases cancelled. Even before the crisis, the realisation rate for approved projects was only 50 per cent.

The crisis and the ensuing political uncertainty have severely dampened foreign investor interest. Foreign investment approvals in 1998 were only 40 per cent of the level of 1997, in spite of the continuing high number of projects receiving approval – suggesting that the size of projects is declining significantly. FDI inflows on a balance of payments basis have actually represented a net outflow of $628 million in the year to October 1998.

This study reviews the role that FDI has played in Indonesia's economic development and traces the shifts in policies towards foreign investors over time. As in many other countries, the Government has taken significant strides in recent years to improve the access of foreign investors. These reforms were already starting to bear fruit before the crisis. Together with further liberalisation measures, they could play an instrumental role in bringing the economy out of its severe slump and in continuing the slow move towards greater openness and outward orientation of the Indonesian economy.

I.   Direct investment trends in Indonesia

Overall trends

Indonesia experienced a boom in inward direct investment from the mid-1980s until the crisis. As a result, it has been the seventeenth largest recipient of FDI inflows world-wide in the 1990s and the sixth among non-OECD countries. As a percentage of GDP, FDI grew almost steadily from 0.13 per cent in 1981 to peak at 2.7 per cent in 1996 (Figure 1). These inflows are nevertheless relatively small given the large size of the economy and the attraction of its abundant natural resources. Compared to some other Southeast

Asian countries, Indonesia is not heavily reliant upon foreign equity, and foreign firms did not play a major role in Indonesian industry until the early 1990s (based on the structure of value added in industry). With few exceptions, the involvement of foreign investors in Indonesia is thus both limited and recent, although it has grown quickly recently.

Figure 1. **Net FDI inflows as a percentage of GDP, 1970-97**

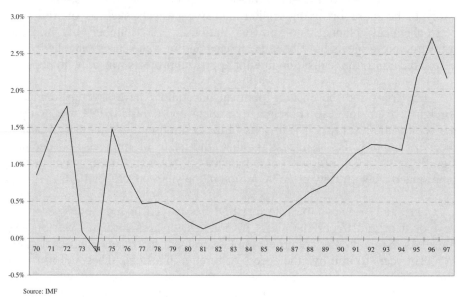

Source: IMF

The growth in foreign investment since the mid-1980s relates both to the improvement of the investment climate and to external developments. More liberal foreign investment laws were introduced or enhanced in the second half of the 1980s, a period which coincided with sharp shifts in the competitive position of firms in both Japan and the first-tier Newly Industrialising Economies (NIEs). Firms from Japan, Chinese Taipei, Korea, Singapore and Hong Kong, China and invested throughout the region in response to the higher costs of operating in their domestic markets owing to the currency revaluations, rising land and labour costs, liberalisation of home country rules on capital outflows and the loss of preferential access for home country exports to leading industrialised countries. Southeast Asia benefited strongly from these FDI flows from elsewhere in Asia. These investments have tended to be export-oriented.

The crisis and the ensuing political uncertainty have severely dampened foreign investor interest. Foreign investment approvals in 1998 were only 40 per cent of the level of 1997, in spite of the continuing high number of projects receiving approval – suggesting that the size of projects is declining significantly. FDI inflows on a balance of payments basis have actually represented a net outflow of $628 million in the year to October 1998.

Approvals data[2]

Data on foreign investment approvals, which exclude oil and gas exploration as well as financial services, reveal that by the end of 1998, cumulative approved foreign investments totalled $217 billion, with over half occurring since 1995. Indonesia experienced an investment boom after 1986, with both approved foreign and domestic investments growing quickly, partly in response to new export opportunities arising from currency realignments in Asia.

Foreign and domestic investments in all sectors except financial services and oil and gas (except refining) require approval by the Investment Co-ordinating Board (Badan Kordinasi Penamanan Modal or BKPM). The approvals data are strongly influenced by investments in oil refineries which tend to be highly capital-intensive and hence exert a strong influence on total capital invested. Of the record $40 billion in 1995, $13 billion was accounted for by proposed refinery projects. Many of these are unlikely ultimately to come to fruition. As of early 1997, BKPM approvals include $15–20 billion of investment for around ten oil refinery projects, which had been proposed against the possibility that the Government might allow domestic distribution of petroleum products by private investors. Even if such deregulation were to proceed, it was generally thought at the time that no more than four new refineries would be required.[3]

The low rate of project realisation is not confined to refineries. In some cases, projects may be withdrawn by the promoters themselves; in others approval may be revoked by the BKPM for not proceeding within the agreed timescale or failing to meet other approval requirements. Projects may be adjusted and implemented with (usually) less and (rarely) more capital outlay than initially planned. While approved investments (both foreign and domestic) remain high, there is some indication that the realisation rate of foreign investment projects has been in decline since 1992-93. It is estimated that the rate of realisation hovered around 50 per cent before the crisis for both domestic and foreign investors.[4]

This slowdown in realised investments was a concern to the Government before the crisis because of its potential impact on future export growth and hence on economic growth more generally. Encouragingly for the Government, the realisation rate has tended to be much higher in the manufacturing sector than in other sectors such as petroleum refining. Moreover, realisation rates have been particularly high among export-oriented manufacturers.[5] The realisation rate is likely to fall further in the wake of the crisis, as a result of the postponement or cancellation of a number of large capital-intensive projects such as oil refineries, power stations and large-scale chemicals and metallurgy plants.

Another indicator of the attractiveness of Indonesia as a location for investment is the extent to which investors expand their operations once they are established. Before the crisis, three out of four foreign investors had applied for an expansion of their initial investment at least once, 60 per cent twice and 25 per cent had expanded three times.[6] These results were perceived by BKPM as proof of Indonesia's sustained attractiveness and of the profitability of foreign investment.

Sectoral distribution

Two thirds of approved foreign investments are in manufacturing, almost half of which is in the chemicals sector, including in oil refining (Table 1). Paper and pulp rank second, highlighting the interest of foreign investors in the processing of Indonesia's vast natural resources. FDI in export-oriented, labour-intensive industries such as textiles and clothing, footwear, or consumer electronics accounted for 15 per cent of total FDI in 1995. The textile industry share has been dropping rapidly and now accounts for only 3.3 per cent of cumulative inflows. Foreign firms are nevertheless important in this sector through non-equity links such as sub-contracting. In contrast, although the electronics sector still accounts for a tiny share of total manufacturing, it has been growing quite strongly recently, mainly as a result of Japanese investments.

In the service sector, most of the investment has been in infrastructure projects (e.g. toll roads) and utilities (electricity, water and gas) as a result of the recent opening to both domestic and foreign private sector participation in these areas. Private participation by both domestic and foreign firms has been encouraged in the power industry under a variety of BOO (build-own-operate) or BOT (build-operate-transfer) arrangements. Domestic business groups have often entered into joint ventures with foreign firms to establish plants. In the power sector, a major development was the signing of a BOO agreement for the construction of the coal-fired Paiton II power station in East Java by PT Java Power, a consortium comprising the German firm Siemens, the UK firm PowerGen, and a unit of the Bimantara conglomerate.

Table 1. **Foreign investment approvals by sector** ($ million)

	1996	*1997*	*1998*	*1967-98*	
Primary	**3 218**	**465**	**998**	**16 900**	**7.8%**
Agriculture	1 306	437	965	6 092	2.8%
Fisheries	80	27	33	639	0.3%
Forestry	135	-	0	637	0.3%
Mining	1 697	2	0	9 532	4.4%
Secondary	**16 075**	**23 017**	**8 389**	**139 241**	**64.3%**
Food	691	573	342	5 663	2.6%
Textiles	514	373	217	7 197	3.3%
Wood	101	70	71	1 475	0.7%
Paper	2 907	5 353	41	25 925	12.0%
Chemicals	7 362	12 376	6 179	65 055	30.0%
Non-metal minerals	793	1 457	237	7 116	3.3%
Basic metals	651	357	394	8 447	3.9%
Metal goods	2 938	2 322	891	17 727	8.2%
Other	74	126	17	636	0.3%
Tertiary	**10 638**	**10 350**	**4 177**	**60 354**	**27.9%**
Construction	297	307	198	1 787	0.8%
Hotels	1 716	463	451	11 200	5.2%
Housing/office building	3 000	1 398	1 271	12 411	5.7%
Transport	695	5 900	79	14 495	6.7%
Utilities/trading/other	4 933	2 283	2 178	20 461	9.5%
Total	**29 931**	**33 832**	**13 563**	**216 494**	

Source: BKPM, as reported to Bank Indonesia

The power sector has been particularly hard hit by the turmoil. As a result of the financial crisis, 13 out of the 29 privately-funded power plants already approved by the Government have been postponed. In early January 1998, 12 infrastructure projects that were postponed or placed under review were cancelled. Similarly, two oil refineries, 29 toll roads, a bridge linking the islands of Java and Madura, and a transport terminal in Jakarta were cancelled.

By 1998, inflows in all sectors were below the peak levels reached in the mid-1990s. Only in agriculture did inflows recover from 1997 levels. The chemicals sector represented one half of approvals in 1998, though many of these projects may never be realised. Large, capital-intensive projects such as pulp and paper are substantially down from earlier levels.

Oil and gas sector

Foreign participation in the oil and gas sector is not considered as direct investment. Yet under production-sharing contracts with the State-oil firm Pertamina, private international oil companies have been the dominant force in the industry, accounting for 95 per cent of crude production (with an estimated $43 billion of export, development and production expenditure over the 14 years to 1995 alone). Outlays by international (in particular American) firms have been the driving force in the development of Indonesia's oil industry. European enterprises have also invested significantly in the development of Indonesia's petroleum sector. British Gas, British Petroleum, Enterprise Oil, Shell Petroleum and Total all operate in oil and gas activities.

Sources of FDI

Overseas private investment in Indonesia originates from more than 40 countries. The major foreign direct investors in Indonesia are shown in Table 2. The ten top investing nations account for almost 90 per cent of all foreign approvals since 1967. With a large domestic market, Indonesia has had more scope to pursue import substitution. It attracted investment from Japan early on to sell in the domestic market but has been less prominent as an export platform for foreign investors. It is also the most resource rich of the countries in the region and has drawn in investment in these sectors. Although the BKPM reports that manufacturing is the main activity for all of the main investors except Singapore, figures for FDI outflows from Japan and the United States to Indonesia show that non-manufacturing is significantly more important than manufacturing for these investors.

Table 2. **Foreign investment approvals by country** ($ million)

	96	*97*	*98*	*1967-98*	*shares**
Japan	7 655	5 421	1 331	**34 778**	21.6%
UK	3 391	5 474	4 745	**24 353**	15.1%
Singapore	3 130	2 299	1 267	**18 360**	11.4%
Hong Kong, China	1 106	251	549	**14 411**	8.9%
US	642	1 018	568	**10 219**	6.3%
Chinese Taipei	535	3 415	165	**12 795**	7.9%
S. Korea	1 231	1 410	202	**8 976**	5.6%
Malaysia	1 393	2 289	1 060	**6 629**	4.1%
Australia	450	187	85	**6 547**	4.1%
Germany	165	4 468	71	**6 309**	3.9%
Netherlands	1 330	319	412	**5 651**	3.5%
Thailand	1 611	19	3	**1 769**	1.1%
France	71	457	8	**1 465**	0.9%
Joint projects among two or more investing countries	5 051	5 529	2 718	**55 225**	
Others	10 233	7 600	3 520	**9 007**	5.6%

*excludes joint projects

Total	**29 931**	**33 832**	**13 563**	**216 494**	

Source: BKPM, as reported to Bank Indonesia

Approvals from almost all countries fell in 1998 compared to a year earlier. Japanese firms were particularly cautious, with investment in 1998 only one sixth of the level of two years earlier. UK firms have been the largest investors since 1995, and their investments have fallen by much less than those of other foreign investors.

Japanese firms have invested more in Indonesia than in any other Southeast Asian country. In 1985, almost half of the total flow of Japanese FDI to East Asia was to Indonesia, mostly in natural resource industries and labour-intensive manufacturing. By 1996, Indonesia still held more Japanese FDI than any other Asian developing country, but its share had fallen to only one quarter of the cumulative stock of Japanese direct investment in non-OECD Asia. In total, six of the top ten investors in Indonesia come from within the Asian region itself.

Investment by firms from Singapore has been encouraged by the establishment of so-called growth triangles. As Singapore's production costs have risen, manufacturing plants have increasingly moved to Johore (Malaysia) and Riau, although the design, marketing and distribution of goods has remained in Singapore. Capitalising on low-cost land and labour in Riau, and Johore's abundance of semi-skilled labour, the Singapore-Johore-Riau triangle has created a wide manufacturing base benefiting from greater scale economies and relying on vertical integration.[7]

Table 3 classifies major home countries by group. OECD countries loom larger in Indonesia than in other neighbouring countries, partly because Indonesia's downstream oil and gas sector is dominated by US and European firms.[8] The emerging Asian economies (NIE3[9]) are the most active investors in the primary (mining excluded) and tertiary sectors and in the less sophisticated manufacturing industries. Much of the NIE investment in the primary and secondary sectors is from Chinese Taipei and Hong Kong, China, while Singapore firms are most important in the service sector. OECD investors, notably Japanese and UK firms, dominate many manufacturing sectors, with OECD investments particularly strong in the chemicals, paper and metal goods sectors.

Although they may be less active than in some neighbouring countries, firms from the NIEs were progressively increasing their investments before the crisis by relocating manufacturing facilities in the face of rising costs in their respective countries. Since the onset of the crisis, Singapore and Hong Kong, China have maintained or increased investments, while Korea and Chinese Taipei have reduced theirs. Korean firms are almost certainly likely to be less active abroad in the near term because of problems at home.

Direct investment from other Asian countries was already important in Indonesia by 1970, exceeding investments by both European and US firms.[10] Developing country investments were overshadowed by Japanese investment between 1977 and 1985 but have recently rebounded sharply. Since January 1992, firms from NIEs have accounted for 40 per cent of approvals in value terms (and 45 per cent in number of projects), compared to 31 per cent for the period 1967-97. Most of these projects have come from South Korea, Singapore and Hong Kong, China. Chinese Taipei has simply kept its share constant over the most recent period. Malaysian and Thai investment was growing immediately before the crisis. The NIEs have invested about three times more than Japan in Indonesia over the past five years.

Table 3. **Foreign investment approvals by country and sector**
(based on cumulative flows, 1967-96)

Sectors	NIE3	Japan	Other OECD
Primary	**31%**	**4%**	**65%**
Food Crops	68%	11%	22%
Plantation	43%	1%	56%
Livestock	49%	2%	48%
Fisheries	61%	30%	9%
Forestry	68%	3%	29%
Mining	5%	0%	95%
Secondary	**28%**	**28%**	**44%**
Food	25%	12%	63%
Textiles/Footwear	43%	39%	18%
Wood	53%	24%	22%
Paper	52%	16%	32%
Pharmaceuticals	8%	13%	78%
Chemical	20%	18%	62%
Non-Metallic Minerals	24%	36%	40%
Basic Metals	13%	49%	38%
Metal Goods	17%	60%	24%
Other	18%	39%	43%
Tertiary	**47%**	**14%**	**39%**
Electricity/Gas/Water	51%	10%	39%
Construction	44%	4%	51%
Trade	83%	13%	4%
Hotels/Restaurants	44%	9%	47%
Transport	24%	13%	64%
Housing/Real Estate/Industrial Estates	66%	17%	17%
Office Building	52%	28%	19%
Other	41%	26%	33%
Total	**33%**	**24%**	**44%**

NIE3: Chinese Taipei, Singapore and Hong Kong, China

Other OECD: Australia, Germany, Korea, the Netherlands, the UK and the US

n.b. The largest investor in each sector is highlighted.

Source: Investment Coordinating Board

The kind of investment that dominates has also changed along with the source of FDI: direct investors from neighbouring Asian economies are coming for reasons that differ from those that were most common in the past and they are likely to have different objectives from OECD investors. The majority of very recent investors from developing Asia come to Indonesia to serve export markets previously supplied from their home base, rather than to serve the Indonesian market. More than half of these foreign firms plan to export most of their output from the host country. These so-called mobile exporters have sought new manufacturing sites primarily to maintain low costs, rather than to escape quota restrictions.[11] Indonesia was an obvious choice, given overcrowding in Thailand and labour shortages leading to rising wages in Malaysia. As indicated in Table 4, with the exception of Hong Kong Chinese investors who are heavily involved in the chemicals sector, firms from Singapore, Korea and Chinese Taipei tend to have much less capital invested in their projects than OECD investors.

Table 4. **Capital intensity of foreign investment projects by country**
($ million, number)

	Total inflows 1967-98	Number of projects	Average capital intensity
UK	24 353	281	86.7
Germany	6 309	142	44.4
Hong Kong, China	14 411	384	37.5
Japan	34 779	1 070	32.5
US	10 219	330	31.0
Netherlands	5 651	206	27.4
Malaysia	6 629	268	24.7
Singapore	18 360	828	22.2
Australia	6 547	345	19.0
Chinese Taipei	12 795	683	18.7
S. Korea	8 976	587	15.3
Others	67 465	1 416	47.6
Total	**216 494**	**6 540**	**33.1**

Source: BKPM

Direct investment abroad by Indonesian firms

Indonesian firms have invested very little abroad so far. Most outward direct investments are realised by large conglomerates, such as Bakrie Brothers (distributive trade), the Lippo or the Salim groups. There are some investments in the former Soviet Union but little else, although Indonesian firms have started investing in neighbouring countries, primarily in Malaysia and Thailand, under the growth triangle schemes. In 1990, for instance, Indonesia's FDI into Malaysia of $400 million made it the third largest foreign investor, largely due to relaxation of foreign exchange controls by Indonesia.[12] Indonesia was again the third largest foreign direct investor into Malaysia in 1993.

II. The evolution of the overall policy environment[13]

Over the past three decades, the Indonesian economy has been gradually opening up, while reducing its dependence on oil as a major source of foreign exchange. The changing conditions prevailing in the oil sector have been a major determinant of successive policy shifts. Although the reforms have brought considerable change in economic orientation, the basic idea of import-substituting industrialisation which dominated the economic strategy right after independence has not been fully discarded. It is now combined with some export-orientation. The long term impact of the crisis on the overall policy environment is not yet clear.

As in the Philippines, the period immediately following independence witnessed rising economic nationalism resulting in declining real incomes, high inflation and spiralling government debt. The change of government in the mid-1960s restored macroeconomic stability and reversed the earlier inward-looking policies. The trade regime was liberalised and a more favourable stance adopted towards private investment, including foreign investment. The import licensing system was completely abolished and, while there were some upward adjustments in tariffs in 1968, import protection was reduced. Most domestic price controls were also eliminated. Some nationalised enterprises were returned to previous owners and a new Foreign Investment Law that provided a 30-year guarantee of non-nationalisation and compensation was enacted in 1967.

Over time, however, certain restrictive measures were reimposed, and import substitution remained the dominant philosophy, as a wide range of locally-made final consumer goods (including light consumer goods and consumer durables) replaced imports. This led to the growth of the textile industry, as well as various engineering goods industries which assembled imported final consumer goods. As a result, although the traditional manufacturing sectors, such as food and tobacco, continued to dominate in the mid-1970s, the textile industry became significant, representing 16 per cent of manufacturing production and almost 30 per cent of employment.

As the domestic market for most basic consumer goods gradually became saturated by the mid-1970s, Indonesia's policy-makers — buoyed by a strong economic performance, vastly increased oil revenues and the boom in primary commodity prices — promoted upstream investment in basic resource-processing and intermediate good industries. This move was strongly influenced by the perceived need to maintain growth of manufacturing in order to improve the balance of Indonesia's trade in manufactured goods, as well as to broaden and deepen Indonesia's industrial structure through backward and forward linkages. As a result, although the traditional sectors of food, beverages and tobacco and textiles still dominated in 1984, sectors such as basic metals, rubber products and chemical products were growing quickly.

Although Indonesia was relatively successful in moderating exchange rate appreciation induced by the oil and commodity boom, the appreciation that did occur increased pressures to protect domestic non-oil producers from imports. At that time, the trade and investment regime was increasingly State-dominated and inward-looking, and the regulations on foreign and domestic investment were gradually tightened (World Bank 1993).

The end of the oil boom era in 1982 ushered in the third phase in Indonesia's industrial growth based on an export-oriented strategy. The drop in oil revenues led to the rescheduling of the ambitious, large-scale, industrial projects which the Government had planned to set up during the second stage of import substitution in early 1983. Recognising the need for greater private sector participation, the Government simplified the cumbersome regulatory framework and reduced the anti-export bias of the highly protectionist trade regime. While the shift to a more liberal and outward-looking policy was still ambiguous in the period 1982-1985, the dramatic decline in the price of oil in early 1986 and the appreciation of the yen, which led to a deterioration in the balance of payments and huge budget deficits, gave the Government the final push to go ahead with reform and liberalisation. Deregulation and outward-orientation have been stressed since the mid-1980s, and export promotion is the major goal of FDI policy.

Trade reform

The trade reform launched in the mid-1980s aimed at alleviating the effects of the high-cost economy on exports. Prior to the reform, extensive protection was granted in particular to State-owned enterprises and upstream import-substituting industries dominated by politically favoured individuals, while downstream labour-intensive industries, with considerable export potential, received low levels of protection.[14] The anti-export bias of the trade regime was due to the high cost of imported inputs as well as to heavy export controls, including bans, quotas or taxes on agricultural and wood products. The devaluation and the maintenance of a low real effective exchange rate also helped to boost exports.

Trade reform packages (involving export incentives, as well as simplified import and export procedures) followed almost annually from 1986 to 1991. On the whole, tariff levels have fallen considerably since 1985 (Table 5).[15] The Government has also moved to dismantle the complex import licensing system and to phase out non-tariff barriers (NTBs).[16] In response to the decline in, and frequent uncertainties surrounding, international oil prices, Indonesia's trade strategy has been to try to stimulate exports through further trade liberalisation, with three reform packages between 1994 and 1996. The coverage of restrictive NTBs has also fallen dramatically.

Table 5. **Average tariffs before and after deregulation**
(per cent)

	pre-1985	1986	1990	1992	1994	1995	1996
Unweighted tariffs	37	27	22	20	19.5	15.4	14.6
Weighted tariffs							
based on imports	22	13	11	11	13.7	12.5	n.a.
based on production	29	19	17	11.8	10.4	8.2	n.a.

Source: Government of Indonesia Official Decrees and World Bank Estimates

In spite of these significant reforms, some important sectors (engineering goods, paper products, and food processing, as well as a number of agricultural goods) are still protected by NTBs. The same holds true for licences which have been maintained on goods equivalent to about one quarter of domestic production. For a number of goods (in particular agricultural goods) import monopolies may be granted to designated importers such as the six State trading companies or to Bulog, the Government's agricultural marketing agency, or to Pertamina. The business licensing system can be said to be a significant barrier to entry of new firms. Moreover, heavy export controls still exist on natural resource-based products, affecting over half of Indonesia's non-oil exports.[17] Extensive local content requirements and sanitary regulations further restrict trade.[18]

A recent illustration of this protectionist trend was given in early 1996 when the Government introduced special 20 per cent tariff surcharges[19] on imports of ethylene and propylene, which are the two main products produced by a recently completed $2 billion petrochemical plant. Another was the national car programme which the Government argued was essential to developing Indonesia's industrial base ahead of AFTA and APEC forum obligations bringing down tariff walls. The car programme has since been abandoned.

Competition policy

Among the various policy initiatives, one area which is deemed insufficient by many observers is competition policy. While greater liberalisation in other domains has significantly improved the potential for foreign investors in Indonesia, there remain numerous obstacles to both foreign and domestic investment such as weak property rights and passive competition policy. The four firm concentration ratio[20] at the three digit industry level for Indonesia's manufacturing sector peaked at 61 per cent in 1987 and declined thereafter to 50 per cent in 1992. While the evolution is towards less concentration, the level is still high and constitutes a barrier to firms interested in the local market. Significant improvements have nevertheless been made in certain sectors such as the footwear and electrical machinery equipment industries, where concentration dropped from 60 and 71 to 20 and 35 respectively.[21]

Table 6 summarises these various obstacles to private investment (both foreign and domestic) and identifies the sectors in which they were prevalent up to 1997. Numerous reforms have been undertaken since the crisis.

The financial turmoil has given new momentum to further initiatives in this area. As a result of successive agreements with the International Monetary Fund, imports of sugar, wheat, soybeans and garlic are no longer to be controlled by Bulog. Bulog's monopoly is now limited solely to rice. Tariffs are to be cut on chemicals (previously excluded from the liberalisation move in order to protect the Chandra Asri petrochemical plant), metals and fish; and export taxes for metal ores and rattan are also being cancelled. Restrictive marketing arrangements for cement, paper and plywood were eliminated in February 1998 while price controls on cement were abolished as early as November 1997.

Table 6. **Obstacles to foreign investment prior to the crisis**

Type of restriction	Sectors in which prevalent
Cartels	Cement, plywood, paper, fertiliser
Price controls	Cement, sugar, rice
Entry and exit controls	Plywood, retail trade
Exclusive licensing	Clove-marketing, soymeal, wheat-flour milling
Public-sector dominance	Steel, fertiliser, refined oil products

Source: World Bank, as reported in the *Far Eastern Economic Review*, 16 October 1997

In addition, domestic trade in all agricultural products was fully deregulated and the Clove Marketing Board was eliminated in June 1998. Moreover, budgetary and extra-budgetary support and credit privileges granted to IPTN's airplane projects were discontinued as of January 1998. Lastly, all special tax, customs and credit privileges for the National Car project were revoked. The enactment of these reforms constitutes a major step towards a more open environment for both foreign and domestic private investment.

Privatisation

State enterprises once dominated the economy, but the private sector now accounts for more than 80 per cent of total national output (as of 1995) and 76 per cent of investment (up from 56 per cent in 1980). Public enterprises dominate the so-called strategic industries[22], and the State is still a dominant actor in the production of petroleum, cement, steel, aircraft, ships, chemicals, fertilisers, and paper, as well as in rubber, palm oil, tea and other cash crops. Public enterprises are generally sheltered from competition by investment licensing, tariffs and non-tariff barriers. Privatisation initiatives have typically had a rather limited impact on the degree of competition prevailing in the economy.

Although still in its initial stage, the privatisation process has recently been boosted further by the need to reduce Indonesia's external debt. The privatisation of State assets is increasingly seen as an important source of funds, since revenues from privatisation are directed to support debt repayment. Privatisation proceeds have exceeded $4 billion in the 1990s. The privatisation process has been accelerating recently; a Presidential decree issued on 8 July 1996 set up a new inter-ministerial team to formulate and implement a coherent privatisation strategy.

So far two telecommunications companies (PT Telkom and PT Indosat), a mining company (PT Tambang Timah), a cement factory (Semen Gresik) and a bank (BNI - Bank Negara Indonesia) have already been privatised. The sale of PT Telekom alone raised $1.68 billion. The Government is now focusing on the State airline, Garuda, which was to be partially privatised by December 1998. Another State commercial bank (BDN - Bank Dagang Negara), as well as steelmaker PT Krakatau Steel, toll road constructor PT Jasa Marga and subsidiaries of state electricity firm PLN (Perusahaan Listrik Negara) are also on the list.

Private foreign investors have been active in the privatisation process. As of March 1997, about a third of the available listed shares of Indosat, Semen Gresik and Tambang Timah were in the hands of foreign investors. The share owned by foreigners hovers around 16 per cent in the case of both PT Telkom and Bank BNI.[23]

In the wake of the financial crisis the Government has committed itself to further privatisations and a master plan for privatisation was nearing completion towards the end of 1998 (privatisation is expected in the cement industry, some areas of telecommunications, mining, plantations, and infrastructure). State-owned banks are to be prepared for privatisation by the year 2001.

III.   Indonesian policies towards FDI

Foreign investors requesting incentives, including tariff exemptions for imports, require approval from the Investment Co-ordinating Board (BKPM) which remains a matter of discretion. Approval has typically depended on an assessment of the suitability of the project, with reference to the Government's sectoral, technology, market and financial policies. The obligation to obtain such a recommendation concerning sectoral policies has since been removed for all sectors except mining, energy, palm oil plantations and fisheries.

All approvals over $100 million must be signed by the President. Investment approvals under that value are signed by the Minister for Investment/Chairman of BKPM. Export performance requirements are no longer a pre-condition for approval. Although domestic investors must also seek approval, they are treated differently. Approvals for investments in oil and gas, mining, banking and insurance are handled by the relevant ministries. Until recently, foreign investors were prohibited from acquiring more than 49 per cent of the shares of a local company listed on the Indonesian Stock Exchange. This restriction now remains only in banking and financial services.

Equity restrictions in certain sectors are contained in a Negative List which has been shortened significantly recently. Foreigners may not own land, but joint ventures established under Indonesian law can obtain title to land for business operations for a period of 35 years, renewable for another 25 years. Based on a 1996 decree[24], certain industrial sectors might be able to obtain fiscal investment incentives. The criteria for granting incentives is currently under consideration.

The policy stance towards FDI in Indonesia has traditionally been conditioned on developments in the oil market. Although FDI regulation was relatively liberal in the early 1970s, Indonesia made little effort to attract foreign investors before the collapse of oil prices in the late 1980s. Since then, the regulation has been more and more liberal with a view to boosting non-oil exports. The overall direction of Indonesian investment policy is to promote investments which increase non-oil exports[25], encourage processing of raw materials into finished goods, use local products or components, transfer technology and skills and save foreign exchange. Investments are also encouraged where local capital is limited or where advanced technology is needed. Most investments are structured as joint ventures to foster the development of domestic industries.

Industries performing a vital function in national defence, such as those producing arms, ammunition, explosives and war equipment are closed to foreign investment (1967 Law). Foreign investment in mining is to be carried out in co-operation with the Government on the basis of a work contract. Such restrictions are in line with Constitutional provisions emphasising the need to preserve the country's independence.

Under Indonesian law, the exploitation of petroleum and gas resources is reserved to the State[26]. The State oil company Pertamina directly operates a number of fields; explores for and produces oil and gas on its own account; operates refineries and supplies petroleum products to the domestic market; and conducts overseas sales of crude oil, refined products and liquefied natural gas. Pertamina also supervises the activities of more than a hundred private foreign oil and gas contractors operating under production sharing contracts. Under such arrangements, the contractors are entitled to be compensated for operating costs and capital investment in the form of retained crude oil, with the balance of oil production ("share oil") being divided between the Government and the contractor at a pre-determined ratio.

To promote foreign investment in manufacturing, the Government has steadily reduced tariffs and restrictions on imports of key manufactured inputs and simplified administrative procedures. Foreign investors are also given a number of investment guarantees and protection. The law guarantees that after-tax profits, depreciation of capital assets and proceeds from sales of shares to Indonesian persons may be repatriated in the original investment currency at the prevailing exchange rate.

In spite of greater opportunities for foreign investors, there remains a discrepancy sometimes between the degree of openness stipulated in the law and the actual scope for foreign investment on the ground. The recent experience of Malaysian investors who were refused the right to invest in Indonesian palm oil industry is one example.[27] The complexity of the approval process also acts as a brake on investment. Both foreign and domestic investors complain about cumbersome and time-consuming licensing procedures, and a survey of Japanese firms ranked the complexity of administrative procedures as the main obstacle to doing business in Indonesia.[28]

Background

Except for a brief window of opportunity following the change of government in the mid-1960s, Indonesia was relatively closed to foreign investors until late 1980s. There had been almost no foreign investment under the Sukarno regime, and those Dutch firms remaining after independence were nationalised in 1958. The Suharto government initially welcomed foreign investment as part of policies designed to restore macroeconomic stability and promote growth. Attracting FDI was not a high priority when compared with recent incentive programmes, but FDI policy was relatively liberal.

The Foreign Capital Investment Act 1967 (subsequently amended by the Foreign Capital Investment Law of 1970) was very generous in providing and safeguarding benefits for the investors. It permitted foreign companies to invest in projects approved by the Government and to operate in Indonesia for a period of up to 30 years with guaranteed rights of profit repatriation and protection against expropriation[29]. Foreign investors in priority sectors were exempted from corporation tax for 2 to 6 years, depending on the location of the facility in Indonesia, on its size and its market orientation.[30] Under this open door policy, 100 per cent foreign ownership was allowed and there was no obligation for foreign investors to transfer a given share of the company's equity to Indonesian interests. The decision to liberalise the capital account in 1971 was also favourable to foreign investors. There was no specific promotion of import substituting firms.

In the course of the 1970s, because oil provided foreign exchange and capital, as well as opportunities to borrow from international banks, there was no real urgency to attract FDI. As a result increasingly severe conditions were placed on foreign investors. Moreover student protests against foreign investment and other manifestations of economic nationalism also discouraged greater openness. The rules governing the employment of expatriates and the importing of machinery and materials were gradually tightened, the range of activities closed to foreign investment was increased and rigid requirements were imposed with regard to local partnerships and equity divestment. Full foreign ownership was prohibited, foreign participation in joint ventures was limited to 80 per cent, and at least 51 per cent of the company's equity had to be transferred to Indonesian nationals within 10 years. This process culminated in the revocation of the tax holiday under the 1984 tax laws, which also lowered the corporate income tax rate. These policies, combined with a major recession, reduced FDI flows in the mid-1980s. Foreign investors returned as the economy recovered and as the new, lower tax rate offset the elimination of tax holidays.[31]

With the tightening resource constraints imposed on the Government by changing external economic conditions, the investment downturn observed in the mid-1980s triggered a comprehensive reappraisal of Indonesia's foreign investment policy, leading to a new investment promotion drive after 1986. The new FDI policy relaxed maximum foreign ownership requirements for export-oriented investments and simplified investment licensing procedures. The first package of deregulatory reforms in 1986 liberalised equity restrictions on foreign ownership for export-oriented joint ventures (defined as those exporting 80 per cent of production, later modified to 60 per cent). Export-oriented investments could have up to 95 per cent foreign equity (compared to 80 per cent previously). In an attempt to do away with its bureaucratic reputation, BKPM also simplified its application forms and promised a reduction of the delays in making decisions.[32] This first package was followed by almost annual reforms, resulting in a considerable relaxation of the terms governing foreign investments.

The salient features of the 1987 package were the easing of investment regulations, the gradual opening of more sectors to foreign investors and the promotion of private over public investment. Since 1987, the number of sectors open to foreign investment has steadily increased, the minimum initial capitalisation requirement for foreign investment projects has been reduced, and the strictures on expatriate employment and the use of imported inputs have been eased.

In 1989, the BKPM scrapped a cumbersome positive list of areas open to foreign investors and replaced it with the Negative Investment List. The Negative List is "effective for three years and subject to annual review if considered necessary according to the needs and development of the situation". The list defines the fields of activity completely closed to domestic and foreign investments, those that are closed to foreign investors only, those where 100 per cent foreign ownership is prohibited and other areas where foreign investment is permitted subject to certain restrictions and limitations. The list opened more than 300 sectors to foreign investors, with only six sectors remaining completely closed to foreigners. Although retailing was closed to foreigners, FDI in this field occurred under the guise of loans and franchise arrangements.[33] Wholly-owned foreign firms are allowed to establish export houses and import firms solely importing goods for further processing and re-export.

Under the new regulations introduced gradually between 1989 and 1994, 100 per cent foreign equity ownership was permitted in most sectors subject to certain strict conditions (*i*) total paid-up capital was at least $50 million; (*ii*) the company was located outside Java; and (*iii*) the company was located in a bonded area and all its output was exported. In the two Indonesian duty-free zones, 95 per cent foreign ownership was allowed. Otherwise, foreign ownership in new projects was limited to 80 per cent for total investment of at least $1 million.

In 1993, there was a step back from liberalisation as the divestment requirement became more restrictive: 51 per cent of a company's equity had to be handed over to local interests within 15 years (compared to 20 per cent as stated in the April 1992 deregulation).

The 1994 reform package

These reforms failed to deliver the expected investment. FDI approvals declined sharply and investors complained of continuing difficulties in operating in Indonesia. In response, the Government undertook further liberalisation in May 1994.[34] According to a GATT Trade Policy Review of Indonesia, this reform was the result of the Government's concern that slower growth of inward FDI was beginning to inhibit export performance[35]. The reform package constitutes a significant step towards a much more conducive and attractive investment environment and reflects the growing competition for FDI faced by Indonesia from neighbouring economies, such as China and Vietnam.

As a result of the 1994 reform package:

    i)   permits 100 per cent foreign ownership throughout Indonesia, although priority will be given to projects in established bonded zones or industrial estates wherever feasible;

    ii)   lifts the previous requirement for wholly foreign-owned companies to have a minimum paid-up capital of $50 million and permits investors to determine capital outlays based on the commercial viability of the project;

iii) significantly relaxes the domestic partnership and divestment requirements introduced in 1974. The obligation for foreign investors to establish joint ventures with local partners and to prepare for the transfer of at least 51 per cent of the company's equity to Indonesian ownership has been abolished. Only a token divestment of as little as 5 per cent is required after 15 years[36];

iv) reduces the minimum equity holding for Indonesian partners in joint ventures from 20 to 5 per cent and requires no further divestment in this case. This increased equity limit also applies to joint ventures in deregulated strategic industries listed below;

v) allows foreign and Indonesian partners to determine changes in the composition of share ownership;

vi) sets 30-year validity for foreign investment licences with a possible 30-year extension additional investment is undertaken.

After 1994, foreign firms or joint ventures were allowed to acquire up to 49 per cent of a listed local company. This minority restriction was eliminated in early 1998 except in banking and finance. Foreign investors were also allowed to enter previously closed strategic sectors, such as ports, shipping, civil aviation, railways, telecommunications, energy sectors, nuclear power, education and other infrastructure projects (water supply), through joint ventures with State enterprises. Full ownership was not permitted. Although the regulation also allowed foreign joint ventures in the mass media, current laws governing the press prevent application of the regulation to this sector.[37]

Liberalisation has gained new momentum during the financial crisis. Retail and wholesale trade have been opened for foreign investment in partnership with Indonesian investors, and a revised and shortened Negative Investment List was issued on 2 July 1998 (Box 1).

Box 1. **Negative Investment List** (Presidential Decree 96/1998)

I. Sectors closed to both foreign and domestic investment

A. Primary sector
  cultivation and processing of marijuana and the like
  exploitation of sponges
  contractors of forest logging
  uranium mining

B. Secondary sector
  manufacture of penta chlorophenol, ddt, dieldrin, chlordane
  production of pulp using sulphite processing or whitening chlor.
  alkaline chloride industries using mercury process.
  manufacturing of cyclamate and saccharine
  processing of mangrove wood to produce finished/semi-finished goods
  liquor/alcoholic beverages
  firecrackers and fireworks
  explosive materials and the like
  manufacturing of weapons and related components
  printing of valuable papers: postage stamps, duty stamps, commercial paper of
    Bank Indonesia, passports

c. Tertiary sector
  casino/gambling

ii. Sectors closed for investment in which part of the shares are owned by foreign citizens or foreign legal entities

A. Primary sector
  freshwater fish and freshwater fish cultures
  forest utilisation right

B. Tertiary sector
  taxi/bus transport
  local shipping
  private television and radio broadcasting services, newspaper and magazines
  operation of cinemas
  spectrum management of radio frequency and satellite orbit
  trade services and its support services
        except:
        retailer (mall, supermarket, department store, shopping centre),
        distribution/wholesaler, restaurant, quality certification services, market
        research services, and after sales services
  medical services: general, delivery, specialist and dental clinics.

Source : BKPM

Incentives

Incentives primarily take the form of import duty exemptions on capital goods used in the production process. Tax holidays were eliminated in 1984 but were restored in July 1996.

All investment projects, both domestic and foreign, approved by BKPM are granted a number of facilities under given conditions. Exemption or relief from import duties is granted for capital goods or raw materials (in the latter case the exemption is restricted to two years of full production). Further tax incentives may also be granted for any industry or project considered as a national priority in terms of export or for the development of a remote area.

Many incentives are also provided to encourage exports of manufactured products: restitution of import duties on goods and materials needed to manufacture the finished products for export, exemption from VAT and sales tax on luxury goods and materials purchased domestically, to be used in the manufacturing of the exported products. Lastly, the company can import raw materials required regardless of the availability of comparable domestic products.

Industrial estates, bonded zones and export processing entrepots

After several unsuccessful attempts to create export-processing zones, the Government created an organisation in the Ministry of Finance that was charged with providing duty exemptions and duty drawbacks for exporters. As a result, an exporter would no longer have to locate in an export-processing zone to qualify for duty-free imports, provided it met certain conditions. In addition, Indonesia created an investment area on Batam island just off Singapore, where export firms were exempt from Indonesian ownership requirements and other regulations.

Although foreign investors may now locate anywhere, priority will be given to the location of projects in established bonded zones or industrial estates[38] wherever feasible. Seven bonded zones have been established.[39] Since April 1996, private firms have been allowed to develop and manage bonded zones, formerly the prerogative of State-owned companies. Perhaps one tenth of foreign investment is located in bonded areas.

Companies located in the bonded areas or having export-processing entrepot status are provided with additional incentives: exemption from import duty and other taxes on imports of capital goods and equipment including raw materials for the production process. They are also allowed to divert products amounting to one quarter of their export volume or shipment of goods to other bonded zones, to the Indonesian customs area, through normal import procedures including payment of customs duties. They are exempted from value added tax and sales tax on luxury goods on the delivery of products for further processing from bonded zones to their subcontractors outside the bonded zones or the other way around as well as among companies in these areas. Another major advantage of the bonded areas is that they offer a one-stop agency.

Growth triangles

To facilitate the movement of labour-intensive activities to Riau, the Batam Industrial Corporation, which is jointly owned by Singaporean and Indonesian public and private sector interests, was created. In addition to securing all necessary permits from the Indonesian Government, the Corporation makes factory premises available on 30-year leases and supplies low-cost labour. Investment is attracted by a number of financial incentives, including a provision that allows foreigners to hold 100 per cent equity in businesses for the first five years, after which 5 per cent must be divested. Major projects in Riau include: the Bintan Beach International Resort, a light industrial estate on Bintan island, a water supply project, and an oil terminal and marine petroleum processing complex on Karimun island.

Batam island has attracted investors mostly in electronics. The largest impact of the triangle has been on the Riau islands which had previously been largely untouched by economic development. Eight industrial estates have been established, the most important of which is the Batam Industrial Park which in 1994 had 32 000 employees and $600 million worth of exports.

IV.   Financial sector reform and restrictions on FDI

From the time of independence until 1965, an increasingly large share of the financial sector came under Government control. The second wave of reform launched in the late 1960s reversed the direction of the process. The New Order gradually took steps to reduce the degree of centralisation and Government control and foreign banks were gradually let in even though their activities remained highly restricted. The need for a reform of the financial sector was felt as a result of the end of the oil boom and the ensuing drop in Government revenue (World Bank 1993).

Banking reform

A major banking reform was launched in 1983 to improve the efficiency of the financial system by easing restraints on the activities of both private and State-owned banks[40]. The reform involved the elimination of the system of credit allocation by Bank Indonesia, the removal of the number of categories of credit for which banks would be refinanced from Bank Indonesia on favourable terms, the clearing of controls on most deposit rates paid by banks and on all loans except these refinanced by Bank Indonesia, and the removal of the remaining subsidies on deposit rates paid by State banks. The elimination of the credit ceilings also spurred competition among commercial banks.

The reform package of October 1988 (*Pakto*) removed most of the remaining impediments to competition, including a 16-year ban on new foreign bank entry. Since the reform, new licences have been issued to allow new entrants, though no new foreign branch banks are allowed. *Pakto* also included prudential measures to strengthen the soundness of the banking system and to reduce further Bank Indonesia's role in the allocation of credit and in the banking sector more generally. In 1991, the Government moved to improve its prudential regulation, more or less in accordance with the Basle standards.

Deregulation had a dramatic impact on the banking sector. More than 40 new private banks were established in the first year following the opening up of licences for new banks and foreign joint ventures. The number of branches increased more than threefold and new private banks proliferated. While 10 foreign banks were operating as fully-owned branches before the reform was implemented, from 1988 to 1996, 31 additional banks penetrated the Indonesian market through joint ventures. Changes in the banking sector following deregulation have led to what the World Bank has called a de facto privatisation of the industry. Before the reform the State banks dominated the system, holding 70 per cent of total bank assets and 69 per cent of outstanding credit. By 1996, the private sector (including private national, joint ventures and branches of foreign banks) accounted for 57 per cent of a vastly increased asset base, 63 per cent of total deposits and about 59 per cent of extended credit.[41]

Out of the 240 banks in operation after the deregulation, 34 are state commercial banks or local government banks (one in each province), 165 are private national banks and 41 are foreign banks (with 10 foreign bank branches and 31 joint-venture banks). 31 foreign joint-venture banks were added to the 10 branches of foreign banks already operating in the country prior to deregulation.

Table 7. **Indonesia's commercial bank network**

Year	1987	1995*
Total number of banks	112	240
- State	7+	7
- Private national	66#	165
- Foreign/joint venture	11	41
- Regional Government	27	27
Total Offices/Branches	1622	5114
Total Assets (Rupiah trillion)	50.1	279.4
Total Deposits (Rupiah trillion)	29.2	195.5
Outstanding Credits (Rupiah trillion)	31.5	216.8

* Excludes Bank Indonesia and rural banks
+ Includes the state development and savings banks which assumed commercial status in 1994
# Includes private development and savings banks which assumed commercial status in 1994

The expansion of the banking sector has not been trouble free, however, with higher than desired loan growth and excessive lending to the property sector leading to a deterioration in the quality of loan portfolios and the accumulation of non-performing loans, particularly among State banks. Moreover the large number of banks in the market results in insufficient scope for economies of scale. In response to increasing banking fragility, Indonesian authorities were taking measures to monitor the performance of the banking sector before the crisis. Banks were urged to align their annual credit growth plans to indicative targets set by Bank Indonesia and to ensure that credit growth for property (excluding low cost housing) and consumer credit in 1996 did not exceed total bank credit growth. New credit guidelines were tailored to each bank. Bank Indonesia had also sought to bring about consolidation within the banking sector through merger of weaker banks with stronger counterparts, but with limited success. The financial turmoil in 1997 may stimulate this process, with Bank Indonesia being less reluctant to allow some insolvent banks to declare bankruptcy.[42]

Restrictions on FDI in banking

Foreign investment in the banking sector is monitored by the Ministry of Finance, not the BKPM. The relaxation of barriers to entry in the banking industry under *Pakto* also applied to foreign institutions, but they remain subject to strict requirements. Foreign financial firms that entered the domestic market prior to 1972 are allowed to maintain full ownership of their Indonesian branches. Moreover wholly foreign-owned branches are permitted to provide the same services as domestic banks. All other foreign investors must establish through joint ventures with local banks. Joint ventures are allowed in banks, finance, insurance and securities companies. Foreign banks must have a local partner with at least 15 per cent of the equity, and the domestic partner must be a national bank that has received a sound credit rating for at least 20 months. The foreign bank must have a representative office in Jakarta, be reputable in the country of origin, and be from a country with a reciprocity agreement with Indonesia (Nasution 1995). Moreover, these banks are only allowed to operate in a limited number of cities.[43] Foreigners may acquire up to 49 per cent of domestic banks listed on the Jakarta Stock Exchange (JSE).

Foreign joint venture banks must have a minimum paid-in capital of rupiahs 100 billion, while the requirement for domestic banks is only rupiahs 50 billion. They are also subject to a higher capital adequacy ratio than domestic banks (12 per cent), a measure which is deemed to be an effective barrier to entry protecting domestic banks. Furthermore these banks are required to extend 50 per cent of their credits to export-related activities. Foreign banks are prohibited from attracting deposits from State-owned enterprises, and the number of foreign employees is restricted.

Conversely, according to officials at Bank Indonesia, the requirement that a minimum 20 per cent of total credit be extended to small-scale businesses may not be applied as strictly to foreign banks as is the case for their local competitors, because the former are thought to be in a better position to finance large businesses.[44] Moreover, foreign joint venture banks are entitled to engage in foreign exchange business without a waiting period, whereas local banks must wait two years before they can receive approval to engage in foreign exchange activities.

Overall competition in the private banking sector is far from free and the positive impact foreign banks may have exerted on the rest of the system has probably been hindered by the unhealthy state of local banks. As a result of the liberalisation move triggered by the financial crisis, foreign banks have more access to the market, but it is not yet clear whether they will be granted national treatment. Restrictions on branching of joint-venture banks and sub-branching of foreign banks were lifted in February 1998, and the Government submitted to Parliament a set of amendments to the banking law that would eliminate the legal restrictions on foreign ownership of listed banks.

Other finance

The *Pakto* reforms have been followed by a number of other packages focusing on the securities market and other specialised financial institutions. In the wake of economic restructuring since the mid-1980s, high rates of investment and growth in manufacturing and services have stimulated increased demand for long-term capital. To meet this need, reform of Indonesia's capital markets (especially the Jakarta stock exchange) has aimed at increased mobilisation of domestic savings and the attraction of foreign portfolio funds.

Beginning in 1987, the reform initially focused on widening investment flexibility and freeing up more sources of investment, including allowing foreign investors to purchase up to 49 per cent of listed shares. The stock market reform, coupled with the listing of a number of State-companies, had a direct impact on the activity of the stock market. Between 1988 and the end of 1995, the number of listed companies grew from only 24 to 239; listed shares expanded from a mere 60 million to nearly 46 billion; market capitalisation surged from Rp 0.5 billion to Rp 152.2 trillion; while the ratio of market capitalisation to GDP rose from less than one per cent to about 37 per cent. This development is particularly important for investment, because it offers alternatives to direct borrowing. Foreign investment in the capital markets has also been robust; foreigners held 27 per cent of Indonesia's Rp 204 trillion listed equities ($87 billion). Foreigners participate in at least 80 per cent of all trades on the JSE. The Indonesian Capital Market Supervisory Agency (BAPEPAM) cleared the way for mutual fund activity in January 1996. Beyond attracting foreigners in the banking sector, financial liberalisation also helped the development of the economy at large through the provision of more diversified sources of financing.

Restrictions on FDI

Financial reforms instituted in 1987 allowed foreign firms to enter the securities market as underwriters, broker-dealers, and investment managers through joint ventures with Indonesian firms. The Indonesian partner must have at least a 15 per cent ownership stake. In addition, foreign-owned joint venture securities firms are subject to discriminatory capital requirements twice the size of their domestic counterparts.

In the insurance sector, only life insurance business was open to foreign participation before 1988. Since then other insurers have been able to enter the market. Foreign firms may insure foreign nationals and foreign companies without having to form a joint venture. In a joint venture, the share of equity held by the Indonesian partner must be at least 20 per cent, and the agreement must stipulate a timetable for transferring up to a minimum of 51 per cent of total equity to the Indonesian partner within a 20 year period.[45] This provision discourages joint ventures, and as a result very few have occurred.

Foreign insurers face a higher initial equity investment requirement than do domestic insurers. They also have to place 20 per cent of total capital in the form of time deposits with an Indonesian commercial bank. The deposit, which is redeemable when the foreign company ceases operations in Indonesia, can be accessed temporarily in case of liquidity crisis with prior approval by the Ministry of Finance. Indonesia has committed itself to eliminate all market access restrictions and national treatment limitations for insurance companies by 2020.

Foreign involvement in the financial sector

Although FDI in the financial sector may be relatively small compared to the vast sums going into the petroleum sector or invested through the BKPM, the importance of financial sector investment comes from the impact it has on asset formation and fund mobilisation, not from absolute amounts.

In financial services, ABN Amro Bank, Deutsche Bank, Crédit Lyonnais and Société Générale, as well as ING Bank are among European enterprises involved in Indonesia's banking sector, while other European firms are active in financing and insurance provision.

Table 8. **Commercial banks' outstanding funds and credits**
(percentage shares)

	1987		1995	
	Total funds Rp 29.3 trn	Total credits Rp. 31.5 trn	Total funds Rp 214.8 trn	Total credits Rp. 234.6 trn
State banks	62.0	68.9	35.4	39.8
Private banks	27.4	23.8	54.7	47.6
Foreign/JV	7.5	4.5	6.3	10.4
Regional govt.	3.1	2.8	3.6	2.2

Source: Bank Indonesia

Foreign banks may be few in number but they are quite large in terms of assets, and above all in terms of efficiency and profitability. The return on assets was much higher in the case of foreign banks (7 per cent) than for private national banks (1.5 per cent in 1996) before the crisis.

The opening up of the banking sector to foreign banks has stimulated competition and enhanced efficiency. Even though a large number of local banks were established after deregulation, they are not in a position to compete either with foreign banks established locally or once the market is open to the outside as a result of the regional integration scheme. As a result, foreign banks are key in the necessary modernisation of the banking sector.

Transfers of technology in the banking industry are deemed to be quite large primarily because of greater expertise of foreign banks. In this sector, technology transfers may come about either through fiercer competition imposed by foreign banks or through labour mobility. High labour turnover in firms with minority foreign interest is an indication that FDI may help technology transfers. The active presence of foreign brokers on the Jakarta Stock Exchange should help accelerate the learning curve. Foreigners are active as portfolio investors and securities firms.

V.   Assessing the role of FDI in Indonesia

Indonesia's changing economic structure

Indonesia is richly endowed with natural resources. The switch away from primary exports was postponed until the mid-1980s, when the country's traditional exports suffered from the oil price shock. Compared to first-tier NIEs, Indonesia had less need to rely on low-skill, labour-intensive sectors since it was in a position to meet its foreign exchange requirements from its exports of primary commodities and oil. Such exports still account for a sizeable share of total exports, even though much less than in the late 1970s. There was initially considerable scope to accelerate growth through diversification and increased processing of natural-resource-based products, such as wood and paper. Indonesia also developed export-oriented manufacturing where lower labour costs gave a competitive edge (textiles, clothing, footwear). The real need to cut dependence on oil and other primary commodities was felt in the late 1980s, after the counter-shock in oil prices and the deterioration in Indonesia's terms of trade. The shift in policy towards export-oriented FDI and the surge in FDI flows dates from this period.

The improved climate for investments and exports led to a surge in investments and high growth in non-oil exports, especially manufactured exports. Figure 2 shows non-oil exports as a share of GDP since 1986. The share doubled in the late 1980s, as deregulation, currency devaluation and a wave of foreign investment combined to promote exports. Until the currency crisis beginning in 1997, non-oil exports had made only slow progress in the 1990s and in 1996 were little changed from 1989. Indonesian industries on average tend not to be heavily export-oriented with exports only accounting for 17 per cent of total manufacturing output in 1990, but performances vary widely across sectors. Some sectors, such as wood and textiles, are clearly more export-oriented than the average.

Figure 2. **Non-oil exports as a percentage of GDP, 1986-97**

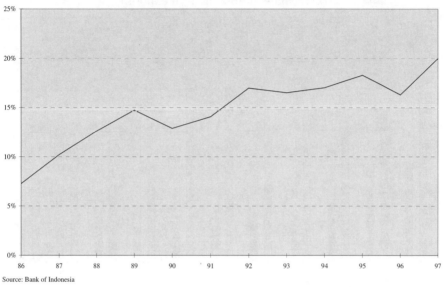

Source: Bank of Indonesia

With the decline in oil prices, non-oil exports have emerged as the prime earner of foreign exchange. While the share of oil and gas in total exports fell from 82 per cent in 1981 to 25 per cent in 1994, manufacturing rose from 11 per cent to 64 per cent. The most dramatic change in the composition of manufactured exports since the early 1970s results from the rise of the textiles and apparel industry (27 per cent of manufactured exports) and of the lumber and furniture industry (with 24 per cent). More recently, the electrical goods sector has emerged, accounting for almost 10 per cent of industrial exports in 1995, compared to about 4 per cent in 1991.

Faced with increased competition from other developing countries and stagnant or slow growth in overseas markets, exports of garments and plywood have suffered in the past few years. Conversely, among other major export categories, footwear, processed rubber and especially electrical goods all increased their shares of export earnings between 1990 and 1996 (Figure 3). This trend was interrupted in 1997 as a result of the currency crisis. The

81

currency depreciation partly restored Indonesian competitiveness in the garments sector. In the past decade, the fastest growth among major non-oil sectors has been in electronics. Exports of electrical appliances grew from $1 billion in 1992 to $3.6 billion in 1996.

Figure 3. **Selected non-oil exports from Indonesia, 1986-97**
(percentage of total non-oil exports)

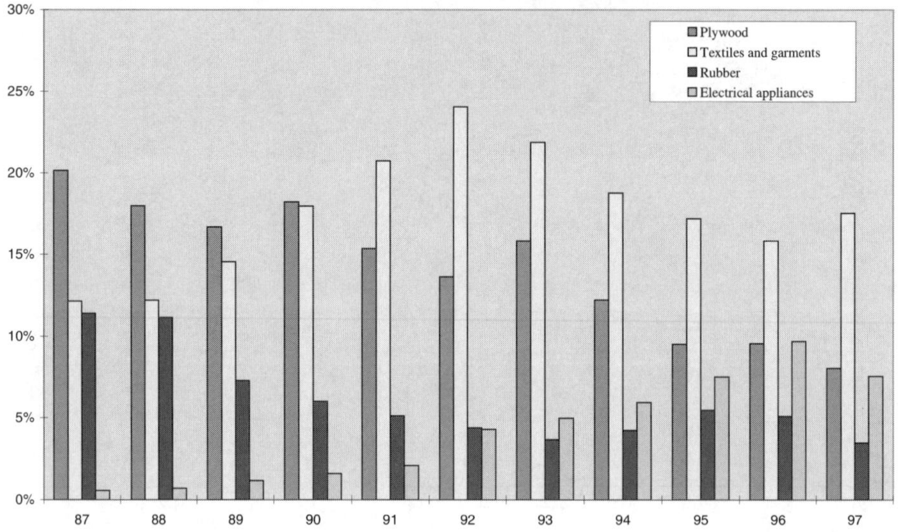

Source: Central Bureau of Statistics

The role of foreign firms in trade performance and growth

Foreign firms have been catalysts for manufactured exports throughout Asia, but in Indonesia the foreign role is often indirect. The main export sectors in manufacturing -- textiles, garments, and wood and wood products -- are dominated by domestic firms rather than foreign ones, but links with foreign buyers are nevertheless close. The impact of FDI on trade performance will increase in the future, as foreign investors are becoming more keen to take advantage of export opportunities. Recent foreign investment projects have tended to be increasingly export oriented, and more clearly so than domestic projects. Over the period 1992-96, about 43 per cent of the new domestic projects were export-oriented, compared to 57 per cent for foreign investment projects. In 1996, almost 70 per cent of foreign investment projects were classified as export-oriented, compared to fewer than half in 1992.

82

In a number of sectors, foreign firms represent over 30 per cent of capital invested, such as beverages, footwear, paper products, other chemicals, plastics, non-electrical machinery, electrical equipment, transport equipment and professional equipment. Out of these sectors, export orientation is evident in the footwear, paper products and electrical machinery sectors. Therefore, the foreign presence is important in the newly-introduced products which are also targeted for export. Most foreign firms in the export-oriented sectors locate in Indonesia for its competitive labour and land costs. In the various sectors which cater to the domestic market, many foreign firms were motivated to maintain markets in the face of import substitution policies and, more recently, to benefit from the potential size of the Indonesian market as its purchasing power increased.[46]

Textiles and footwear

Although figures on foreign investment outlined above indicate that the role of foreign firms may not be directly important as providers of capital, export orientation and technological development, they tend to underestimate the importance of foreign linkages that occur through various channels such as trading houses, buyer-supplier relations, licensing, subcontracting and so on. For instance, trading houses and buyers have been important in providing design and technology information to the predominantly domestically-owned garment subsector, which is also export-oriented.[47] Indonesia is used as a manufacturing base for textile, garment and footwear producers. Footwear production is dominated by foreigners, while textile and garment production is frequently based on sub-contracting arrangements. Companies which source from Indonesia include numerous international brands such as Nike and Reebok.

Textile and garment firms from richer countries have a long history of investing in poorer countries. The earliest non-OECD Asian manufacturing investments in the Southeast Asian region (in Thailand in particular) were by firms driven abroad by export quotas at home. Under the Multifibre Arrangement, textiles were the first labour-intensive industry to fall under voluntary export restrictions. These first round investors never reached Indonesia in any significant numbers, partly because there were no functioning export-processing zones, as the Government hesitated at that time to allow special status for such investors. No general duty drawback or exemption system functioned to allow components to be brought in for inclusion in exported products. The country placed little weight on manufactured exports at that time because oil was generating adequate foreign exchange.[48] Moreover, local conditions may not have been perceived as attractive by foreign investors.

83

Another stream of investors followed whose target markets were the host countries themselves. Tariffs and quotas in the poorer countries limited exports to those markets from Korea, Chinese Taipei and Hong Kong, China. To escape those restrictions, emerging economy firms established plants in order to serve the local market. In many cases, parent firms had exported to the market before they invested. Such investment was associated with small-scale, often second-hand plants, cost-minimising technologies, and price rather than brand name competition. The small-scale, cost-oriented investor serving local markets accounted for most of the flow of FDI from developing countries to other developing countries. Firms of this type are particularly attracted to markets that offer protection from imports.[49]

The latest wave of FDI from East Asian countries in the textile, clothing and footwear sectors is driven by Indonesian cost advantage in labour-intensive production. This is particularly true for the. Although quotas still play a role in investment decisions in the textile industry, sports shoes account for a large number of clothing projects. Managers in those plants do not claim to have invested for reasons of quotas.[50]

In the sporting shoes sector, a potential benefit of the presence of such foreign investors is that they are usually followed by their buyers who soon follow the subsidiaries and set up buying offices in the countries where the new plants are located..[51] Nike, Reebok and Adidas have all established offices in Indonesia, thereby reducing the distance between foreign buyer and prospective Indonesian suppliers. Once buying offices have been established in the country, local firms approach the foreign buyers and offer to match the product quality of the investors from Korea and Chinese Taipei, at lower prices. As a result, domestic firms may erode the advantages with which foreign firms entered.[52] The capital associated with their investment and the direct exports may not be the most significant gain from the mobile exporters, as foreign producers may act as catalysts for the development of local exporters. There is considerable anecdotal evidence that Indonesian firms are taking advantage of access to such buyers to export directly and to sell components to foreign producers to include in their exports. As a result the export diversification and expansion offered directly by the mobile exporters themselves may greatly understate the actual contribution of foreign firms.[53]

Electronics

The large potential contribution of FDI to export performance is exemplified by the emerging electronics industry which is both foreign-dominated and export-oriented. Although still a newcomer, the electronics industry has developed into a significant player in the economy since the late 1980s. The industry is made up of joint ventures between foreigners and Indonesians as well as Indonesian firms manufacturing a broad range of electrical and electronic products (radios, audio cassettes, television sets, telecommunications equipment, radio transmitters, digital telephone lines, and telephone answering machines, as well as various home appliances). In the electronic sector, foreign producers account for about 80 per cent of exports.[54] The home appliances and electronics industry was fundamentally import substituting until the late 1980s, with domestic production operating behind relatively high tariffs on imported finished products and largely geared to the domestic market, but eventually turned into an export-oriented industry as a result of deregulation.[55]

The removal of import restrictions and the reduction of import tariffs have lowered production costs, enhanced efficiency and boosted competitiveness. Most parts used in the production of exported electronic goods are now imported duty free. Moreover, a more favourable investment climate has also attracted foreign producers, particularly those from Japan and other East Asian countries compelled to relocate from high to lower cost areas in order to maintain competitiveness in serving international markets. Among the 400 or so firms operating in the sector, the large foreign joint ventures have brought volume production, technology and access to overseas markets. Wholly local producers tend to be much smaller. Consumer electronic products account for over half of the industry's output, with the balance shared almost equally between business and industrial products and components.

The reorientation towards overseas markets is reflected in the rapid growth of the industry's contribution to the country's foreign exchange earnings. Electrical and electronic appliances were the third largest source of export earnings in 1995, after plywood and garments, but ahead of footwear and processed rubber. Indonesia is not yet ready to produce parts and components locally, however, because this involves both large volume production and a relatively high level of technology. Major foreign joint ventures source over 60 per cent of the components they need for production in Indonesia from a home base or from plants in nearby ASEAN countries. Very preliminary steps have been taken by Japanese and Korean firms to source locally (NDIO 1997). While still high, the import dependence of Indonesian exporters is much smaller than in Malaysia, perhaps partly because the electronic sector is not as heavily export-oriented in Indonesia.

Petrochemicals

The large foreign involvement in the petrochemical industry may contribute significantly to growth in a number of sectors, such as food (through fertilisers), textiles and garments (through polyester production and the production of other synthetic fibres) or through plastic production. According to the State Minister for Investment, petrochemical projects accounted for around 30 per cent of the total cumulative foreign investment approved as of the end of 1995. Some protection is being granted to the industry, supposedly in order to develop Indonesia's industrial base ahead of the ASEAN Free Trade Area and APEC forum obligations. In the oil and gas sector, even though FDI is not permitted except in oil refining and oil and gas support services sectors, transfers of technology are quite large, owing to extensive use of production sharing agreements.

Automobiles

The Indonesian automotive sector is still highly restrictive, although some reforms have been undertaken as a result of the crisis. The sector was removed from the Negative Investment List in 1995, but local content requirements and other important restrictions remain.

While in the 1960s, Indonesia imported completely built-up (CBU) automobiles to meet the domestic need for motor vehicles, the Government eventually took successive steps to develop its own automotive industry. This strategy is consistent with those of other ASEAN countries which all regulated vehicle imports and foreign investment to protect domestic markets and localise production. To that end, CBUs were banned altogether in the early 1970s (until 1993) and imports were restricted to those in completely knocked down (CKD) form in order to encourage the setting up of vehicle assembly plants, mostly supported by Japanese car-makers. Beginning in the mid-1970s, imports of full CKDs had to be gradually replaced with automobiles using locally manufactured components (the so-called deletion programme) which saw the construction of component plants alongside assembly facilities.

Local content requirements should be reduced to 20 per cent for all CKD units and components after 2003 in line with ASEAN regional integration efforts. Import duties on CKD commercial vehicles will be 15 per cent and 25 per cent for passenger cars. Import duties on CBU passenger cars will be lowered from 125 to 40 per cent with an additional surcharge of 50 per cent for non-ASEAN countries[56]. In response to the financial crisis, the Government made the commitment to phase out the local content program for motor vehicles by the year 2000.

In February 1996, the Government made yet another move towards the creation of a fully-fledged domestic auto industry by launching a new policy for the development of a national car. The policy provided for a single company to build the national car, the Timor, with a three year exemption from import duties and luxury sales tax, provided it complied with the following local content rules: 20 per cent local content in the first year, 40 per cent in the second year, and 60 per cent in the third year. The Timor was the result of a joint-venture between Timor Putra Nasional and Kia Motors Corporation of South Korea. Given the lack of supporting industries or industrial experience on the part of the local company, reaching the objectives set by the Government turned out to be extremely difficult.

The programme discriminated against foreign producers and the policy of waiving duty and luxury tax only on units imported from the Korean company was seen as violating the fundamental WTO principle of non-discrimination. As a result, Japan took steps to bring Indonesia before a WTO panel over the car programme, a move that was followed by both the European Union and the United States. Japanese firms currently supply more than 90 per cent of the Indonesian market. As a result of the crisis, special tax, customs and credit privileges granted to the National Car were discontinued in January 1998.

Industrial upgrading and FDI

Overall, Indonesian exports are bunched at the upper and lower ends of the skill and technology range. The predominance of commodities with low technological content in the export mix (plywood, textiles and garments) reflects the country's low position in the global production system.[57] Despite increases in the range of the exported commodities in the past few years to include electronic goods, Indonesia still relies heavily on its traditional comparative advantage based on cheap labour.

The figures for total exports in higher segments hide a fairly large import content. For instance, the development of the electronics sector and of exports from this sector is fuelled by imported parts. Most parts used in the production of exported electronic goods are imported duty free. The large import content of exports resulting from a lack of competent and competitive part suppliers is a problem in Indonesia. The continued heavy reliance on imports of both capital and intermediate goods suggests that Indonesia has not yet started to upgrade in the medium technology sectors.

Table 9 shows groups of commodities according to the level of skill, technology, and capital content. The most dramatic increases in exports can be observed in Group II (labour-intensive and resource-based industries with low skill, technology and capital content) and Group V (but in this latter group the inclusion of refined oil products in the chemical industry may bias the result).

Moreover, unlike Malaysia, Indonesia has been extending its market shares more in less dynamic than in highly dynamic products.[58]

In the past, Indonesia's efforts at upgrading were concentrated in a limited number of sectors, such as the steel and aircraft industries. Indonesia entered the aviation industry with the establishment of state-owned aircraft manufacturer PT Industri Pesawat Terbang Nusantara (IPTN) in 1976. The company switched from the production of very simple aircraft designs in its early days, to a more advanced and wholly-Indonesian designed and built commuter aircraft (N-250) and was intent on designing the country's first jet aircraft. In July 1996 IPTN entered into a contract to manufacture components and to assemble and overhaul industrial gas turbines produced in Indonesia by a leading American gas turbine manufacturer. In spite of these advances, the success of IPRN has been equivocal and has been called into question by the recent crisis. Roughly 70 per cent of parts for the N-250 are imported and the aircraft has not yet been granted certification from American regulators. As the budgetary and extra-budgetary support and privileges to IPTN projects were eliminated in January 1998, the fate of the project and of the company as a whole is made even more uncertain.

The predominance of simple assembly and finishing operations and the low level of technological capabilities have given rise to the fear that China, Vietnam and other neighbouring countries with relatively low wage levels could eliminate these sources of growth momentum, unless measures are introduced to deepen the domestic industrial base and improve the quality of the labour force, management and infrastructure. A joint response is also envisaged through the establishment of the so-called ASEAN Investment Area.

A proposed revision of the Alien Business Law reduces the number of categories closed to foreign investment to 34 from 63 and raises the ceiling on foreign shareholdings in restricted areas to as much as 75 per cent. Among the sectors where further liberalisation has been proposed are brokerage services, wholesale and retail trade, construction, non-silk textiles, garments, footwear, hotels, beverage production and auction businesses.[59]

Under the new law there will be two lists of protected businesses, the first dealing with national security or exploiting natural resources, the second including those sectors where Thai firms are not considered to be sufficiently competitive. In the first list, it is not always clear what the exact relationship is between some of these sectors and national security. Such sectors include advertising, pharmaceuticals of all types, newspapers, printing and broadcasting, transport, mining and quarrying, as well as many sectors which the Government wishes to reserve for Thai nationals such as Buddha image production.

Exemptions can be sought in certain cases from the Ministry of Commerce and the Cabinet, especially where they involve the transfer of technology, employment creation and other benefits to the nation. The new draft law requires a minimum Thai holding of between 25 and 40 per cent in 11 activities. The 25 per cent limit applies to restricted businesses, while businesses related to national security will need a minimum Thai holding of 40 per cent and two fifths of the seats on the board.

Technology transfer

Successful industrial upgrading is a sign of the process of technology transfer at work. Indonesia's relatively weak performance in upgrading is matched by a poor record of technology transfers resulting from FDI. A number of studies find that technology transfer has taken place mainly through on-the-job training and has been limited to basic technological capabilities.[60] Otherwise, FDI and its related technology transfer have not generally been effective at developing indigenous industrial technological capabilities, in stark contrast to the performance of economies such as Singapore.[61]

Studies offer several possible explanations for this poor performance. Thee (1998, p. 20) suggests that frequent shifts in foreign investment policies have given conflicting signals to foreign investors of what was expected of them. Furthermore, the emphasis on export-oriented investment may have had the unintended effect of discouraging technology transfer. Sjöholm (1998, p. 6) suggests that foreign export-oriented affiliates may have been reluctant to enter into joint ventures with minority ownership because such exports have to meet international quality standards and hence rely on relatively new or sophisticated proprietary technologies.

A significant dampening factor on transfers is likely to have been the weak absorptive capacity of the local workforce and of local firms. Indonesia faces serious shortages of tertiary and vocational education graduates in various sectors, and these shortages have become more acute since Indonesia shifted to export promotion over a decade ago.[62]

Table 9. **Commodity structure of exports from selected ASEAN countries, 1965-94** (per cent)

Commodity group	Indonesia				Malaysia				Thailand			
	1967	1975	1985	1994	1965	1975	1985	1994	1965	1975	1985	1994
Group I	**96.7**	**95.8**	**75.9**	**42.0**	**94.8**	**81.0**	**63.6**	**23.6**	**98.0**	**85.7**	**63.3**	**28.7**
Food	27.0	22.7	14.6	11.7	6.9	7.7	6.1	3.6	55.2	64.0	47.4	22.7
Other primary commodities	69.7	73.1	61.3	30.3	87.9	73.3	57.5	20.0	42.8	21.7	15.9	6.0
Group II	**0.2**	**0.4**	**16.4**	**43.6**	**1.5**	**5.6**	**7.0**	**12.0**	**1.6**	**11.1**	**22.5**	**27.1**
Wood and paper products	0.0	0.1	10.0	17.3	0.7	2.6	1.5	4.1	0.1	1.3	1.3	1.1
Textiles, clothing, footwear	0.2	0.3	6.1	24.7	0.5	2.7	4.5	6.2	0.5	6.6	16.7	20.4
Non-metallic mineral products	0.0	0.0	0.4	1.0	0.3	0.3	0.5	1.1	1.0	3.2	4.2	4.0
Toys and sports equipment	0.0	0.0	0.0	0.6	0.0	0.0	0.4	0.7	0.0	0.0	0.3	1.6
Group III	**0.1**	**0.3**	**0.4**	**3.0**	**0.3**	**0.8**	**2.2**	**3.0**	**0.1**	**0.8**	**1.7**	**3.3**
Iron and steel	0.0	0.0	0.3	1.0	0.1	0.2	0.5	0.8	0.0	0.3	1.0	0.7
Fabricated metal products	0.1	0.2	0.0	1.1	0.2	0.4	0.5	1.1	0.1	0.5	0.6	1.5
Ships and boats	0.0	0.1	0.0	0.2	0.0	0.1	1.2	0.6	0.0	0.0	0.0	0.2
Other[a]	0.0	0.0	0.0	0.7	0.0	0.1	0.1	0.5	0.0	0.0	0.1	0.9
Group IV	**2.5**	**1.4**	**1.0**	**3.9**	**2.3**	**5.7**	**20.7**	**29.8**	**0.1**	**1.6**	**9.6**	**20.7**
Rubber and plastic products	0.0	0.0	0.1	0.9	0.5	0.7	0.6	1.3	0.0	0.4	1.3	2.8
Non-electrical machinery	2.5	0.8	0.2	0.6	0.7	1.6	2.1	3.6	0.0	0.2	1.8	3.7
Electrical machinery	0.0	0.6	0.8	2.1	0.2	3.1	17.9	24.5	0.1	1.0	6.3	12.7
Road motor vehicles	0.0	0.0	0.0	0.4	1.0	0.4	0.2	0.4	0.0	0.0	0.2	1.5
Group V	**0.5**	**2.1**	**6.3**	**7.5**	**1.2**	**6.9**	**6.5**	**31.6**	**0.1**	**0.9**	**3.0**	**20.2**
Chemicals and pharmaceuticals	0.5	1.4	5.9	3.2	1.1	1.0	1.6	3.1	0.1	0.6	1.4	3.0
Computer , office equipment	0.0	0.0	0.0	0.9	0.0	0.9	0.2	10.0	0.0	0.0	0.8	9.5
Communication equipment[b]	0.0	0.1	0.0	2.5	0.0	0.6	3.3	13.8	0.0	0.1	0.1	4.2
Other[c]	0.0	0.6	0.4	0.9	0.1	4.4	1.4	4.7	0.0	0.2	0.7	3.5

Source: UNCTAD, Trade and Development Report, 1996.

a Transport equipment other than road motor vehicles, ships and aircraft; and sanitary and plumbing products.
b Telecommunications and sound recording and reproducing apparatus and equipment; and semiconductors.
c Aircraft and associated equipment; and scientific instruments, including watches and photo equipment.

NOTES

1.   The Generalised System of Preferences or GSP allows for preferential market access for certain exports to the United States and other developed markets from designated developing countries.

2 .   Owing to a low rate of project realisation, approvals data often exaggerate the importance of FDI inflows.

3.   Allen (1996)

4.   Realised investment ratios are necessarily approximations since realised investments cannot easily be compared with approvals because of the time lag for a project to come on stream, in particular for large and capital-intensive projects such as cement plants or oil refineries.

5.   Allen (1996)

6   Expansion can proceed through the investment of further capital in the existing enterprise, establishing another company or through the purchase of shares of other companies through the stock market.

7.   Thant and Tang 1996.

8.   Approximately 27 per cent of total foreign investment in Indonesia originated from EC countries. The omission of Indonesia's petroleum sector from BKPM data results in a substantial understatement of the US share because it is the major investor in this sector. According to some estimations (Hill 1984), for the period 1980 to mid-1983 the shares were 14.1 for the US and 27 per cent for Japan when oil was excluded, but 58.4 and 10.9 per cent, respectively, when oil was included.

9.   Hong Kong, China; Singapore; and Chinese Taipei.

10.   A Korean company, the Nam-Bang Development Corporation, invested in the forestry industry in Indonesia as early as 1969 (Lee 1994).

11.   Wells (1993).

12. Thant & Tang (1996).

13. This section draws on Pangestu in Nicolas and Krieger Mytelka, 1995.

14. Mc Intyre (1993).

15. In the early 1990s, tariff levels ranged from 0 to 100 per cent with an average rate of 20 per cent compared with 37 per cent before 1985. In line with the Government's efforts to promote an open economy, the reforms in the tariff structure have ensured that imports in sectors representing over half of the domestic output face tariffs of 10 per cent or less. Tariffs exceeding 40 per cent primarily apply to motor vehicles, with rates of up to 275 per cent and alcohol, with rates of up to 170 per cent. Altogether these items account for no more than 1 per cent of the total [Fane 1996].

16. The share of imports subject to NTBs fell from 43 per cent in 1986 to 13 per cent in June 1991, and the promotion of domestic production behind NTBs has declined from 41 per cent to 22 per cent.

17. Fane (1996).

18. Thant & Tang (1996).

19. Surcharges are usually preferred to tariffs by Indonesian authorities because the former are considered temporary and have to be renewed every year.

20. The concentration ratio measures the market share of the four largest firms in the industry.

21. Ramelan Karseno (1997)

22. A number of manufacturing industries are designated strategic commodity industries, under the supervision either of the Ministry of Industry or the Strategic Industries Management Agency (BPIS) [Fane 1996].

23. Data provided by BAPEPAM.

24. Government Regulation no 45 of 1996

25. Export-oriented FDI was attracted into the primary sector very early on in Indonesia. Efforts to direct such investments to the manufacturing sector in the 1970s and intensified in the 1980s, with fiscal incentives, relaxed ownership requirements, etc.

26. This provision is in accordance with article 33 of the 1945 Constitution which states that "land and water and the natural riches contained therein shall be controlled by the State and shall be made useful for the people".

27. The official reason given for the rejection of the Malaysian investment was the promotion of small-scale industries, although pressure from large local oligopolies involved in plantations also played a role.

28. Thee (1998)

29. In the late 1950s a number of Dutch firms were nationalised by the Government of President Sukarno.

30. Wells (1993).

31. Wells (1993).

32. In the past, decisions often took one or two years; reform has reduced the decision time to a still considerable few months at most (Wells 1993).

33. Fane (1996).

34. Peraturan Pemerintah, PP Government regulation 20/1994

35. Fane, 1996.

36. Article 7 of the 1994 regulation does not set a minimum divestment requirement.

37. NDIO (1996).

38. An industrial estate area is developed and managed by a private company and includes all necessary infrastructure (water, electricity, drainage and other important facilities).

39. One in Jakarta, and the others in Batam island, Ujung Pandang (South Sulawesi), Pasuruan (East Java), Semarang (Central Java), Bekasi and Bogor (West Java).

40. The context for this financial reform was far from ideal : fiscal and current account deficits were quite high at the time. In addition, Indonesia reversed the recommended textbook sequence and started with the financial sector reform prior to completing reform in the real sector. Finally, in the absence of foreign exchange controls, there was a high risk of capital flight.

41. Bank Indonesia (1996)

42. *Far Eastern Economic Review*, 22 May 1997.

43. The largest cities and Jakarta: Medan, Bandung, Semarang, Surabaya, Denpasar, and Ujung Pandang, as well as Batam Island.

44.   Mandatory lending to small-scale businesses was raised to 20 per cent in March 1997 in an attempt to distribute wealth more equitably. 60 per cent of Indonesia's private capital is still in the hands of 2 per cent of the population.

45.   Dobson and Jacquet (1998).

46.   Pangestu (1995).

47.   Garments accounted for 55 per cent of textile exports in 1995.

48.   Wells (1993).

49.   Wells (1993).

50.   Wells (1993).

51.   Wells (1993)

52.   This has already happened in Mauritius for instance where local textile producers have driven out Hong Kong Chinese producers.

53.   Wells (1993).

54.   Allen (1996).

55.   NDIO (1997).

56.   Automotive tariffs were excluded from Indonesia's most-favoured nation tariff liberalisation programme announced in May 1995. A separate schedule was established that would reduce automobile tariffs to 20 per cent by 2010.

57.   Prabatmodjo, (1997).

58.   UNCTAD (1996).

59.   Letter of Intent by the Thai Government to the IMF, 25 August 1998.

60.   Saad (1995), p. 212.

61.   Thee (1998), p. 14

62.   Thee (1998), p. 14.

REFERENCES

Allen, Nancy, "Foreign Direct Investment and Export: Should Indonesia Play a Tax Incentive Game", *mimeo*, Department Keuangan Republik Indonesia, Badan Analisa Keuangan dan Moneter, November 18, 1996.

Bank Indonesia, *Annual Report*, various issues.

BKPM, *Indonesia: A Brief Guide for Investment*, Jakarta, 1996.

Caves, Richard, "International trade, international investment and imperfect markets", Special Papers in International Economics, no. 10, Princeton, 1974.

Chant, John and Mari Pangestu, "An Assessment of financial reform in Indonesia, 1983-90", in Caprio, Gerard, Izak Atiyas and James Hanson, *Financial Reform: theory and experience,* Cambridge, Cambridge University Press, 1994.

Dobson, Wendy and Pierre Jacquet, *High Stakes: the Global Financial Services Talks,* Institute for International Economics, Washington, D.C., 1998.

Fane, George, "The Trade Policy Review of Indonesia", *World Economy*, 1996.

Fujita, Kuniko and Richard Child Hill, "Auto Industrialization in Southeast Asia: National Strategies and Local Development", *ASEAN Economic Bulletin*, vol.13, n°3, March 1997.

Gundlach, Erich, "Globalization as a Challenge for Developing Countries: A Bird's Eye View on Perspectives for Indonesia", *The Indonesian Quarterly*, vol. XXV, n°1, 1997.

Healey, Derek, *Les exportations japonaises de capitaux et le développement économique de l'Asie*, OECD, Paris, 1991.

Hill, Hal and Brian Johns, "The Role of Direct Foreign Investment in Developing East Asian Countries", *Weltwirtschaftliches Archiv*, vol. 120, 1985, pp. 355-81.

Lee, Chung H., "Korea's Direct Foreign Investment in Southeast Asia", *ASEAN Economic Bulletin*, vol. 10, n°3, March 1994.

MacIntyre, Andrew J., "Indonesia, Thailand and the Northeast Connection", in Higgott, Richard et al. (eds.), *Pacific Economic Relations in the 1990s - Co-operation or Conflict?*, Lynne Rienner, Boulder, 1993.

Nasution, Anwar, "Financial Sector Policies in Indonesia, 1980-1993", in Zahid, Shahid N., *Financial Sector Development in Asia - Country Studies*, Asian Development Bank, Manila, 1995.

National Development Information Office, *Direct Investment - Strengthening the Foundations for Sustained Economic Growth*, Indonesia Economic Brief, Indonesia NDIO, Jakarta, 1996.

National Development Information Office, *Capital Markets and Portfolio Investment - Mobilizing Long-Term Capital for Economic Development*, Indonesia Economic Brief, Indonesia NDIO, Jakarta, 1996.

National Development Information Office, *Indonesia Source Book 1996*, Indonesia Economic Brief, Indonesia NDIO, Jakarta, 1997.

Oman, Charles, Douglas Brooks and Calm Foy (eds.), *Investing in Asia*, OECD Development Centre, Paris, 1997.

Pangestu, Mari, "Indonésie : la diversification d'une économie pétrolière", in Nicolas, Françoise and Lynn Krieger Mytelka, *L'innovation, clef du développement - Trajectoires de pays émergents*, Masson/Ifri, Paris, 1995.

Pramatbodjo, Hastu, "Towards Trade Liberalisation - A brief note on the Industrial Technological Competence of Indonesia in the Mid-90s", *The Indonesian Quarterly*, vol. XXV, n°1, 1997.

Ramelan Karseno, Arief, "Perspectives on Government Policy for Industrial Competitiveness in Indonesia", in Masuyama, Seiichi, Donna Vandenbrink and Chia Siow Yue (eds.), *Industrial Policies in East Asia*, ISEAS and NRI, Singapore, 1997.

Rinakit, Sunardi, "Indonesia in the Face of Globalization: Some Socio-Economic Adjustments", *mimeo*, presented at the Asia Pacific Agenda Project held in Bali on January 10-12, 1997.

Saad, Ilyas, "Foreign direct investment, structural change, and deregulation in Indonesia", in *The New Wave of Foreign Direct Investment in Asia*, Nomura Research Institute and ISEAS, 1995.

Sjöholm, Fredrik, "Joint ventures, technology transfer and spillovers: evidence from Indonesian establishment data", paper presented at an International Symposium on Foreign Direct Investment in Asia, Tokyo, 22-23 October 1998.

Thant, Myo and Min Tang, *Indonesia-Malaysia-Thailand Growth Triangle: Theory to Practice*, Asian Development Bank, Manila, 1996.

Thee, Kian Wie, "Foreign Direct Investment and Technological Development in Indonesia", paper presented at an International Symposium on Foreign Direct Investment in Asia, Tokyo, 22-23 October 1998.

UNCTAD, *World Investment Report*, various issues.

UNCTAD, *Trade and Development Report 1996*, United Nations, New York and Geneva, 1996.

Wells, Louis T. Jr, "Mobile Exporters: New Foreign Investment in east Asia", in Froot, Kenneth (ed.), *Foreign Direct Investment*, Chicago University Press for NBER, Chicago, 1993.

Chapter 2

MALAYSIA

Introduction and summary

In the four decades since independence, Malaysia has seen its economy expand and diversify at an impressive rate. Growing on average seven per cent each year in real terms before the crisis, the economy is now six times as large and GDP per capita three times as high as it was in 1970. The economy has also successfully diversified away from commodities and into manufacturing, reversing the relative roles of agriculture and manufacturing. This structural transformation is even more pronounced in terms of trade, as exports have shifted from commodities, primarily rubber and tin, to manufactured products, mostly electronic goods. Driven largely by growth in these manufactured exports, the volume of Malaysian exports is now nearly three times as high as a percentage of GDP as 25 years ago. Because manufactured exports have tended to be less volatile than commodity trade, the move towards manufacturing has meant that economic growth in Malaysia has been relatively stable, in spite of the vulnerability to externally-induced fluctuations created by the country's openness and trade dependence. Until recently, real growth rates had rarely dropped below six per cent over almost three decades.

Foreign firms have played a major role in this process of growth and diversification and foreign investment has been a key part of the outward-oriented development strategies of successive Governments. Malaysia sought to attract foreign investors interested in an export platform long before it became fashionable in the developing world. The combination of Malaysia's relatively early pursuit of mobile investors and its as a location for this sort of investment in earlier decades has contributed to the relatively high share of investments in the non-OECD area which Malaysia has traditionally received. Foreign investors are prominent in many parts of the manufacturing sector. In the electronics sector which has been the driving force behind exports, foreign investors control almost 90 per cent of total fixed assets and paid-up capital.

In spite of the prominent role of foreign multinational enterprises (MNEs) in the economy, however, Malaysia's openness to foreign direct investment (FDI) has always been selective, with the selection based more on the motive for the investment rather than on the sector of the investor. Investments intended to serve the domestic market have faced restrictions on the level of foreign ownership as part of the major focus of Malaysian economic policies to redistribute income in favour of the majority *Bumiputera* population. Income redistribution has been a feature of Malaysian policies since the ethnic riots of 1969.

Malaysia has a dualistic policy towards inward investment. Any firm which exports a high percentage of its output, contributes significantly to technology transfer or offers some other clear benefit to the host economy faces relatively few restrictions on its activities and receives fiscal and other incentives. Foreign MNEs interested in the local market, however, are sometimes prohibited from investing if there is already a local producer and even when permitted face numerous restrictions. The most important of these is the limitation on foreign equity participation. These policies, together with a lack of transparency in the approval process, add considerable uncertainty to any proposed foreign investment in Malaysia.

The Malaysian authorities actively screen both greenfield investments and take-overs. Foreign investments require the approval of either the Malaysian Industrial Development Authority (MIDA) or the Foreign Investment Committee (FIC), or sometimes both. Restrictions may be placed on an investor as a condition for receiving a manufacturing licence. These include the location, equity structure, distribution pattern, use of local professional services, construction date, quality standards, pricing, use of local raw materials, and technical and marketing agreements. All investments in natural resource sectors, except petroleum, require the approval of state governments.

Unlike in many other Asian developing countries, Malaysia does not have a "negative list" of sectors in which foreign investment is prohibited. The Constitution provides guarantees against nationalisation without compensation, and legal disputes can be settled through ICSID to which Malaysia adhered in 1966. Profits, dividends, interest, royalties and fees, as well as capital repatriation, are freely allowed, subject to the nominal permission of the Central Bank and after withholding taxes have been paid. Although the capital controls introduced in late 1998 are not directed against FDI, they add to the uncertain environment and raise concerns about possible future limits on capital repatriation by foreign affiliates.

Non-Malaysian companies or individuals require approval from state authorities to acquire non-industrial real estate. Some states are reluctant to allow property to pass to foreign nationals and will sometimes prohibit such sales outright.

Several key public utilities that were recently privatised have also been opened to foreign investment. These include the national shipping line, the national airline, and the telecommunications and electricity utilities. Foreign investment is also permitted in mining and forestry. Investment in the oil and gas sector is a Federal matter and is managed by the State oil company, Petronas, through production sharing arrangements. The national defence and the media sectors are closed to foreign investment. A few sectors are also reserved to member states of the Federation.

In spite of the obstacles, Malaysia has attracted substantial inward investment, mostly in export processing zones. It was in the right place at the right time when it adopted an export-oriented development strategy based on multinational-affiliated production in the early 1970s. American firms in Singapore were interested in shifting some activities offshore, and neighbouring Malaysia was an obvious choice. Building on this initial experience in electronics, Malaysia was equally well-placed, when it liberalised its investment regime after 1986, to take in the Japanese and Chinese Taipei corporate diaspora driven to make investments overseas by appreciating currencies and rising wage costs at home. At that time, Malaysia offered numerous advantages relative to other possible locations in the region, including a workforce which was relatively skilled, productive and English-speaking, a better infrastructure, greater industrial experience, particularly in electronics, and proximity to Singapore which had emerged as the regional hub for MNEs in the electronics sector. The foreign investment regime for export-oriented production was also more liberal than in most other ASEAN member countries.

Over ten years later, Malaysia faces growing competition to attract investment both from within ASEAN and from China, as these countries have opened up to foreign investment and have begun to offer the same incentives for exporters as Malaysia. The immediate success of the new Philippine regime for free trade zones and the rapid rise of investment in China show the potential for investment diversion away from Malaysia. Furthermore, productivity increases have not kept pace with wage rises in Malaysia, and the rise in relative unit labour costs can partly explain the steep drop in investment in 1994-95. A disproportionate share of companies leaving Malaysia come from Chinese Taipei – particularly those in the iron and steel industry – as these firms seek out lower wage locations in Vietnam and elsewhere. Investments from Chinese Taipei fell 50 per cent in 1995 and almost the same again in 1996.

Much of the decline in recent flows has been in labour-intensive, export-oriented projects, while projects which are not primarily export-oriented have grown quickly in the 1990s and have tended to be less volatile. In a competitive local environment unhindered by trade barriers or dominant national producers, this domestic market oriented investment can have a strong impact on the competitiveness of Malaysia as a location for investment. This indirect influence on export performance through the activities of foreign MNEs providing goods and services for the local market may be greater in the long run than any measures designed to increase exports from export processing zones. Local market oriented investments have been found to have greater linkages with the local economy and hence allow greater scope for technology transfer. This investment relates not just to manufacturing but also to services, including banking, and infrastructure.

To attract further investment of this type would require a modification of longstanding policies enshrined in the New Economic Policy which limit foreign ownership in non-export projects to 30 per cent. An important precedent has been set in this area as a result of the crisis: with few exceptions, foreigners may now hold up to 100 per cent of the equity in MIDA approved manufacturing projects. This measure is to expire at the end of December 2000, although existing projects will not be required to restructure after this period.

This liberalisation is designed to encourage FDI in manufacturing in Malaysia in the short term. It could usefully be extended to other sectors such as services and could also be placed on a more permanent basis. There is reason to question whether these equity restrictions can continue to meet the development needs of the Malaysian economy. Not only has the *Bumiputera* share of ownership of share capital not changed since the early 1980s, but foreign equity limits discourage inward investment and may actually impede technology transfer by making the MNE more reluctant to transfer proprietary information to its affiliate.

Foreign investment has played a prominent role in the past in Malaysian economic development. It will likely continue to do so in the future, given Malaysia's experience in promoting itself as a location and the advantages which it still offers potential investors. Nevertheless, it may be an opportune time to ask whether further reforms might not bring about not only a resurgence in FDI flows but also closer linkages between foreign MNEs and the local economy and hence a greater contribution of FDI to the future development of the Malaysian economy.

I.   Direct investment trends

Overall trends in inflows

Malaysia began to attract foreign direct investment long before other countries in the region. Since 1990, it has been the fifteenth largest recipient of FDI inflows world-wide and fourth among non-OECD countries after China, Brazil and Singapore. As a percentage of GDP, inflows grew from less than one per cent in 1968 to peak at almost nine per cent in 1992 (Figure 1). Inflows in the first three quarters of 1998 were less than inflows in the fourth quarter of 1997 alone, according to the Bank Negara. Figures from the Malaysian Industrial Development Authority (MIDA) show that applications by foreign firms fell 12 per cent in local currency terms in 1998, after declining 18 per cent in 1997. Given the depth of the economic slump in Malaysia, these declines can be considered moderate and contrast forcefully with the 68 per cent drop in investment applications by domestic firms. Much of this decline in applications has come from Japanese firms.

Figure 1. **Malaysian FDI inflows as a percentage of GDP**

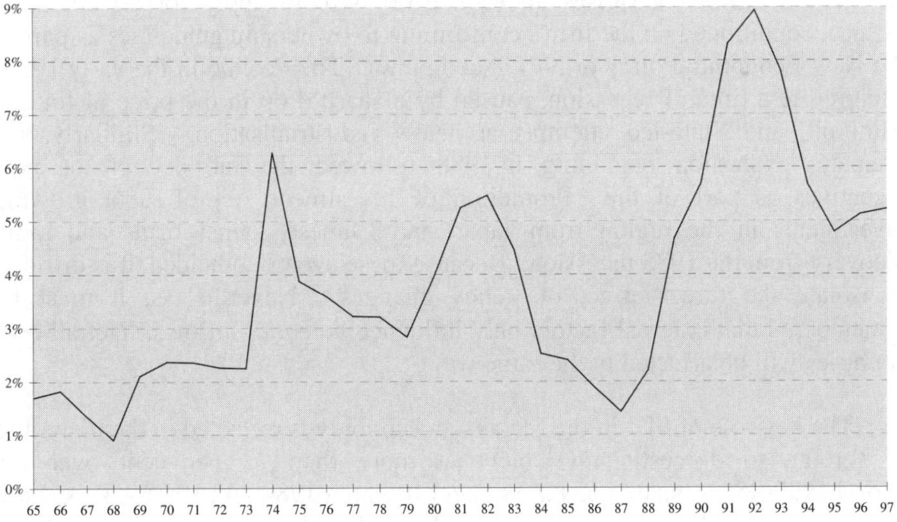

Source: IMF

103

The Government attributes the recent decline in inflows to the economic slowdown in Japan, to the growing competition for FDI, particularly from China, and to Malaysia's own revised policy of being more selective in approving foreign investment projects.

Variations in the level of inflows over time relate to both internal and external factors. Internal influences include changes in Government policies towards inward investment which will be discussed later, fluctuations in the growth of the Malaysian market and changes in relative unit labour costs. External factors include currency appreciation in home economies, such as Japan and the Newly Industrialising Economies (NIEs) of Asia, particularly Chinese Taipei, as well as the loss of GSP[1] status at home and rising wage costs in the NIEs.

Given the various and interconnected links between the factors listed above and FDI, it is difficult to establish a direct causal relationship between policy changes and inflows of FDI. Relative economic performance, for example, will induce policy changes while also directly affecting investors' perceptions. Nevertheless, there are certain observations which can be made about the factors behind the volatility seen in Figure 1. The growth of inflows in the early 1970s corresponds to the rise in the electronics sector, particularly in the Free Trade Zones (FTZs). The decline in inflows in the second half of the 1970s coincides with a sharp drop in economic growth in the mid-1970s and with the promulgation of the Industrial Co-ordination Act (ICA) which required all manufacturing enterprises above a given size to apply for an operating licence, conditioned on the firm's conforming to ownership guidelines as part of the New Economic Policy or NEP (see below). The decline in the early 1980s occurred at a time of recession, caused by a sharp drop in the price of tin and palm oil, and State-led attempts at heavy industrialisation. Similarly, the dramatic expansion beginning in 1988 followed the introduction of new incentives as part of the Promotion of Investment Act of 1986, growing investments in the region from Japan and Chinese Taipei firms and rapid recovery from the 1985 recession. Because these events coincided, it is difficult to isolate the direct effect of policy changes. Nevertheless, it must be remembered that external factors only influence *potential* inflows. Not all host countries will be affected in the same way.

The key role of FDI in the Malaysian economy is reflected in the high ratio of foreign to domestic investment at more than 22 per cent over the period 1990-95, compared to 8.8 per cent between 1984 and 1989.[2] This sharp increase reflects the surge in FDI since the mid- to late 1980s. Malaysia has a higher ratio of FDI to gross fixed capital formation than any other ASEAN member country except Singapore.

On average, over the period 1985-96, foreign investment has accounted for more than half of the capital invested in the manufacturing sector[3], with the degree of foreign participation varying widely across sectors. The ratio of foreign to total capital is particularly high in the electrical and electronic products sector (88 per cent) and in the scientific and measuring equipment sector (98 per cent), well ahead of the textile industry (with 61 per cent), and the rubber products sector (48 per cent). By contrast, the wood and wood products sector is clearly dominated by local firms (about 65 per cent), as well as the food manufacturing sector (70 per cent) and the chemicals and chemical products sector (66 per cent).

With few exceptions, much of the foreign investment in Malaysia until the 1980s was intended to supply the domestic market. Second in importance was access to raw materials, followed by low labour costs. Malaysia ranked second only to Singapore in ASEAN as a favourable investment climate.[4]

Sectoral distribution of FDI

In the 1960s, FDI was concentrated in import-competing industries partly in response to the investment incentives provided by the Malaysian Government and partly because investors wished to maintain their share of the Malaysian market for consumer goods in the face of tariffs. Although it was certainly more costly for these firms to produce locally rather than to export to Malaysia, the cost differential was largely absorbed by the implicit subsidy provided by tariff protection. While foreign investment in the Malaysian manufacturing sector has traditionally been domestic-market-oriented, Government efforts since the early 1970s have sought to encourage greater manufactured exports. Foreign-controlled subsidiaries have on the whole had a slightly higher export propensity than local firms since the mid-1970s.

Foreign investors have gradually shifted away from primary products to labour-intensive manufacturing activities and more recently to more capital-intensive manufacturing. This shift has, not surprisingly, been reflected in the economy as a whole. Each wave of foreign investment corresponds more or less to a shift in sectoral concentration. The changing sectoral concentration of FDI also coincides with changing objectives of the Government. Employment creation was initially a major objective[5], together with the need to integrate the country into the international division of labour and to foster exports; more recently the objective has shifted away from employment concerns to upgrading the domestic technological capacity, hence a more selective approach to FDI.

Table 1. Foreign investment in Malaysia by industry
(end December 1996, in million ringgit; per cent)

	Paid-up capital		Fixed assets	
Food	1,320	7%	1,265	3.8%
Beverages & tobacco	459	2.6%	362	1.1%
Textiles	1,849	10.4%	3,856	11.6%
Leather	36	0.2%	42	0.1%
Wood	613	3.5%	1,482	4.5%
Furniture	115	0.6%	169	0.5%
Paper, publishing	157	0.9%	363	1.1%
Chemicals	1,427	8.1%	2,686	8.1%
Oil & coal	859	4.8%	2,564	7.7%
Rubber products	505	2.9%	1,094	3.3%
Plastic products	575	3.2%	908	2.7%
Non-metallic mineral products	1,003	5.7%	2,065	6.2%
Basic metal products	880	5.0%	1,152	3.5%
Fabricated metal products	702	4.0%	871	2.6%
Machinery	713	4.0%	1,022	3.1%
Electrical & electronic products	5,379	30.4%	11,397	34.3%
Transport equipment	669	3.8%	1,060	3.2%
Scientific equipment	297	1.7%	505	1.5%
Miscellaneous	159	0.9%	394	1.2%
TOTAL	**17,717**		**33,257**	

Source: MIDA

From an early date, the relatively high-technology electronics industry assumed a prominent place in the country's industrial structure. Because this industry is dominated by foreign investors, the presence of foreign MNEs has clearly shaped the industrial profile of the Malaysian economy. The first MNE to establish in the country in electronics was a Japanese firm in consumer electronics in 1967, initially to take advantage of the domestic market. This was followed by investment by semiconductor firms beginning in 1971 primarily for export production.

By any measure of foreign investment, the electrical and electronic products sector now ranks first in Malaysia (with 30 per cent of total foreign paid-up capital and 34 per cent of total fixed assets), well ahead of the chemicals and chemical sector product, petroleum and coal and textiles (Table 1). Unlike most other developing or industrialising countries in Asia,

Malaysia did not move from textiles to electronics. The textile and garment sector accounts for a mere five per cent of total FDI in the country. Rather than building on traditional, low-skilled, labour-intensive industries, as in many other Asian economies, Malaysia went directly from a raw materials producer to a major manufacturer of electronic products.

In the early days of the electronics industry in Malaysia, the activities performed were highly labour-intensive, consisting primarily of assembly of various components, sub-systems and equipment.[6] Current production includes such items as semiconductors, but the local value added as a per cent of gross output in electronics remains small and actually declined from 28 per cent in 1981 to 22 per cent in 1992.[7]

Changes in the sources of FDI.

Historically Singapore and the United Kingdom were the most important investors in Malaysia's manufacturing sector, but with the rise of MNE exports in electronics, Japan, Chinese Taipei and the United States have all become prominent (Table 2). OECD countries represent around 60 per cent of total investment in Malaysia. Chinese Taipei, Singapore and Japan have been the major foreign investors since 1986 in terms of number of projects, well ahead of the United States and Hong Kong, China (Figure 2). In terms of capital, Japan ranks first ahead of Chinese Taipei, the United States and Singapore.

Table 2. **Foreign investment stock by country**
(paid-up capital; RM million, per cent)

	1983		1996	
Australia	79	2%	312	2%
Chinese Taipei			2 970	15%
Germany	86	3%	546	3%
Hong Kong, China	304	9%	599	3%
Japan	525	16%	6 369	33%
Netherlands	42	1%	766	4%
Singapore	1 052	32%	3 455	18%
Switzerland			172	1%
UK	582	18%	893	5%
US	181	6%	1 469	8%
Others	426	13%	1 951	10%
Total	**3 277**		**19 502**	

Source: MIDA

Figure 2. **Foreign investment approvals by country, 1985-96**

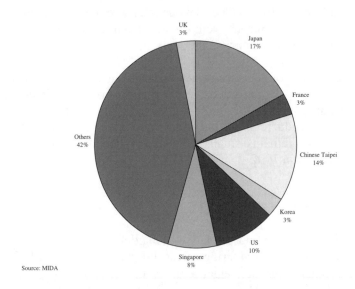

Source: MIDA

Firms from Chinese Taipei are generally recent investors, mostly in labour-intensive activities and in real estate. They have been driven overseas partly by rising costs and an appreciating exchange rate at home and the loss of preferential GSP status at home but not in Malaysia. This investment in has been facilitated by the links established with the Chinese community in Malaysia. An unknown – though possibly significant – share of regional investment in Malaysia may come through affiliates of OECD companies located in Singapore or Chinese Taipei. Certain Japanese investors, for example, have invested in Malaysia through their affiliates in Chinese Taipei. The active involvement of Singaporean firms in Malaysia is also due to the existence of the Johor-Singapore-Riau growth triangle which has promoted a regional division of labour.

Home country differences in investment behaviour

Investors from different home countries choose different sectors in which to invest based on their own competitive advantages. Japanese firms are heavily involved in electrical and electronic products (with 50 per cent of total Japanese involvement), as well as in transport equipment, chemicals and basic metal products. More than 30 per cent of investments from Chinese Taipei are in electronics, in spite of a substantial presence by the Taipei textile giant,

Hualon, which has 28 plants in Malaysia. Singaporean firms are active in many sectors, with a strong emphasis on food, beverages and tobacco. Investors from the United States focus on electrical and electronic products (with more than 30 per cent of their total investments) as well as on chemicals and chemical products (about 15 per cent). The Netherlands is also among the top foreign investors in Malaysia in terms of stocks, because of its traditionally heavy involvement in the petroleum sector.

Table 3. **Foreign investment by country and by industry**
(percentage of paid-up capital as of 31 December 1996)

	NIE3*	Japan	Other
Food	45%	11%	34%
Beverages & tobacco	45%	5%	50%
Textiles	72%	16%	14%
Leather	50%	0%	50%
Wood	68%	17%	15%
Furniture	67%	18%	15%
Paper, publishing	57%	16%	27%
Chemicals	26%	26%	48%
Oil & coal	10%	9%	81%
Rubber products	15%	12%	73%
Plastic products	31%	41%	28%
Non-metallic mineral products	31%	31%	38%
Basic metal products	45%	35%	20%
Fabricated metal products	44%	31%	25%
Machinery	23%	38%	39%
Electrical & electronic products	30%	52%	18%
Transport equipment	25%	38%	37%
Scientific equipment	13%	51%	36%
Miscellaneous	28%	28%	44%
TOTAL	**36%**	**33%**	**31%**

*NIE3: Chinese Taipei, Singapore and Hong Kong, China.
Source: MIDA

Table 3 provides a measure of the foreign investment stock based on paid-up capital. For each sector, the share is divided among the NIEs (Singapore, Chinese Taipei and Hong Kong, China), Japan, and other – principally OECD – investors. Each group accounts for roughly one third of the investment stock. A clear pattern emerges, with the NIEs dominant in the more labour-intensive, less technologically-sophisticated sectors. The only possible exception is fabricated and basic metal products, and scientific equipment. Japanese investors prevail in many of the remaining sectors, such as machinery and electronics. Firms from other OECD countries are the largest investors in oil and coal, and rubber and plastic products where they tend to have a competitive advantage over Japanese firms.

The focus on labour intensive production by NIE firms can be seen by comparing the capital/labour ratios for investors from different countries (Table 4). Investments from OECD countries are the most capital intensive, while NIE investments are more labour intensive. In between these extremes, the high capital intensity for Indonesian investment stems from its concentration in the chemicals sector. Japanese investments are the least capital intensive of all the OECD countries in the group, reflecting their focus on relatively labour-intensive assembly operations in the electronics sector and the fact that smaller firms are relatively more important in outward Japanese investment in Asia than for other OECD countries. The same applies for investments from Chinese Taipei.

Table 4. **Sources of foreign investment in approved manufacturing projects**
(based on cumulative paid-up capital, 1991-95; RM million, number)

	Capital per employee	Average capital investment	Average employment
France	177.97	1.36	131
Australia	31.91	0.42	76
US	48.82	0.21	228
UK	21.78	0.18	122
Indonesia	76.15	0.14	530
Japan	14.20	0.09	154
Chinese Taipei	15.73	0.09	180
Hong Kong, China	9.34	0.04	211
Singapore	4.92	0.03	144

Source : MIDA

Forms of FDI

Until the mid-1980s, most foreign investment was in the form of joint ventures with State-owned enterprises, such as the Heavy Industries Corporation of Malaysia (HICOM) or Petronas, the national oil company. Joint ventures between State-controlled companies and foreign firms were promoted as a way to reduce the importance of ethnic Chinese in Malaysian industry, as required by the objectives of the New Economic Policy. The weakness of the local private sector explains the heavy involvement of the State at that time (see below). On the whole, there has been a clear switch from the domination of majority Malaysian-owned ventures to a greater percentage of majority foreign-owned ventures in the 1990s, although joint ventures nevertheless remain common (Table 5). The steady decline in the share of wholly Malaysian-owned projects relates to the reversal in the stance of governmental policies from regulating inward investment in the 1970s and early 1980s to more active, though selective, promotion of FDI since 1987.

Table 5. **Distribution of called-up capital by degree of participation,**
1984-1995 (per cent)

	1984	1987	1991	1995
Wholly Malaysian-owned	40.1	27.5	13.4	23.3
Wholly foreign-owned	2.3	28.6	29.9	36.1
Joint ventures				
- Malaysian majority	47.0	27.5	26.7	18.9
- Foreign majority	9.2	13.9	28.5	21.3
- Equal participation	1.3	2.7	1.5	0.4

Source: MIDA, taken from Ali and Yean (1993) and MITI (1996)

Malaysian direct investment abroad

Before the crisis, Malaysian companies were starting to invest in other Asian economies (Japan, Singapore, China, Philippines, Indonesia, Myanmar, Vietnam) as well as outside the region (United States, United Kingdom, some Middle Eastern countries), albeit usually only small amounts. So far these investments have mainly concentrated in textiles, wood products, rubber products, transport equipment and in the oil industry. Malaysian textile plants have been established in Mauritius, palm-oil refineries in Egypt, and rubber product plants in China.[8] Petronas, the national oil company, is also aggressively investing in oil field development in Iran and Vietnam. Altogether, Malaysian direct investment abroad rose from RM 1.3 billion in 1992 to RM 6.6 billion in 1996.

As in other countries within the region, Malaysia boasts a certain number of conglomerates. Sime Darby, a company established in the colonial past, is by far the largest multinational in Malaysia in terms of foreign assets.[9] Building on its earnings during the years of rapid growth at home, it has a substantial presence throughout the region, such as in Philippine plantations or in Australia and recently purchased a small manufacturer in the United Kingdom. The aim of this investment is partly to acquire technology. In the words of Sime Darby's Chief Executive, "we aim to bring the...plant up to state-of-the-art manufacturing standards and expand operations into continental Europe. Later we plan to bring the technology we are investing in back to this region and set up a similar operation here."[10] Similarly, the Malaysian infrastructure company Intria, which is leading a project to build the world's longest bridge in Uruguay, acquired a financially-troubled British civil-engineering group to help in its venture in South America.[11]

The aim of acquiring foreign technology through outward direct investment is not only a corporate strategy, it is also an explicit policy of the Government.[12] A similar strategy was initially used for resource-based industries, in particular rubber and tyres. The purchase by *Perusahaan Otomobil Nasional Berhad* (Proton), Malaysia's "national" car producer, of a majority stake in Lotus, the UK sports car and engineering group, in 1996 clearly fits in this recent tradition. According to the Prime Minister, Dr. Mahathir, Lotus is to help with the design, engineering and technology for new Proton models, through design and engineering centres in both the United Kingdom and Malaysia.[13] Proton cars are currently dependent on technology and high cost items such as transmission systems provided by Mitsubishi of Japan. Lotus also has expertise in composite materials which can contribute to Malaysia's move into aerospace.

In addition to these significant purchases by Malaysian companies, the holding company for State-owned assets, *Khazanah Nasional*, has a new mission to enhance the technological capacities of the Malaysian economy by encouraging outward investment. Accordingly, "it will seek to buy or form strategic links with foreign companies that have technologies needed by the country".[14] These links could presumably involve either inward or outward investment. One such example involves a proposed joint venture between *Khazanah* and two Asian firms to manufacture advanced semiconductor wafers in Malaysia. The *Khazanah Nasional* is chaired by the Prime Minister. In another example, the Government – through *Khazanah* – took control of an Australian small aircraft manufacturer and now plans to manufacture the aircraft entirely in Malaysia as part of its long-term plan to develop its own aerospace industry.[15] Two other projects involve joint ventures between Malaysian companies and foreign small aircraft manufacturers to produce in Malaysia.

The Government has encouraged outward investment not only for its role in technology transfer but also for its contribution to Malaysian exports[16] and hence in cutting the current account deficit. Outward investment may also provide advantages in terms of economies of scale for Malaysian companies too reliant on their small domestic market. It is felt that outward direct investment can also contribute to structural transformation and to a move to higher value-added activities by shifting production of declining industries to more suitable locations abroad.

As a result, the Government has offered tax incentives for outward investment. With the 1991 Budget, Malaysian firms with overseas investment were given a 50 (later raised to 70) per cent income tax abatement for profits that were repatriated to Malaysia. Malaysian firms were given incentives especially in areas in which they have special expertise (such as in resource-based manufacturing and processing of agricultural products). A further liberalisation of the tax treatment of reverse investments was introduced in 1995, with a full exemption of income tax.

The Malaysian government attitude to outward investment has shifted dramatically over time. Previously stigmatised as disloyal[17], outward investments have become a means to enhance the technological sophistication of the Malaysian economy. It remains to be seen how effective this strategy will be, especially given the high costs involved in acquiring a foreign company. Such a strategy was employed by Japanese firms in the early stages of their investment in the United States to channel technology back to Japan.[18] Its effectiveness can only be judged over time and has likely been severely curtailed as a result of the crisis. At least one major Malaysian investor has sold off some foreign assets as a result of the crisis.

II.   Malaysian development strategy: growth and equity

Malaysian policies towards FDI are such an integral part of its development strategy that it is not possible to discuss FDI policies without understanding first how this overall strategy has evolved. The Malaysian development strategy can be separated into four broad phases: import substitution but relatively non-interventionist development from 1957 to 1970; substantial intervention beginning in 1970 to redress growing imbalances in the distribution of wealth among ethnic groups; State-led heavy industrialisation in the early 1980s; and adjustment and liberalisation since the second half of the 1980s.[19]

Foreign direct investment was perceived very early on as a possible instrument of economic development and modernisation in Malaysia. As a result, Malaysia has maintained a selectively liberal foreign investment regime, in keeping with the economic openness of the country, the pro-private sector stance of the Government for most of the period under study (with the exception of the early 1980s) and the export-oriented industrialisation strategy of successive development plans.

1957-70: import substituting industrialisation

From independence in 1957 until the social unrest in the late 1960s the major emphasis was on the agricultural sector. The Government promoted import substitution during this phase, aimed at reducing the dependence on imported consumer goods, but the protectionist bias was not considered to be strong. Instead of direct industrial intervention, the Government chose to create a favourable investment climate through various financial incentives and the provision of infrastructure. Foreign firms set up manufacturing plants in Malaysia in order to preserve their share of a market previously supplied by exports but now protected by import barriers[20]. Such investment occurred primarily in food, beverages and tobacco, printing and publishing, building materials, chemicals and plastics.

During this first phase of Malaysian development, foreign investment in manufacturing was welcomed as a substitute for imports but did not have the same overwhelming importance in the local economy which it has since acquired. By 1970, the manufacturing sector still represented only 13 per cent of GDP and was dominated by foreign firms who owned 60 per cent of corporate equity at the time. Even though FDI was favourably perceived in Malaysia, there was no aggressive promotion of foreign involvement as such in the economy until the mid-1980s.

The import substitution policy was constrained by the small size of the domestic market and, faced with growing unemployment and ethnic unrest, including the *Bumiputera* riots in 1969, the Government was forced into a dramatic change in policy as part of the New Economic Policy.

1970-1980: the early years of the New Economic Policy

The New Economic Policy (NEP) was put in place in 1971 as a response to the ethnic conflict. It aimed to eliminate the identification of race with economic function so as to foster national unity and to eradicate poverty and increase the weight of the *Bumiputeras* in national income. The *Bumiputeras* were expected to manage and own at least 30 per cent of total commercial and industrial activities by 1990. Moreover, employment at all levels, in particular

114

the modern and urban sectors, should reflect the ethnic composition of the population. The NEP implied a much stronger involvement of the Government in resource allocation, production and trade, primarily through public enterprises. A first step taken was to nationalise a number of foreign-held companies in order to transfer them eventually to the *Bumiputeras*. In the 1970s, the Government took over several major foreign-owned corporations in the mining and plantation sectors through mergers and stock market purchases financed in part through external borrowing.[21] Much of the regulation and intervention in the economy still revolves today around the NEP.

This period also saw a shift from import substitution to export promotion. The production of light manufactures was encouraged through various incentives (tax holidays, indirect subsidies to pioneer industries, etc.). Along these lines, under the Free Trade Zone Act passed in 1971, export processing zones were established to encourage investments, particularly from export-oriented manufacturing companies. These zones played a key role in the shift to export-oriented manufacturing. At the same time, tariff rates were gradually reduced across the board, except for some products associated with the development of heavy industries.

Malaysia came to rely even more than before on foreign capital. The policy was two-pronged: in addition to the opening of specific sectors to foreign investors, the Government sought to increase its control over the economy according to the goals set by the NEP. The *Industrial Co-ordination Act* (ICA) was passed in 1975 to regulate investment activities in the country in accordance with the NEP. It was formulated to complement previous regulations in an attempt to promote exports and encourage job creation with a view to increasing *Bumiputera* participation in industrial development. The ICA empowered the Minister of Trade and Industry to impose a number of constraints on domestic and foreign investors in order to achieve the twin NEP objectives of growth and equity. Among other things, the ICA imposed a licensing requirement for all projects involving shareholders' funds over RM 250 000 or employing at least 25 full-time workers[22]; the granting of the licences was made conditional upon compliance with NEP guidelines stipulating that at least 30 per cent of equity of licensed firms was to be owned by *Bumiputera* interests.

In accordance with the NEP goals, the Government is widely believed to have tried to favour industrialisation under foreign MNE auspices in preference to the likely alternative of domestic ethnic-Chinese dominance.[23] One of the objectives of the NEP and of the ICA was to give the mainly rural *Bumiputera* population more weight in industrial and commercial activities and to offer them jobs in industry. The principal way of getting the *Bumiputeras* involved in industrial activities was through the establishment of State-owned or State-controlled firms which eventually concluded joint ventures with foreign firms.

In terms of promoting redistributing ownership of corporate assets, the NEP and the ICA helped to raise the *Bumiputera* share from under two per cent in 1969 to almost 19 per cent by 1983 (Table 6). Much of this increase came at the expense of foreign-controlled share capital, however. Other ethnic groups in Malaysia actually increased their share over the same period. Very little progress has been made since the early 1980s, and the target of 30 per cent *Bumiputera* ownership has not been achieved.

Over the period 1970-80, the share of manufacturing in GDP gradually increased from 13 to 20 per cent. Oil also contributed to an increasing share of export revenues. The commodity price boom of the late 1970s and the second oil shock encouraged policy-makers to launch a major State-led development effort.

Table 6. **Ownership of share capital (at par value)**
of limited companies, 1969-92

	Bumiputera	Foreign	Other	*of which:* Chinese	Indian
1969	1.5	62.1	36.4	22.8	0.9
1970	2.4	63.4	34.2	27.2	1.1
1971	4.3	61.7	34.0		
1975	9.2	53.3	37.5		
1980	12.5	42.9	44.6		
1982	15.6	34.7	49.7	33.4	0.9
1983	18.7	33.6	47.7		
1985	19.1	26.0	54.9	33.4	1.2
1988	19.4	24.6	56.0	32.6	1.2
1990	19.2	25.4	55.4	45.5	1.0
1992	18.2	32.4	49.4	37.8	1.1

Source: MIDA

Early 1980s: the State-led attempt at industrial upgrading

Frustrated at the pace of economic development and buoyed by the rise in both oil and rubber prices, the Government embarked on a heavy industrialisation strategy under the lead of State-owned companies (HICOM in

116

particular). The Proton national car project was launched at this time. In parallel, import substitution was revived in an attempt to emulate the Japanese and Korean experiences (hence the so-called Look East Policy, a term coined in 1981).

Like many other emerging economies, Malaysia experienced major difficulties in the first half of the 1980s as a result of recession in industrial countries. The Government initially maintained its industrialisation strategy, but as the recession proved longer and deeper than initially expected, the counter-cyclical policy was no longer tenable. The current account and budget deficits both deteriorated (reaching 14 per cent and 19 per cent of GDP respectively in 1982). Indebtedness rose as a result, and economic growth slackened. An adjustment programme in the early 1980s managed to reduce budget and balance of payments deficits to six per cent and two per cent of GDP respectively by the end of 1985. The commodity price collapse imposed further strain on the economy at the end of 1985.

Mid-1980s to 1996: adjustment and liberalisation

The 1984-86 recession exposed a number of structural weaknesses and triggered a new round of market liberalisation and a more active promotion of the private sector. Following heavy criticism of the ICA and in response to the sharp decline in FDI inflows in the early 1980s, the ICA was liberalised by raising its minimum equity requirement for a manufacturing licence from RM250 000 to 1 million, then to 2.5 million, and by exempting companies employing fewer than 75 full-time employees. Prior to 1987, when the ICA was first liberalised, only small manufacturing firms were exempted from the requirement to obtain a license under the ICA of 1975, while larger firms had to abide by strict rules on equity, employment structure, etc.. Private sector interests currently call for a further increase in the minimum equity requirement from RM 2.5 million to RM 5 million. The key issue is to determine how liberalisation would affect domestic SMEs vis-à-vis locally-based SMEs set up by foreign investors. The current deregulation of the ICA has already provided easy access for foreign investors to compete in the domestic market by setting up local SMEs exempt from the ICA. [24]

The new policy was defined in the *Promotion of Investments Act* of 1986 (see below). The pattern of growth shifted during this period, with local demand playing a larger role than before. These policies are still in place today. The period since the mid-1980s has also seen a growing emphasis on privatisation to improve the efficiency of the industrial base and to curtail public spending (see Section IV). Because trade policy has always complemented the approach to FDI in Malaysia, Box 1 examines these policies.

Box 1. **Trade regime**

Malaysia's trade regime is deemed by the WTO to be relatively liberal: the country has few trade barriers, import permits are generally not required, and import duties are rather low (although they range from 0 to 300 per cent, they do not exceed 10 per cent on most goods). A ten per cent sales tax is levied on most imports, but imports of products not available locally and used for export production are exempt from both the duty and sales tax. US semiconductor companies operating in Malaysia have benefited from this provision. Malaysia has moreover agreed to substantial tariff reductions on a wide range of products to comply with WTO standards. State-trading activities are also slowly being privatised.

A number of sectors, such as automobile, steel, rubber and tyres are still heavily protected for infant industry motives. Although mild by developing countries standards, the protective measures are considered by some to have significantly promoted industrialisation in Malaysia at the expense of imports (Ariff 1993). Effective rates of protection in these sectors have been very high, although nominal rates have been lower because of low tariffs on imported inputs.

The effect of these various policy directions can be seen in the trend in exports of goods and services. Exports as a percentage of GDP fell in the 1960s as a result of declining commodity prices and import substitution policies. Following the shift to export-orientation in the early 1970s, the export share grew quickly, if erratically, at first but then showed only a slight upward trend until the mid-1980s when the confluence of external and internal factors caused the export share of GDP almost to double in the next ten years. Much of this growth was fuelled by substantial export-oriented investments by foreign MNEs in the electronics sector.

In a departure from its traditional outward orientation, the Malaysian government imposed foreign exchange controls in 1998 as a means of mitigating the impact of international financial instability on the economy. While foreign exchange controls might be viewed as a step backwards from the gradual liberalisation of the economy since the mid-1980s, certain existing restrictions on FDI have been lifted at the same time (see below). Both of these have been announced as temporary. At the same time, however, both challenge long-standing policy orientations.

III.   Malaysian policies towards FDI

Malaysia has two distinct policies towards inward investment. Any firm which exports a high percentage of its output, contributes significantly to technology transfer or offers some other clear benefit to the host economy faces relatively few restrictions on its activities and receives added fiscal and other incentives. At the other extreme, foreign MNEs interested in the local market are sometimes prohibited from investing if there is already a local producer and even when permitted face numerous restrictions. The most important of these is the limitation on foreign equity participation which is designed to redress what was seen as a socially unacceptable imbalance in income distribution affecting the *Bumiputera*. This dualistic policy, together with a lack of transparency in the approval process for investors oriented towards the local market, adds considerable uncertainty to any proposed foreign investment in Malaysia.

The following sections look at restrictions and at incentives for foreign investors. The financial sector is considered separately.

Restrictions on inward investment

The Malaysian authorities actively screen both greenfield investments and take-overs. Foreign investments require the approval of either the Malaysian Industrial Development Authority (MIDA) or the Foreign Investment Committee (FIC), or sometimes both. The Ministry of International Trade and Industry (MITI) which includes MIDA may place restrictions on an investor as a condition for receiving a manufacturing licence. These include the location, equity structure, distribution pattern, use of local professional services, construction date, quality standards, pricing, use of local raw materials, and technical and marketing agreements.[25] All investments in natural resource sectors, except petroleum, are approved by state governments.

In addition to the oil sector which is reserved to the Federal government, a few sectors are also reserved to member states of the Federation. Most other industries are potentially open to foreign investment. Unlike many other Asian developing countries, Malaysia does not have a "negative list" of sectors in which foreign investment is prohibited. The Constitution provides guarantees against nationalisation without compensation, and legal disputes can be settled through ICSID which Malaysia signed in 1966. Profits, dividends, interest, royalties and fees, as well as capital repatriation, are freely allowed, subject to the nominal permission of the Central Bank and after withholding taxes have been paid.

119

Non-Malaysian companies or individuals require approval from state authorities to acquire non-industrial real estate. Some states are reluctant to allow property to pass to foreign nationals and will sometimes prohibit such sales outright.

Several key public utilities that were recently privatised have also been opened to foreign investment.[26] These include the national shipping line, the national airline, and the telecommunications and electricity utilities. Foreign investment is also permitted in mining and forestry. Investment in the oil and gas sector is a Federal matter and is managed by the State oil company, Petronas, through production sharing arrangements. The national defence and the media sectors are still closed to foreign investment.

Mergers and acquisitions

Foreign equity investments in Malaysian companies exceeding RM 5 million or 15 per cent of paid-up capital require the approval of either MITI or the FIC or both, depending on how the acquisition is financed. The approval of the Central Bank may also be required. The FIC guidelines applying to the proposed acquisition of assets or any interests, mergers or takeovers are as follows:

Against the existing pattern of ownership, the proposed acquisition should result directly or indirectly in a more balanced Malaysian participation in ownership and control;

1. The proposed acquisition should lead directly or indirectly to net economic benefits in relation to such matters as the extent of Malaysian participation, particularly *Bumiputera* participation, ownership and management, income distribution, growth, employment, exports, quality, range of products and services, economic diversification, processing and upgrading of local raw materials, training, efficiency and research and development;

2. The proposed acquisition should not have adverse consequences in terms of national policies in such matters as defence, environmental protection or regional development;

3. The onus of providing that the proposed acquisition is on the acquiring parties concerned.

Greenfield investments

In keeping with the objective of ensuring increasing Malaysian participation in manufacturing activities, the Government encourages projects to be undertaken as joint ventures between Malaysian and foreign entrepreneurs. There is no export requirement imposed on foreign investors, but export performance determines the level of foreign equity participation that will be allowed. Foreign equity participation is governed by the following guidelines:

   i) no equity condition is imposed on projects that export at least 80 per cent of output (changed from 50 per cent in the 1992 legislation);

   ii) the level of equity participation for other export-oriented projects is as follows:

   - for projects exporting between 51 per cent and 79 per cent of their production, foreign equity ownership of up to 79 per cent may be allowed, depending on factors such as the level of technology, spin-off effects, size of the investment, location, value-added and the utilisation of raw materials and components;[27]

   - for projects exporting between 20 per cent to 50 per cent of their production, foreign equity ownership of between 30 to 51 per cent is allowed, depending on the factors as mentioned above;

   - for projects exporting less than 20 per cent of their production, foreign equity ownership is allowed up to a maximum of 30 per cent.

Foreign equity ownership up to 100 per cent may nevertheless be allowed for projects producing high technology goods or priority products for the domestic market as determined periodically by the Government. These guidelines do not apply to sectors subject to specific joint-venture equity policies, where foreign equity ownership is limited to 30-60 per cent (see below).

Requirements are also maintained on the distribution of Malaysian equity. Where foreign equity is less than 100 per cent, the balance of the equity to be taken up by Malaysians should be allocated as much as possible to *Bumiputeras*, in accordance with the inter-ethnic redistribution goal. The minimum share reserved to *Bumiputeras* depends on the initiators of the project as well as on the scope of foreign involvement.

As a result of further relaxation of the stringent NEP rules, any company set up with foreign capital is now exempted from the NEP equity restructuring requirement provided it is export-oriented and employs at least 350 full-time

Malaysian workers in proportions corresponding to the racial composition of the country (Ariff 1991). The Second Outline Perspective Plan and the successor to the NEP, the National Development Plan (NDP) introduced in 1991 dropped most limits on minimum percentage of *Bumiputera* participation in approved projects. Yet the basic objectives of growth with equity are still retained. This is supposed to come about through deregulation and through Government initiatives to support the development of facilities to make Malaysia attractive to investors.

In spite of a generally favourable stance towards export-oriented FDI, particularly in the electronics sector, the Government is not taking a hands-off approach in all respects. "National unions in other industries are permitted, but the government...has forbidden the formation of a union in the important electronics sector since 1972 and restricted workers to Japanese-style in-house employee associations."[28]

The more selective approach to FDI in the pre-crisis period

Until recently the major objective of the authorities in charge of FDI had been to encourage inflows in export sectors as a way of providing employment. That policy proved remarkably successful, with employment in the electronics sector growing from 600 in 1970 to 85,000 in 1984 and to almost 300,000 by the end of 1994. Because of Malaysia's tremendous success in attracting investment and severe labour shortages, the Government started to become more selective and to move away from an emphasis on labour-intensive basic manufacturing and component assembly processes towards more capital-intensive, high-technology processes and highly-skilled service occupations. A number of provisions reflected this strategic shift. Except in certain strategic sectors, incentives were reduced and the focus shifted to encouraging domestic investment. Special incentives were given to semiconductor producers in an attempt to move up the production ladder, such as by setting up silicon wafer plants.

Applications for new manufacturing projects also had to pass a capital-labour ratio threshold, while existing manufacturing units below this threshold were encouraged to leave Malaysia and move to Indonesia or other low-wage countries in ASEAN. Projects with a capital investment per employee ratio of less than RM 55,000 were defined as labour-intensive and hence were not considered for a manufacturing licence or for tax incentives by MITI, although this limit was not imposed too strictly. Projects could be exempted from this guideline if value added was more than 30 per cent, or if the project undertook activities or products listed as promoted activities and products of high technology, etc. Foreigners were nevertheless required to source locally if

122

products were available domestically. The only exception was for Free Zones or where local quality was too low or prices too high.

The more selective stance toward FDI could be seen in the decline in the number of approvals for projects funded by foreign companies. In 1995 MIDA received foreign investment applications worth RM 12.9 billion in the manufacturing sector but approved only projects worth RM 9 billion (although some projects might have been approved subsequently).[29] In addition, the Seventh Malaysia Plan (1996-2000) encouraged the growth of clusters of interdependent workshops and discouraged low-capital, low-productivity and low value-added ventures. This stance was also reflected in the Industrial Linkage Programme, launched in June 1996, which aimed to encourage the development of SMEs and which also hoped to encourage the rapid evolution of industrial clusters or groupings of SME suppliers gathered around large customer industries. Under the Multimedia Super Corridor Project (MSC), for example, a package of incentives was offered to information technology firms willing to set up operations in the corridor (south of Kuala Lumpur). In an unprecedented incentives package, these firms were exempted from local ownership requirements, existing restrictions governing the employment of expatriates, and income tax for up to 10 years. Moreover they were granted duty-free imports of multimedia equipment and were offered competitive telecommunications tariffs. MSC infrastructure contracts were also open to companies willing to use the zone as a regional hub.

In order to enhance further the importance of the manufacturing sector in the economy, the 1997 Budget included several incentives, mainly in the form of easier entry approval for expatriates, opening of foreign currency accounts and foreign equity ownership to encourage the setting up of International Procurement Centres (IPCs) which would undertake procurement of raw materials, components and finished products for sale to related and unrelated companies in Malaysia and abroad.

The heavy emphasis on training and education (especially in science and technology) led to the opening of the country to foreign institutions.

Post crisis changes in FDI policy

The Minister of International Trade and Industry has announced changes to the current policy on equity for the manufacturing sector, applicable from 31 July 1998 to 31 December 2000. These changes allow flexibility in the equity holdings of investors, both local and foreign, in all areas of manufacturing, with the exception of specific activities and products where Malaysian SMEs already have the capabilities and expertise.

The relaxation in the Equity Policy is as follows:-

a) With the exception of activities and products in a specific exclusion list[30] (which are subject to the prevailing specific equity guidelines), all new projects in manufacturing, including for expansion and diversification will be exempted from both Equity and Export Conditions. This means that project owners can hold 100 per cent equity irrespective of the level of exports.

b) This policy will apply to all applications received from 31 July 1998 to 31 December 2000, as well as applications already received, but for which decisions are pending.

c) All projects approved under the new policy will not be required to restructure their equity after the period.

d) The Government will review this policy after 31 December 2000.

To encourage greater industrial linkages and domestic sales, the Government has relaxed the export conditions imposed on manufacturing companies effective from 1 January 1998 to 31 December 2000. All existing companies which had previously received incentives based on their level of exports can now apply to MITI for an approval to sell up to 50 per cent of their output in the domestic market. The products eligible to be considered for increased domestic sales are those which presently do not face an import duty and those which are not available locally or in inadequate local supply. This temporary relaxation of export conditions will not affect the current equity structures and incentives of existing companies. The relaxation is also extended to new companies approved before 31 July 1998 once they commence operation. A company that has been approved with a certain equity participation will not be required to restructure its equity at any time, provided that the company continues to comply with the original conditions of approval and retains the original features of the project.

The limits on foreign equity holdings have also been relaxed in sectors other than manufacturing. The Government increased to 51 per cent (up from 30 per cent) the equity foreigners are allowed to hold in wholesale and retail companies. Foreign equity holdings in the local licences of basic telecommunications companies have been raised from a previous maximum of 30 per cent to a new maximum of 49 per cent. Malaysia is prepared to consider applications to raise the foreign equity holdings up to a maximum of 61 per cent, provided that the companies concerned shall reduce their foreign equity holdings to a maximum of 49 per cent within 5 years.

In contrast to these measures aimed at making Malaysia more attractive to foreign investors, the imposition of currency controls in the fall of 1998 may deter foreign investors. These controls require the following:

- the repatriation by 1 October 1998 of all ringgit held abroad;
- an end to offshore trading in ringgit instruments and to domestic credit facilities for overseas banks and stockbrokers;
- the retention of the proceeds of the sale of Malaysian securities in the country for a year;
- payment in foreign currency for imports and exports; and
- central bank approval for the conversion of ringgit into foreign currency.

The aim of these controls is to stabilise the exchange rate and insulate the domestic economy from adverse global developments. The Government claims that these changes will have no impact on the business operations of traders and investors or on the normal conduct of economic activity as it will continue to guarantee the general convertibility of current account transactions, free flows of FDI and repatriation of interest, profits and dividends and capital.

It remains to be seen whether the Government's optimism will be justified. Against the benefits from currency stability much be weighed the potential damage from policy uncertainty. In late 1998, the Parliament passed an amendment to the Companies Act which would limit dividend payments to the company's net profit in the current fiscal year or average dividend payments over the past two years, whichever is greater.[31] Many existing investors may not be much affected by this amendment, but potential investors might worry about what it presages for future policies.

Incentives for inward investment

In contrast to many neighbouring countries, Malaysia's FDI policy has always relied rather heavily on tax holidays. In the 1960s, the industrialisation policy was built around the *Pioneer Industries (Relief from Income Tax) Ordinance* of 1958. Under the ordinance, firms granted "pioneer" status were given an initial tax relief (from the prevailing 40 per cent company tax) for 2 years, with an extension to 3 or 5 years depending on the amount of capital investments. Losses could be carried over into the years after pioneer status had ended. The initial law was amended in 1965, with higher qualifying levels of capital investment. These laws applied to both domestic and foreign firms, but pioneer status firms were largely foreign, with about 70 per cent of the value added of pioneer firms produced by foreign-owned firms.[32]

In late 1968, the *Investment Incentives Act* replaced the Pioneer Industries Ordinance with the two objectives of creating employment and diversifying the economy.[33] The Federal Industrial Development Authority (FIDA), predecessor to the MIDA, was established in 1965 and activated in 1967 to attract and develop export-oriented industries.[34] The Act was meant to encourage more FDI into export-oriented manufacturing through tax holidays to approved firms for up to eight years. Additional incentives were granted for non-pioneer industries under this Act, including investment tax credits, accelerated depreciation allowances, and export incentives. In addition, tariff protection and exemption from import duties and surtax were granted to facilitate the establishment of new manufacturing enterprises.[35] These provisions signalled a strategic switch in emphasis from import substitution to export orientation. Export promotion was then perceived as the only way to overcome the problem of internal market saturation which was seen as the main barrier to manufacturing expansion. The authorities did not simply target export-oriented firms, they favoured specific industries over others. As a result of investment missions to capital-exporting countries, specific companies in the fast-growing semiconductor industry were identified and targeted as likely candidates for investment.[36]

Following a recession in the mid-1980s and in an effort to revive inflows of FDI into Malaysia, the authorities offered generous incentives and more liberal conditions under the *1986 Promotion of Investment Act*. Companies undertaking activities in manufacturing, agriculture, tourism, research and development and technical and vocational training became eligible for tax incentives.

Pioneer status (tax holidays) or an investment tax allowance (ITA) are given to companies undertaking the following activities: i) promoted products or activities, ii) high-technology products or activities, iii) strategic products of national importance, iv) research and development, v) technical or vocational training (ITA only) and vi) small-scale industries (pioneer status only).

A company given pioneer status is exempted from taxation on part of its statutory income. The extent and period of tax exemption depends on the activities in which the firm is involved. The general rule is an abatement of 70 per cent of the statutory income for five years, the rest being taxed at the prevailing corporate tax. A corporation carrying out a project of national and strategic importance involving heavy capital investment and high technology will be granted full income tax exemption for ten years. A high technology company producing promoted products in new and emerging technologies will be fully exempted for five years.

A company eligible for an ITA will enjoy an allowance of a given percentage for qualifying capital expenditure within five years from the date it was first incurred. The allowance can be set off against part of the statutory income in the year of assessment. Moreover, certain expenses incurred by resident companies for the purpose of seeking opportunities for the export of manufactured products and agricultural produce are eligible for double deduction. Finally, an infrastructure allowance is available to any resident company in Malaysia engaged in manufacturing, agricultural, hotel, tourist or other industrial or commercial activity in the Eastern corridor of the Malaysian Peninsular.

The Income Tax Act 1967 also offers other types of incentives in addition to those provided under the PIA 1986. Non-tax incentives, in the form of export credit refinancing facilities, export credit insurance and guarantee schemes, as well as industrial technical assistance fund are also provided to spur the private sector. The PIA began at a time of massive outflows of FDI from Japan and the NIEs and hence it is difficult to ascertain its precise impact on FDI inflows. Lim and Nesadurai (1997, p. 201-2) suggest that it had a positive influence on inflows. At the very least, it helped Malaysia in the competition for Japanese investment at the time.

Profits are freely remittable and exchange controls have, until recently, been minimal. These provisions have been highly attractive for foreign investors. Malaysia also encourages sequential investing through the provision of a reinvestment allowance of 60 per cent on capital expenditure incurred (raised from 50 per cent in the 1996 Budget). A second round of pioneer status/investment tax allowance is also granted to companies setting up separate expansion projects to produce similar products or undertake similar activities (UNCTAD 1995). Expansion projects in promoted areas such as the Eastern Corridor of Peninsular Malaysia are eligible for even better treatment.

Free zones

Free Zones are areas designed for export-oriented manufacturing establishments (exporting at least 80 per cent of their output) or for engaging in trading, breaking bulk grading, repackaging, relabelling and transit. Free Zone investors enjoy minimal customs controls and formalities in their import of raw materials, parts, machinery and equipment as well as in the exports of their finished products. The country now has 12 Free Zones.[37] Sales of components to firms located in zones are considered as exports and may receive incentives. Goods sold into Malaysia by companies in Free Zones for home consumption are subject to the same duties that apply to foreign imports, unless they are to be used as direct raw materials or components by manufacturers in Malaysia.

In order to encourage the dispersal of industries and to enable companies to establish factories for the manufacture of products mainly for the export market, where the establishment of Free Zone is neither practical nor desirable, the Government has allowed the setting up of licensed manufacturing warehouses.

In the free trade zones, 100 per cent foreign ownership is allowed if firms are export-oriented. The official incentive package includes: duty-free imports of raw material and capital equipment; streamlined customs facilities; subsidised provision of infrastructure; and corporate income tax incentives.

Free Zones tend to be almost completely dominated by foreign capital. Penang's customs free industrial zones have been the focus of investments by international electronics companies. Firms located in Free Zones dominated Malaysian manufactured exports in the early 1980s, overtaking the resource-based industries processing raw materials for export. As there was no pressure placed on these foreign firms to set up joint ventures with domestic firms unless they produced for the local market, fully foreign-owned firms clearly dominate. As of 1978, 94 per cent of firms in Free Zones were foreign-controlled.[38] Most of Malaysia's export-oriented foreign-owned industry is now located there.[39]

Restrictions on FDI in the financial sector

The early stages of economic reform in Malaysia were not accompanied by liberalisation of the financial sector. Instead, there was even greater control and supervision of the financial system because of difficulties arising from mismanagement, over-exposure to some sectors, and bad debts during the recession. Malaysia went through a banking crisis in 1985-88 due to speculation in the property sector. As a result, real sector liberalisation preceded financial reform, and it was only with economic recovery after 1987 that the Government took further steps toward financial liberalisation. A major impact of the reform was to reduce the degree of concentration in the commercial banking industry. While the 10 largest banks accounted for more than 80 per cent of the industry's total deposits and loans and almost 80 per cent of all assets before 1978, these shares were greatly reduced as a result of liberalisation although they remain high compared to other countries.

Foreigners in the banking sector

Malaysia's strong growth performance in the past attracted intense pressure to allow unlimited foreign participation in the Malaysian financial sector. In preparation for foreign competition, Bank Negara encouraged mergers and consolidation of the domestic financial industry which it considered to be overcrowded. Regional liberalisation of the financial sector should occur within the next decade. So far, however, important restrictions on expansion and operations by foreign banks still exist.

The banking industry is dominated by a small number of domestic institutions controlled by the Federal government or by quasi-governmental entities. The Government has a majority share in the three largest banks. There are 35 licensed commercial banks, of which 13 are foreign bank branches. They hold a sizeable share of the banking market, with 30 per cent of the total deposits and loans, and 46 per cent of total trade financing in the country (Table 7). Moreover foreigners have equity participation in 12 domestic banks, seven finance companies and one merchant bank. Foreigners also have an interest in 11 of the 59 stockbroking firms. There are also 29 foreign banks that have established representative offices in Kuala Lumpur, but they are not permitted to conduct normal banking business.

Table 7. **Foreign and domestic commercial banks**

	1992		1996	
Total deposits (RM million)	112 547		243 969	
Domestic Banks	87 312	(77.6%)	192 496	(78.9%)
Foreign Banks	25 235	(22.4%)	51 473	(21.1%)
Total loans (RM million)	105 729		228 240	
Domestic banks	77 598	(73.4%)	175 282	(76.8%)
Foreign banks	28 131	(26.6%)	52 958	(23.2%)

Source: Bank Negara Malaysia, *Annual Report*, various issues.

Malaysia has issued no new commercial banking licences, except those restricted to offshore activities, since 1982. As a result, almost all foreign commercial banks currently operating in Malaysia had established themselves as branch banks of an overseas bank before or shortly after the country reached independence.[40] Acquisition of existing domestic banks is not a viable option for foreigners, because ownership in domestic banks is limited to 10 per cent for an individual, 20 per cent for others, with a maximum foreign investment of 30 per cent in any one entity[41].

Under the Banking and Financial Institutions Act 1989, a licence to carry on banking business may be issued only to a Malaysian incorporated company.

As a result, foreign incorporated banks operating as branches of parent companies were required to convert into locally incorporated institutions by September 1994 if they wanted to continue their operations in Malaysia. Although foreign banks are still allowed 100 per cent foreign ownership, the forced incorporation imposes heavy costs on them. By the end of 1994, 14 out of the 16 foreign banks had initiated steps to establish locally-incorporated companies that would take over their banking operations in Malaysia.[42]

In addition to the limitations on entry and the incorporation requirement, there are other important restrictions on the operations and expansion by foreign banks which do not apply to domestic banks. Unlike domestic banks, foreign commercial banks may not establish new branches. For regulatory purposes, offsite ATMs are considered to be separate branches, thus limiting the ability of foreign banks to compete by offering the same range of services as their domestic competitors.[43] These restrictions were not lifted by the local incorporation of foreign existing branches because they applied to all banks with more than 50 per cent foreign ownership. Foreign banks were also restricted to providing no more than 40 per cent of the domestic borrowing by foreign companies. Foreign-controlled companies are estimated to comprise 10 per cent of the total market for domestic banking credit and tend to be natural consumers for foreign banks.

Foreign financial institutions are also adversely affected by the restrictions limiting the number of expatriate employees to two per cent, but domestic banks are subject to even more stringent restrictions on hiring expatriates. New guidelines offering a more flexible approach to the employment of expatriate staff were adopted in 1994 which allow banking institutions greater flexibility in employing expatriate staff under certain conditions. First, banking institutions with foreign equity of at least 20 per cent may be allowed to recruit one expatriate and those with foreign equity exceeding 50 per cent may be allowed to recruit two. Secondly, banking institutions may recruit foreign specialists or experts, subject among other things to an acceptable programme to train local staff. There are also restrictions applying to the board of directors.

By contrast, the lending guidelines requiring that 20 per cent of the loans be extended to *Bumiputeras* are imposed by Bank Negara on all banks, domestic and foreign alike. Similarly, foreign-controlled banks are granted the same treatment as domestic banks with regard to money market instruments, access to the Central Bank discount window, etc.

Other financial sectors

In insurance, no new licences have been granted since 1985. Existing foreign branches are required to incorporate locally, while further entries are limited to equity participation in existing locally-incorporated companies. Approval is required for equity participation exceeding five per cent. There is an individual shareholding limit of 20 per cent and an aggregate limit of 30 per cent, but exception can be made up to 49 per cent. There are ten fully foreign-owned companies and an additional eight have foreign equity exceeding 50 per cent. Foreign equity ownership amounts to 44 per cent of the capital funds of the industry. Foreign companies account for 40 per cent of gross premiums and 52 per cent of total assets.

As a result of the financial crisis, restrictions on foreign equity participation in the insurance sector have been relaxed. While new foreign entrants into the local insurance industry will be restricted to an equity stake of 30 per cent, foreigners with an existing presence in the local industry will be allowed a maximum of 51 per cent foreign equity participation under the following circumstances:

> *i)* a foreign direct insurer operating in Malaysia as a branch, and which locally incorporates its operation in compliance with the Insurance Act of 1996, can retain up to 51 per cent of the equity of the locally-incorporated entity;

> *ii)* an existing foreign owner of a locally-incorporated insurer which has yet to restructure can retain up to 51 per cent of the equity of the restructured company, provided aggregate foreign shareholding does not exceed 51 per cent; and

> *iii)* the present foreign shareholders which were the original owners of locally-incorporated insurance companies that have restructured in line with requirements under the National Development Policy, can increase their shareholdings to 51 per cent provided aggregate foreign shareholdings do not exceed 51 per cent.

These restrictions do not apply to foreign professional reinsurers that are allowed to operate as branches in Malaysia, or in the case of locally-controlled reinsurance joint ventures, the foreign partner may retain up to an aggregate of 49 per cent of the equity in the joint venture.

In the securities industry, foreigners had interest in 11 of the 59 stockbroking firms as of 1994. Foreign corporate ownership, which was limited to 30 per cent, has since been increased to an aggregate total of 49 per cent of paid-up capital of an existing member company. A member company with foreign participation is treated no differently from other member companies. Further liberalisation measures allow increased foreign equity participation in both insurance companies and fund management companies.[44]

Prior to the crisis, foreign fund managers were subject to the general equity participation limit of 30 per cent. Foreign banks and securities firms were allowed to engage in fund management activities in the same way as local banks and securities firms. Because of the equity participation limit, however, a number of foreign fund managers chose to operate offshore, especially in Singapore. In the wake of the financial crisis, fully or majority foreign-owned fund management companies will be allowed.

Restrictions in other sectors

At the conclusion of the Uruguay Round trade negotiations in 1994, several service sectors were to be liberalised to varying degrees, including professional, computer and related services, telecommunications, audio-visual, research and development, rental and leasing, construction and related engineering, hotels and restaurants, and maritime and air transport.[45] In the shipping sector, the Government allows the operations of shipping agents with majority foreign equity and has relaxed the cabotage requirement for certain ports.[46]

Several sectors are subject to specific joint-venture equity policies, where foreign equity ownership is allowed to maximum levels of 30-60 per cent. These industries mainly produce supporting parts and components, including plastic packaging materials, compounds, injection moulded components and parts for the electrical, electronic and telecommunications industries, paper packaging products, metal fabrication and foundry products. The aim of the policy is to enhance Malaysian participation in these sectors.

According to one source, "the Government is active in oil, utilities, transport, banking and public services, and operates the country's many industrial estates. Private participation in these sectors is not formally restricted, but non-*Bumiputeras* may find barriers to entry unless they are associated with *Bumiputera* firms which sometimes contribute only their names."[47]

IV.   Privatisation

Rationale

Following from the NEP, public sector activities expanded throughout the 1970s with the creation of more than 900 public enterprises by 1982, up from only 23 in 1957. The public sector's share of GDP grew from 24 per cent in the 1960s to around 30 per cent in the 1970s and peaked at 48 per cent in 1981. As a result of fortuitous circumstances, notably high commodity prices for Malaysian resources, the Government was able to avert the inevitable structural problems created by growing public sector deficits.

Following the recession of the mid-1980s, however, there was an obvious need to curtail public spending and to reduce the weight of the public sector in the economy. An active policy of privatisation was thus implemented, beginning in 1983 which included the relaxation of regulations on foreign equity participation and other provisions of the ICA 1975. Privatisation formed part of a broad range of macroeconomic stabilisation and liberalisation programmes, including financial deregulation, as well as trade and domestic market liberalisation.

Despite some criticisms, it has been argued by some that the Malaysian privatisation drive has been on the whole successful in fulfilling its various objectives.[48] Privatisation has probably been most successful in contributing to the NEP objective of *Bumiputera* wealth acquisition. It is said to be instrumental in speeding up income and ownership redistribution, especially since all privatised projects must have at least 30 per cent *Bumiputera* participation.[49] This policy of privatisation with redistribution follows logically from the nationalisation move in the 1970s, the purpose of which was to reduce the economic domination of the ethnic Chinese and to facilitate the eventual transfer of these firms to the *Bumiputeras*. Privatisation is also credited with having reduced the Government's financial burden.

Moreover, the impact of privatisation on the growth, depth and sophistication of Malaysian capital markets has no doubt exceeded the authorities' expectations.[50] The market capitalisation of privatised companies on the Kuala Lumpur Stock Exchange at the end of 1995 amounted to RM125 billion or 22 per cent of total market capitalisation. The Malaysian equities market is both large and active. The level of capitalisation exceeded 340 per cent of GDP in 1993 (compared to about 75 per cent ten years earlier).[51] These indicators are much higher than those achieved in comparable emerging markets, such as Thailand (four per cent) or Chile (13 per cent).

A number of criticisms have been raised against the privatisation process, such as a general lack of transparency, sometimes without even the formality of an open tender system or prior public announcement.[52] The North-South Highway concession, for example, was criticised by some observers for a lack of effective transparency and the fact that the concession was awarded to certain officials of the Malaysian government. Other critics have claimed that in many of the larger privatisations the Government has either retained a majority stake or allowed local business interests connected with the Government to retain control.[53] An example is the issue of the country's first and only television broadcasting licence in 1983 to Sistem Televisyen Malaysia Berhad, whose major shareholders then included Fleet Group, the ruling party's (United Malays National Organisation - UMNO) holding company, the UMNO-controlled Utusan newspaper publishing group, and other groups close to the Prime Minister (Jomo 1994). These criticisms are likely to have discouraged foreign firms from bidding in the privatisation process.

Means

In Malaysia, privatisation is often understood to include cases where less than half of the assets or shares of public enterprises are sold to private shareholders and where the Government retains control. Such was the case for the privatisation of the Malaysian airlines company, MAS (Malaysian Airlines System Berhad). Although the Government holds only 48 per cent of the shares, it continues to retain direct control over the company as the single largest shareholder. Moreover a substantial amount of MAS stock is held by Bank Negara Malaysia, the central bank of Malaysia, giving the public sector as a whole a continued majority ownership (Jomo 1994). The Government still retains majority interest in strategic corporations, such as Proton, Telekom Malaysia and the national electric utility Tenaga Malaysia, as well as an important holding in the Malaysian International Shipping Company.

More generally, even if the Government does not keep a majority interest, it may still retain strategic control through a so-called golden share. The partial or complete sale of equity is the most common method used in Malaysia, accounting for 46 per cent of projects privatised in 1991-95.[54] Build, Operate and Transfer (BOT) projects and sale of assets are the two other common means of privatisation, with 10 and 16 per cent of the projects respectively.[55] The BOT approach is most frequently used for infrastructure projects, such as the construction of highways, power plants, and water supply schemes,[56] while the sale of assets is primarily used in the privatisation of quarrying operations. The sale of assets involves the transfer of the assets but not of management and personnel.

The scope of privatisation

Between 1991 and 1995, 204 projects were privatised, mostly in the field of infrastructure. Federal government projects (56 per cent) slightly exceeded those of state governments (44 per cent). Two thirds of the privatisations represented existing projects, while the rest were new projects, sometimes proposed by the private sector itself. The sectoral distribution of privatisation projects can be seen in Figure 3. Construction accounted for the largest share, followed by manufacturing.

The Government has stated explicitly that the aim of the privatisation is not to maximise the value of the assets being sold but rather to fulfil numerous economic and social policy objectives. The privatisations in 1991-95 nevertheless raised RM14 billion from the sale of assets and saved RM52 billion in capital expenditures.

Figure 3. Sectoral distribution of privatised projects, 1991-95

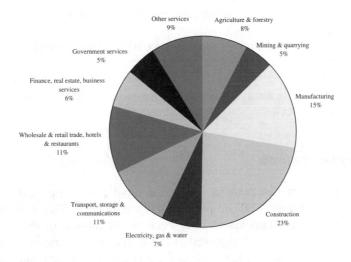

Source: Economic Planning Unit

135

The telecommunications sector was opened to allow establishment of independent telecommunication network services, as the State-run company, Telekom Malaysia, was deprived of its former monopoly status. The appearance of several entrants into the market prompted the Government to insist that they should merge to reduce overcrowding in the market, but this policy has since been reversed.[57] Nevertheless, only acquisitions are permitted, while no new licences are granted. Several new entrants have formed alliances with foreign operators: an American company, US West, owns a 20 per cent stake in Biniariang, an unlisted Malaysian telecommunications company; and Swiss Telecom purchased 30 per cent of Mutiara Telekom for $285 million in 1996.

Power supply has also been subject to privatisation initiatives, mainly through BOO (Build Own Operate) schemes. Five power productions projects have been allowed on a BOO scheme, but problems have recently arisen with the independent power producers (IPP). The Government has been keen to eliminate power outages such as the 16-hour blackout in August 1996 which affected the whole peninsula. The IPPs were originally given permission to set up following a similar blackout in 1992. With the help of these IPPs, Malaysia has overcome the problems leading to these blackouts, but demand for power is growing quickly.

Petronas Gas was privatised in 1996 in one of the biggest deals in the history of the country's privatisation programme. The sale of Petronas Gas for $1.1 billion represented the first time international investors were allowed to participate through an American Depository Receipt placement.

The Government has identified a further 1000 companies with total paid-up capital of RM27 billion for future privatisation (ERT 1996). According to an estimate by the University of Malaya, the private sector is expected to provide over three quarters of total infrastructure spending under the current five-year plan to the year 2000.[58]

The role of foreign firms

The Malaysian Government does not have a specific policy either to restrict or to promote FDI in privatised enterprises. The role of foreign investors nevertheless appears to have been rather limited in the privatisation process, at least when compared to the Latin American experience.[59] *Bumiputera* participation in the equity of a privatised company must follow the 30 per cent rule established in the NEP. Because of dilution of this share over time in privatised companies as the *Bumiputera* engaged in profit taking rather than continuing to hold the shares, the Government stipulated a three-year moratorium on all concession companies with respect to divestment of equity by *Bumiputera* and non-*Bumiputera* after privatisation.

In addition, efforts to increase direct and active participation of *Bumiputera* contractors through privatisation were implemented through the imposition of a condition in the concession agreement requiring at least 30 per cent of contract work to be reserved to *Bumiputera*. Some privatised entities were required to conduct training programmes tailored to the needs of the company, as well as to provide practical training to new labour market entrants.

In the Seventh Malaysia Plan covering the period 1996-2000, the Government outlined a number of aims which were likely to impose a further burden on potential foreign investors. These included ensuring greater participation of local companies, especially in the privatisation of infrastructure projects; promoting greater local content in privatised projects to ensure expansion of local industries and services; expanding *Bumiputera* participation in the management of privatised companies, as well as implementing marketing arrangements and vendor development programmes.

V.   The role of FDI in Malaysia's economic development

Case studies

The automobile sector: lessons from the Proton experience

The automobile sector provides a good example of the perils for foreign investors of selling in the local market. When high tariffs were imposed in the 1960s, a number of foreign producers were permitted to take minority stakes in local companies to assemble cars for the local market. Once the Government launched its own national car project in the mid-1980s, foreign producers were effectively squeezed out of the market.[60] Tariff protection remains, with the automobile sector one of the most highly protected in Malaysia, but national car producers receive much more favourable treatment. In retrospect, import substitution based on foreign investment in this sector can be seen as a temporary stage to give Malaysia time to accumulate sufficient financial resources and experience to develop its own producers.

Malaysia has three national car projects: Proton (a joint-venture with Mitsubishi), Perodua (a joint-venture with Daihatsu) producing a minicar, the Kancil, and a recent joint-venture with Citroen. Production of its first car, the Proton Saga, began in July 1985, with Mitsubishi Motors Corporation and

Mitsubishi Corporation[61] providing assistance in product development and plant construction, operation and management. Because of the 1986 recession, Malaysia suffered a 40 per cent drop in demand for passenger cars compared to the peak level reached in 1982. Although the Saga was originally intended to satisfy domestic demand, the recession pushed it towards exporting. Initially exports were destined for neighbouring markets, but by 1989 the Saga was exported to the United Kingdom (where Malaysia benefits from GSP status) and Singapore. By 1994, Proton had a local market share in Malaysia of 74 per cent (compared to 11 per cent in 1985) and exported about 20 per cent of its production. Its share fell back to 66 per cent in 1996.

Five years after beginning production, Proton had reached local content levels of 65 per cent (compared to an initial level of 42 per cent), but it still relied on imports for those parts requiring heavy investment and a high technological content. Because these imports tend to come from Japan, the rise of the yen has eroded profits at Proton. The Government announced plans to begin producing its own engine blocks in 1994. Proton has built up its local supply network from 17 to 134 companies, which now manufacture over 3000 Proton components. As a result, local content now amounts to 80 per cent. Although Proton does not yet manufacture transmissions and engines, it produces locally cylinder blocks and crankshafts with Mitsubishi's help.[62] Dissatisfaction with the speed of technology transfer from Japan has led Proton to seek out additional foreign partners, such as Citroen which participated in the elaboration of the Proton Tiara. The acquisition of Lotus (UK) in 1996 (described earlier) is another part of this strategy of technological upgrading.

In spite of continued growth in exports, Proton suffered large losses until 1989 and operates well below the minimum efficient scale for car plants.[63] It had record profits in 1996 but has since been hit by the financial turmoil in Southeast Asia since 20 per cent of its costs are denominated in yen which has appreciated sharply against the ringgit.[64]

Proton has traditionally owed its high profits partly to high tariffs on imports of foreign cars. Although tariffs were abolished on completely built-up (CBU) commercial vehicles, CBU passenger car imports remain tightly regulated and subject to tariffs ranging from 140 to 200 per cent[65]. Import levies on completely knocked down (CKD) parts favour national over non-national cars: 13 per cent on parts for Proton and 42 per cent on parts for other producers.[66] Foreign companies assembling cars locally, such as Toyota, Nissan and Honda, face a 42 per cent duty on imported kits. In addition, foreign car assemblers must charge a profit margin of 16-17 per cent over their costs. Beginning in 1992, foreign assemblers were required to increase the local content in their operations in Malaysia or else face high import barriers. The aim was to rationalise the industry since many producers could no longer compete effectively without recourse to imports. The local content requirement is set at 30 per cent with a number of designated items (tyres, batteries, etc).

Foreign car assemblers which had previously formed minority joint ventures with their local distributors in the late 1960s to produce behind protective tariffs have been unable to compete against what has become effectively a protected, monopolistic and subsidised State enterprise. Some investors considered their treatment to be "a betrayal of earlier inducements to foreign firms to invest in car-assembly in Malaysia".[67] The Government had recommended that these firms merge into larger and more efficient plants, move into reconditioning old cars, or diversify into components, but it expected that some of them would eventually close down.[68]

Effects of policies

Before the Proton project was launched in 1982, the automobile industry displayed all the symptoms of the ill-effects of tariff protection. There were 15 assembly plants operating in a small market and hence with low capacity utilisation and local content of only eight per cent.[69] There was some industrial growth and employment creation, but few exports and limited skills development or technology transfer. Any improvement over this earlier situation has come at a high cost for consumers because of tariff protection and for taxpayers from the subsidies offered to national producers. By squeezing out many of these assemblers, the Proton project has necessarily improved capacity utilisation, and, on the back of quasi-monopoly profits at home, the company has begun to export.

If the benefits from Proton were to be compared instead with the potential gains which might have ensued from the alternative policy of tariff reductions and industry rationalisation, the national car project would appear in a less favourable light. The project has nevertheless created a *Bumiputera* industry where none existed before, but the principal high technology components still come from Japan. It remains to be seen whether national producers will become autonomous and internationally competitive – and at what cost. Proton sales have plummeted during the crisis, as a result of the severe contraction in demand in this sector throughout the region.

Electronics

Electronics and electrical appliances account for about 60 per cent of manufactured exports.[70] Within the electronics sector, components are still the major sub-sector, with more than 40 per cent of total exports, ahead of

139

consumer electronics (with 38 per cent and industrial electronics with 22 per cent). Components represented almost three quarters of total electronic exports in the mid-1980s.[71] Even if the concentration of electronic output and exports in electronic components has gradually decreased, leading to a more balanced distribution between components, consumer electronic products and industrial electronic products, the lack of diversification in exports is bound to lead to some vulnerability to fluctuations in the world market. The slowdown in the worldwide demand for semiconductors in 1996, which led to a slump in export revenues in Malaysia, is such an example.

Furthermore, because manufacturing is still concentrated in labour-intensive assembly work, imports of intermediate goods swallow up no less than 85 per cent of manufactured export earnings. Manufactured exports are produced mainly by foreign-owned enterprises engaged primarily in component assembly in Malaysia.[72] Strong import intensity is a characteristic of the high-skill and high-technology segments of manufactured exports. It is estimated that a typical electronics assembly plant in a Free Zone sources as much as 60 per cent of its material inputs from overseas.[73] According to UNCTAD, imports of parts of automatic data processing equipment were more than 95 per cent of the export value of finished products in Malaysia in 1994. This figure is so high partly because electronic parts account for a large share of total electronic exports. Yet, even in terms of the ratio of imported parts to total exports (of both finished products and parts), the import content is still much higher than in the first-tier NIEs.[74] Although the local content of Malaysian manufactured exports has increased significantly over the years, it remains a matter of concern for the authorities. Various measures were recently put in place to keep imports in check, but it is too soon to assess their impact.

In Penang, sixty per cent of the workforce is employed in electronics, but the value added in electronics is well below that found in other sectors, including such basic industries as flour milling. "Low value-added electronic components – where Malaysian factories usually add about 30 per cent of the value of a product – still account for about 40 per cent of the country's electronic sector, although that is down from as high as 80 per cent in 1986."[75] According to Salleh, "while some products are close to the forefront of technology...there has been little deepening in the product design and technologies of the products themselves".[76]

Moreover, in Malaysia, the majority of exports of automatic data processing equipment consist of parts: finished products accounted for only 30 per cent of total exports of the sector. All this suggests that a large share of Malaysian exports in these sectors consists of intermediate products that are re-exported after processing, so that the high technology character of exports may often be primarily a reflection of that of the imported inputs.[77] With assembling activities still dominant, the potential for positive spillovers remains limited.

Although foreign firms in electronics have reportedly often upgraded their production in line with rising labour costs, the trend is not ubiquitous. Rising labour costs in Penang, where wages are higher than those found in most other parts of Malaysia, together with a slowdown in electronics exports throughout Southeast Asia, have contributed to a number of closures of electronics affiliates of foreign companies. Wage rises have apparently grown twice as fast as productivity increases, and the costs of power and land rent have also been rising.[78] The Government has also been discouraging further labour-intensive investments in the area.

A number of foreign investors have recently pulled out of Malaysian production and established elsewhere. A major Taipei producer of disk drives, for example, has shifted production from Penang to China.[79] Philips Electronics is to move its activities to southern China, affecting 1,500 jobs. Matsushita is moving an air conditioning factory to Indonesia. Inventec, one of the first investors in Penang, has moved two thirds of production of certain goods to China. The remaining third were to be displaced in 1998.[80] Some closures, by both Taipei and OECD firms, have resulted more from slack demand than from any developments in Malaysia, but the relocations described above all suggest a weakness in local cost competitiveness in this sector.

FDI as an instrument of economic restructuring

Foreign investment has played a key role in economic restructuring in Malaysia, contributing to development through its catalytic role in structural changes that have turned Malaysia from an agricultural and primary producer into a major manufacturer. In the early 1970s, more than 80 per cent of exports were commodities such as tin, rubber and oil. By the early 1990s, manufactured goods (mainly electronics) represented 70 per cent of total exports. This transformation is echoed to a lesser extent in terms of overall economic activity. The share of GDP represented by agriculture fell from 41 per cent in 1960 to only 13 per cent today, while manufacturing increased from 8 to 35 per cent.

The Government has made this shift an important objective of its development strategy, and much of the actual work of structural transformation has been undertaken by foreign investors, either on their own or in co-operation with a local partner. Malaysia was successful in attracting electronics assembly when large MNEs were looking to relocate activities to low-wage countries.

The strong export orientation of manufacturing is reflected in the percentage of manufactured exports to output, exceeding 65 per cent in 1995, compared to 53 per cent only in 1993. Export orientation is stronger in foreign-owned firms than in domestic ones. Foreign affiliates accounted for an estimated 46 percent of exports and 32 per cent of employment in the late 1980s, and for 60 per cent of exports and 49 per cent of employment in manufacturing.[81] Free Zones have played a major role in this respect, accounting for more than half of total manufactured exports within 10 years of their creation. Foreign firms have been particularly important in the electrical and electronic sector which account for two thirds of total manufacturing exports, compared with only one quarter in 1975 (Figure 4 and Table 8). Only a few Malaysian companies, mainly engaged in resource-based industries or their downstream derivatives, are strong exporters with an international market niche. Foreign firms are not much involved in the processing of primary commodities.

Figure 4. **Manufactured exports as a percentage of GDP, 1970-97**

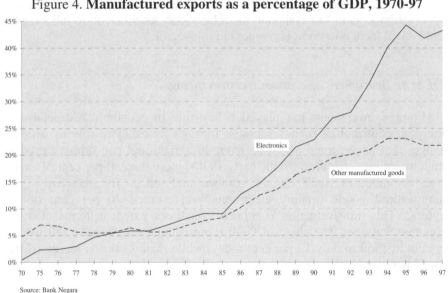

Source: Bank Negara

Table 8. **Malaysian manufactured exports, 1997** (RM million, per cent)

Food, beverages, tobacco	4 470		2.5%	
Petroleum products	3 372		1.9%	
Chemicals and chemical products	8 137		4.5%	
Textiles, clothing and footwear	7 616		4.3%	
Rubber, wood, paper and pulp products	11 196		6.3%	
Metal manufactures	5 661		3.2%	
Electrical and electronic products and parts	119 025		66.5%	
Semiconductors		40 887		22.8%
Electronic equipment and parts		39 889		22.3%
Consumer electrical products		17 777		9.9%
Industrial electrical products		12 001		6.7%
Electrical industrial machinery and equipment		7 739		4.3%
Household electrical appliances		732		0.4%
Transport equipment	4 959		2.8%	
Others	14 509		8.1%	
Total	**178 945**		100.0%	

Source: Department of Statistics, Malaysia

FDI as a driving force behind regional integration

Foreign direct investors have played a pivotal role in the growth of intra-regional trade in Southeast Asia. To the extent reductions in tariff barriers, sub-regional growth triangles, brand-to-brand complementation schemes[82] and the like allow MNEs to rationalise production, the result has been a growth in vertically-integrated trade among affiliates in the region.

In the electronic sector, the pattern of exports has changed as a result of an increasing cross-border division of labour among East Asian countries as intra-Asian trade in electronic machinery and parts has grown since the early 1980s. The pattern of trade between Malaysia and Japan has also changed since the mid-1980s. High technology electronic parts, such as integrated circuit boards and audiovisual parts, are increasingly exported from Japan to Malaysia for assembly by local Malaysian affiliates, while products such as colour television sets are increasingly exported from Malaysia to Japan.[83]

In the case of electronic parts, the pattern of affiliate sales is evolving to take advantage of greater regional integration. The share of the sales directed to the host country has also increased, reflecting large amounts of direct investment by part suppliers following the direct investment by assemblers. Thus subsidiaries in Asian countries purchase increasing amounts of parts from other subsidiaries in the same country. The share of parts sold to the rest of Asia (excluding Japan) has also risen over the last decade. Third countries in Asia are becoming important markets for the products of subsidiaries.

As regional integration has progressed, MNEs have been able to rationalise their production facilities. Some, such as Matsushita, have chosen to locate certain activities in Malaysia. While Matsushita used to have several firms scattered throughout Southeast Asia producing a full range of products destined for protected local markets, it has since reduced the range of products coming from one single factory and instead turned each subsidiary into a regional production centre. Malaysia has become a base for regional exports for the company.[84]

In contrast, Malaysia's participation in the regional division of labour in the automobile sector remains limited. Because of its national car project, Malaysia has always been rather reluctant to take part in the brand-to-brand complementation (BBC) scheme under which all parts of the same brand produced in the ASEAN region are considered as local and therefore face reduced tariffs. Intra-regional trade in automobile parts is not yet very substantial, except in a few cases like Toyota's production of steering gears in Malaysia for export to subsidiaries in the rest of the region. Intra-regional trade may however improve as the BBC scheme is replaced by the ASEAN industrial co-operation scheme, in which approved products may get preferential tariff rates of 0-5 per cent. For the time being, in the automobile sector, MNEs tend to sell mostly in the domestic market, unlike in the electronics sector.

Technology transfer

As repositories of much of the world's most advanced technologies, MNEs can potentially transfer substantial amounts of technology to their affiliates abroad. Technology can flow to the host country through many different channels, including imports of capital goods as part of the investment; affiliate licensing of the parent's technologies; the acquisition of skills by employees, and relations with local suppliers.

The Malaysian experience described in the case studies of the automobile and electronics sectors suggests that such transfers are by no means automatic. Some skills and expertise has been absorbed by employees in foreign affiliates which they can take with them when they change jobs, but in other areas, both the Government and academic experts have found the degree of transfer to be disappointing. According to a study of the Malaysian electronics sector, Malaysian has acquired substantial operational and process adaptation knowledge and experience in the production process, but there has been little deepening of product design and development. Most firms in the sector are heavily engaged in assembly and testing activities.[85] Furthermore, despite a long presence of electronics firms, the level of local content remains low. It is estimated that between 5 and 33 per cent of the production of television sets involves local components, for example. But even this production is most likely to come from a foreign-owned firm.

The causes of poor technology transfer depend on the circumstances. In a sector protected by high tariffs, such as automobiles, the lack of spillovers follow directly from the poor record of innovation by both foreign and domestic firms and can be found in many countries which have followed such protectionist policies. Sheltered behind protective tariffs, producers have little incentive to develop local technological capabilities, preferring instead to share in the economic rents accruing from protection. In a dynamic sector such as electronics in which affiliates must be competitive in world markets, the reasons for poor technological performance are very different. The principal cause is likely to be the enclave nature of this export production which divides Malaysian-controlled activities and the MNE sphere of manufacturing for export. The lack of linkages arises for two reasons in this case. First, export platforms are generally a separate customs territory from the host economy which impedes flows of both goods and information between the two: any purchases or sales to the host economy are treated as international trade. Second, since exporters must compete in third markets, they require inputs which meet high standards or which are technologically sophisticated. In many cases, these inputs are supplied by the parent company or from affiliates in other countries. The indirect effect of placing foreign investors in such enclaves may be to promote integration with neighbouring countries at the expense of linkages with local firms. "If a customs barrier must be crossed to reach suppliers, it might as well be an international barrier to reach already developed suppliers in Singapore."[86]

Various policy measures have been tried recently to strengthen backward and forward linkages and to bridge the gap between MNEs and local firms. Such is the purpose of the provisions allowing easier trade between Free Zones and the rest of the economy for instance. While Free zones remained segregated in the first 15 years (1972-87) with few backward linkages with the rest of the local economy, they have gradually become better integrated as more backward and forward linkages have been allowed, with more inputs being bought from foreign-owned plants and joint ventures.[87]

The extent of technology transfer depends also on the ability of local workers and firms to absorb such technology. This deficiency has been viewed as a contributing factor to Malaysia's lack of success at technological upgrading. While Malaysia's comparative advantage in low-wage activities is eroding, the country as a whole lacks graduate scientists and skilled technicians who would be in a position to initiate technological upgrading. Not only is there a lack of domestic R&D, there is also growing evidence of severe skills shortages. "Employers blame...the Government's policy of funding university education in Bahasa (the local language) for Bumiputeras (Malays) – which they say produced too many social science and arts graduates – while many Chinese were forced to pay for their own education abroad and returned with technical qualifications and a useful knowledge of English."[88] Thailand and the Philippines both have a higher proportion of students in tertiary education than Malaysia (7 per cent of 20-24 year olds compared to 28 per cent in the Philippines and 16 per cent in Thailand). The Government is making a concerted effort to revamp the education system, but the results will not be seen for some years.[89]

This lack of industrial upgrading is not specific to FDI-dominated sectors. Although the locally-controlled resource-based industry has grown quickly, there has been very little progress in increasing value added. Even in the palm oil industry, where Malaysia has successfully created a niche in the global market, many of the processed exports are basic products, such as refined palm oil and olein and basic by-products such as refined stearin.[90]

146

NOTES

1. The Generalised System of Preferences or GSP allows for preferential market access for certain exports to the United States and other developed markets from designated developing countries.

2. By way of comparison, the ratio for Mexico is less than 10 per cent for the most recent period.

3. Based on data from MIDA, the Malaysia Industrial Development Authority, which is the screening agency for domestic and foreign investment projects in Malaysia. Since MIDA data only include larger investments covered by the Industrial Coordination Act (see below) and since the SME sector can be presumed to be mostly local, this measure overestimates the degree of foreign participation in manufacturing, which probably does not exceed 30 per cent (Ghazali Atan in Jomo 1994). Moreover, as there is bound to be a sizeable discrepancy between investment projects approved by MIDA and those actually implemented by the applicants, the MIDA data necessarily overstate the foreign equity participation (Ariff 1991).

4. Allen (1979), cited in Cable and Persaud (1987), p. 106.

5. Within the New Economic Policy, a major objective was to provide urban industrial jobs for the Bumiputeras.

6. O'Connor in Jomo (1993).

7. UNCTAD (1997), p. 91.

8. "Foreign investment in Malaysia surges ahead", *Financial Times*, 19 March 1991.

9. UNCTAD (1996), p. 34. Sime Darby, formerly a British company, was bought up by the Malaysian government at the time of the NEP and eventually privatised in 1988.

10. "Sime Darby looks outside Asia to spread its wings" *Financial Times*, 2 May 1995.

11.   *Far Eastern Economic Review*, 12 December 1996.

12.   This strategy is in stark contrast to South Korea's strategy of outward investment, whose objective is to counteract weak domestic demand and sputtering exports (FEER 1.5.97). Also pushing Korean companies abroad is the need to match Western competitors in reducing production costs through global sourcing and in marketing efforts.

13.   "Malaysia plans world car export drive" *Financial Times*, 18 November 1996.

14.   "Malaysia seeks expertise through foreign companies", *Financial Times*, 3 December 1996.

15.   "Starting small, aiming high", *Financial Times*, 18 February 1994.

16.   Outward investment is thought to ease the access of Malaysian products to foreign markets (GATT 1993).

17.   Lim and Nesadurai (1997).

18.   Caves (1982).

19.   These broad phases were suggested by Salleh and Meyanathan (1993).

20.   Many British firms previously exporting reportedly seized this opportunity to consolidate market monopolies by establishing branch plants behind protective tariff barriers (Jomo 1990).

21.   Lim and Pang (1991), p. 39.

22.   Exemptions from the licensing requirement were given to a limited number of sectors such as rice and rubber milling, crude palm oil processing etc. (Meyananthan and Salleh 1993).

23.   Jomo (1993, p. 297). A similar analysis is developed by Bruton (1992), who argues that developing the manufacturing sector meant - to Malaysian policy-makers - building large-scale Western firms, hence the necessary resort to Western multinationals, because the foreign firms would then provide sufficient competition to the Chinese to prevent their gaining undue dominance.

24.   Lim and Nesadurai (1997).

25.   EIU (1996).

26. Until then most sectors were open to foreign investment, with the exception of postal services, telecommunications and other public services (Lim and Pang 1991).

27. These firms may be allowed to have 100 per cent foreign ownership if the share of fixed assets (excluding land) is at least equal to RM50 million or if value-added amounts to a minimum of 50 per cent and if products are not competing with locally produced goods on the domestic market.

28. "Economic health curbs worker militancy", *Financial* Times, 28 August 1992.

29. "Becoming Choosy", *Far Eastern Economic Review,* 25 July 1996.

30. The Exclusion list includes: paper and plastic packaging, plastic injection moulded components, metal stamping, fabrication and electroplating, wire harness, printing and steel service centres.

31. "Turning off the tap", *Far Eastern Economic Review*, 12 November 1998.

32. Bruton (1992).

33. The national unemployment rate was around 8 per cent in the late 1960s, while the contribution of manufacturing to GDP remained small, below 10 per cent.

34. Jomo (1990)

35. In 1971 amendments were made to the Investment Incentives Act of 1968 to encourage industries to utilise more local labour.

36. UNCTAD (1995)

37. 10 FIZs and 2 FCZs.

38. Meyananthan and Salleh (1993).

39. Lim and Pang (1991), p. 98.

40. The Bank of Nova Scotia was the last one to start business in Malaysia in 1973.

41. In the WTO financial services agreement, Malaysia committed to raise the foreign equity participation in domestic banks to 51 per cent.

42. Bank Negara (1994)

43.   As at end of 1993, foreign banks had 178 ATMs, compared with 1380 for domestic banks.

44.   MITI (1996, p. 149).

45.   ERT (1996).

46.   MITI, p. 149

47.   ERT (1996), p. 162.

48.   Meyanathan and Salleh (1993); Ibrahim (1996).

49 .   Ibrahim (1996).

50.   *Ibid.*

51.   The turnover ratio reflects the intensity of trading on the market, in other words it is an indicator of the depth of the market. Concentration ratios also point in the same direction, indicating that the Malaysian equities market is a mature market.

52.   "Malaysian tenders touch a sore point", *Financial Times*, 20 November 1996.

53.   "A fillip for capital markets", *Financial Times*, 28 August 1992.

54.   It was used in the privatisation of Cement Industries of Malaysia Berhad (CIMA), Telekom Malaysia Berhad, or Edaran Otomobil Nasional Berhad (EON).

55.   Projects privatised under the BOT method include the North-South Highway and the Second Crossing to Singapore.

56.   Under this method, the private sector constructs the facility using its own funds, operates it for a concessionary period and finally transfers it to the Government at the end of the stipulated period.

57.   "Foreign telecoms operators eye Malaysia", *Financial Times*, 18 July 1996.

58.   "Malaysian tenders touch a sore point", *Financial Times,* 20 November 1996.

59.   World Bank (1996) and OECD (1996). For East Asian countries as a whole, the share of privatisation-associated FDI to total FDI inflows was about 1.5 per cent for the period 1989-94, compared with 14.2 per cent for Latin American economies (UNCTAD 1996).

60.   Lim and Pang (1991) suggest that the decision to develop a national car project rather than to allow foreign producers to rationalise to become more efficient was based partly on the fact that foreign firms were generally in joint ventures with local firms owned by Malaysian Chinese. In contrast, the Proton was to be a *Bumiputera* project.

61.   The Japanese share, which was originally 30 per cent in 1988 when the two Japanese companies were invited to take a 15 per cent stake each, has since been reduced through restructuring to 20 per cent. The Government sold off 30 per cent of the company in 1992. The shareholders involved in the multiparty joint venture include : HICOM Berhad (27.5 per cent), Khazanah Holdings Berhad (17.5 per cent), Mitsubishi Corporation (8.6 per cent), Mitsubishi Motors (8.6 per cent), Government Agencies (9.5 per cent), and other local and foreign investors (28.5 per cent) [Fujita and Hill 1997].

62.   Fujita and Child Hill (1997).

63.   *Malaysia: Growth, Equity, and Structural Transformation*, World Bank, Washington DC, 1993.

64.   "Currency pain mounts in Malaysia", *Financial Times*, 22 August 1997.

65.   These tariffs are to be eliminated in 2003.

66.   Fujita and Child Hill (1997).

67.   *Far Eastern Economic Review*, 14 February 1985, cited in Lim and Pang (1991), p. 181.

68.   Lim and Pang (1991), p. 181.

69.   Lim and Pang (1991), p. 178.

70.   The share in total merchandise exports of telecommunication and sound recording apparatus and equipment and electrical machinery, apparatus and appliances has risen from 24.5 per cent in 1988 to 38.7 per cent in 1995 (MITI 1996).

71.   O'Connor in Jomo (1993).

72.   Lim and Nesadurai (1997).

73.   Jomo and Gomez (1994).

74.   UNCTAD (1996).

75.   "Where chips eclipse smelters", *Financial Times*, 30 August 1994.

76.   Ibid.

77 .   UNCTAD (1996).

78.   "Penang finds it tough staying on top", Financial Times, 14 August 1996.

79.   "Where chips eclipse smelters", *Financial Times*, 30 August 1994.

80.   "Malaysia skills shortage hits home", *Financial Times,* 20 August 1997.

81.   World Bank (1997).

82.   The brand-to-brand complementation scheme (BBC) was launched in 1988 to allow MNEs with affiliates in several Asean countries better to integrate their regional operations.

83.   Itoh and Shibata (1996).

84.   "Matsushita's Chinese Burn", The Economist, 20 September 1997.

85.   Salleh (1995), p. 145. See Sieh Lee and Loke (1998) for similar findings.

86.   Lim and Pang (1991), p. 100.

87.   Harrold et al. (1996).

88.   *Financial Times,* 28 August 1992.

89.   *Financial Times,* 7 January 1994.

90.   Lim and Nesadurai (1997).

REFERENCES

Ali, Anuwar and Tham Siew Yean, "Domestic Investment and Foreign Direct Investment: Striking the Right Balance", *mimeo*, paper presented to the MIER 1993 National Outlook Conference held in Kuala Lumpur, 7-8 December 1993.

Allen, T.W., "The ASEAN Report", *Asian Wall Street Journal*, Hong Kong, 1979.

Ariff, Mohamed *The Malaysian Economy - Pacific Connections*, Oxford University Press, New York, 1991.

Athukorala, Premachandra and Jayant Menon (1995), "Developing with foreign investment: Malaysia", *Australian Economic Review*, Q1, pp. 9-22.

Bank Negara Malaysia, *Annual Report*, various issues.

Bruton, Henry J., *Sri Lanka and Malaysia - The Political Economy of Poverty, Equity and Growth*, Oxford University Press, New York, 1992.

Cable, Vincent and Bishnodat Persaut (eds.), *Developing with Foreign Direct Investment*, Commonwealth Secretariat, 1987.

Caprio, Gerard, Jr, Izak Atiyas and James A. Hanson, *Financial Reform: Theory and Experience*, New York, Cambridge University Press, 1996.

Caves, Richard, *Multinational Enterprise and Economic Analysis*, Cambridge, 1982.

Economist Intelligence Unit (EIU), *Investing, Licensing and Trading Conditions in Malaysia*, May 1996

European Round Table (ERT), *Investment in the Developing World: New Openings and Challenges for European Industry*, Brussels, 1996.

Pang, Chan On and Kok Cheong Lim, "Investment Incentives and Trends of Manufacturing Investments in Malaysia", *The Developing Economies*, Vol. XXII, n°4, December 1984.

Fujita, Kuniko and Richard Child Hill, " Auto Industrialization in Southeast Asia: National Strategies and Local Development ", *ASEAN Economic Bulletin*, vol. 13, n°3, March 1997.

Harrold, Peter, Malathi Jayawickrama and Deepak Bhattasali, "Practical Lessons for Africa from East Asia in Industrial and Trade Policies", *World Bank Discussion Paper*, n°310, 1996.

Hensley, Matthew and Edward White, "The privatisation experience in Malaysia", *Columbia Journal of World Business*, Spring 1993.

Ibrahim, Al'Alim, "The Malaysian privatisation experience" in *Privatisation in Asia, Europe and Latin America*, OECD, 1996.

Itoh, Motoshige and Jun Shibata, "The Role of Cross-Border Division of Labor and Investment in Promoting Trade: Two Case Studies from East Asia", in Quibria, M. G. and Malcolm Dowling, *Current Issues in Economic Development - An Asian Perspective*, Oxford University Press, New York, 1996. Pp. 276-98.

Jomo, K.S. and E.T. Gomez, "Rents and Development in Multiethnic Malaysia", in M. Aoki *et al.* (eds.) *The Role of Government in East Asian Economic Development: Comparative Institutional Analysis*, Clarendon Press: Oxford, 1997.

Jomo, K.S. (ed.), *Malaysia's Economy in the Nineties*, Pelanduk Publications, Petaling Jaya, 1994.

Jomo, K.S. (ed.), *Industrialising Malaysia - Policy, performance, prospects*, London, Routledge, 1993.

Jomo, K. S., *Growth and Structural Change in the Malaysian Economy, 1990*.

Lim, Linda and Pang Eng Fong, *Foreign direct investment and industrialisation in Malaysia, Singapore, Taiwan and Thailand*, OECD Development Centre, Paris, 1991.

Lim, Imran and Helen Nesadurai, "Managing the Malaysian Industrial Economy: The Policy and Reform Process for Industrialisation", in

Masuyama, Seiichi, Donna Vandenbrink and Chia Siow Yue (eds.), *Industrial Policies in East Asia*, ISEAS and NRI, Singapore, 1997.

MIDA, *Malaysia - Investment in the Manufacturing Sector*, Kuala Lumpur, 1996.

MITI, *Annual Report 1995-96,* Kuala Lumpur, 1996.

Meyanathan, Saha Dhevan and Salleh, Ismail Muhd, *The Lessons of East Asia: Malaysia Growth, Equity and Structural Transformation*, Washington, D.C., The World Bank, 1993.

Nicolas, Françoise and Lynn Krieger-Mytelka (eds.), *L'innovation, clef du développement - Trajectoires de pays émergents*, Paris, Masson, 1995.

OECD, *Privatisation in Asia, Europe and Latin America*, OECD, Paris, 1996.

OECD, *Foreign Direct Investment - OECD Countries and Dynamic Asian and Latin American Economies*, OECD, Paris, 1995.

Salleh, Ismail Muhd., "Foreign direct investment and technology transfer in the Malaysian electronics industry", in *The New Wave of Foreign Direct Investment in Asia*, NRI and ISEAS, 1995.

Sieh Lee, Mei Ling and Loke, Wai Heng, *FDIs in Asia: Firm level characteristics*, International Symposium on Foreign Direct Investment in Asia, Economic Planning Agency, Japan, 1998.

Siew Yean, Tham, "Determinants of Productivity Growth in the Malaysian Manufacturing Sector", *ASEAN Economic Bulletin*, vol. 13, n°3, March 1997.

Sivalingam, M and Siew-Peng Yong (1993), "TNCs and industrialization in Malaysia: organizational behaviour and local and regional impacts", *Regional Development Dialogue*, 14, 4 (Winter), pp. 40-64.

World Bank, *Global Development Finance 1997*, vol. 1, Washington, D.C., 1997.

Zainal, Aznam Yusof, et al. "Financial Reform in Malaysia", in Caprio, Gerard, Izak Atiyas and James Hanson, *Financial Reform: theory and experience,* Cambridge, Cambridge University Press, 1994.

Chapter 3

PHILIPPINES

Introduction and summary

For four decades following independence, the Philippines followed an inward-looking development strategy punctuated by balance of payment crises. Foreigners were prohibited in sectors designated as strategic by the Government and, in other sectors, were sometimes welcomed as part of an overall import substitution policy but generally faced numerous restrictions, notably prior approval for all equity shares over 40 per cent and capital controls. Reflecting the prominence of special interest groups in the economy, local firms could petition the Government for the inclusion of their industry on the Negative List of restricted sectors. Foreign investment in the Philippines was also hampered by the heavy involvement of the State in the economy. Despite the perceived need to correct the policy biases impeding sustained economic growth, the pressure for reform was stalled by political uncertainties.

In spite of this increasingly hostile environment, the Philippines had some initial success in attracting FDI as part of its import substitution strategy. Considerable foreign investment occurred in the Philippines during the 1950s, geared to replacing imports of final consumption goods which had already found acceptance in the local market. Many wholly-owned foreign subsidiaries were thus established in light manufacturing in such sectors as textiles, pharmaceuticals, household appliances, car assembly, tyres and food products. Foreign participation in the manufacturing sector grew accordingly in the period 1950-67.

This strategy was successful in attracting investors initially because the local market was not yet saturated and the Philippines was still a relatively rich economy within Southeast Asia. But eventually, small market size and sluggish economic growth, combined with rising nationalist economic policies, brought inflows to a halt. Cumulative inflows during the 1960s and early 1970s were negative, indicating net disinvestment from the Philippines. Investments from

157

the United States, historically the major source of investment, were also reduced after the expiration of preferential access of American capital in the Philippines. Except for a brief spurt after 1974, this pattern continued until the mid-1980s.

Because of this poor record in attracting investment, FDI has not until recently been the engine of growth that it has been in many other ASEAN countries. Given a historically languid economy, inadequate infrastructure and an inhospitable legal environment based on nationalistic economic policies, the Philippines was not attractive as a host country. As a result, many multinational enterprises chose to go elsewhere in the region where conditions were radically different.

In the past decade, the Philippines has done much to reverse this legacy of inward-looking policies and poor FDI performance through far-reaching liberalisation and economic reform. It has been one of the most aggressive privatisers in Asia and has made frequent use of build-operate-transfer (BOT) projects to develop the nation's poor infrastructure. Several major State-owned firms or assets have also been partly privatised, including Petron, the national oil company, the Philippine National Bank, National Steel, Philippine Shipyard and Fort Bonifacio. The Government has introduced greater competition into many sectors by breaking up monopolies and cartels, through deregulation and the removal of barriers to entry (including for foreign investors) and through steep tariff reductions within the framework of the ASEAN Free Trade Area. The foreign exchange market has also been deregulated. These reforms have been accompanied by greater political stability.

Among these economic reforms, numerous restrictions on foreign investment have been eliminated or reduced. Except for a clearly delimited list of activities, foreign investors may operate in most sectors of the Philippine economy. The scope for foreign involvement in a number of key sectors is now greatly improved, including in telecommunications, air transport, shipping, oil refining and marketing, banking and insurance, and mining. In addition, the energy sector has encouraged substantial foreign participation through the use of BOT schemes, resulting in a significant improvement in infrastructure in certain areas. Future market opening might include the retail sector.

The Government has also moved aggressively to imitate the success of other economies in the region in attracting export-oriented investors. As in many ASEAN countries, the Philippines seeks to target specific industries deemed to be important to economic development. The Board of Investment, which is the agency in charge of promoting investment, identifies priority areas to be included in the Investment Priorities Plan (IPP).

The promotion and expansion of FDI has been aided by the return of the former US military bases of Clarke and Subic Bay to Philippine control and their conversion into economic zones. Their success in attracting investors is due to the high quality of their infrastructure, the availability of skilled labour and the incentives offered. The Philippine economic zones in general have already attracted large amounts of foreign investment, often in electronics. The rapid increase in exports of electronic goods from the Philippines is the direct result of foreign investment in these zones.

The structural reforms initiated since the mid-1980s have begun to bear fruit. Once dubbed the "sick man of Asia", the Philippines achieved growth rates in the run-up to the crisis on a par with the Asian tigers and has so far suffered less than some neighbouring countries from the Asian financial crisis. As a result of reforms and the resurgence of economic growth in the early 1990s, there was a spectacular rise in FDI into the country. Inflows in the 1990s have been on average over seven times higher than in the two preceding decades. Furthermore, the range of sectors and source countries involved has increased substantially.

This surge in FDI inflows in the 1990s and the fact that FDI inflows have remained relatively stable so far during the crisis are both partly related to the policy liberalisation thrust described above, but other external factors are also at work. The Philippines was starting to benefit before the crisis from the erosion of location advantages in some of its neighbouring economies, leading first to FDI from Japan and the newly-industrialising economies of Asia and then from other ASEAN countries, such as Malaysia.

The quality of inward investment is also changing. In the new, more open environment, the natural attractions of the Philippines as a location for production – a well-educated and English-speaking workforce, an ample supply of managerial talent and a large domestic market – can play their dominant role as a magnet for investment. The improved provision of infrastructure will contribute to this attractiveness in the future. While FDI was traditionally attracted either by high tariffs on imports or by large natural resource endowments, the new wave of foreign investments is clearly much more export-oriented and the Philippines is now in a better position to compete with some of its neighbours.

Further scope for reform

In spite of what has already been achieved through deregulation, privatisation and trade and investment liberalisation, there remains scope for further reforms. What follows is a list of areas where policies and practices continue to impede potential foreign investors interested in locating in the Philippines

- *Lack of transparency in the approval process.* The Board of Investment responsible for screening investments seeking incentives has not yet moved sufficiently in the direction of an investment promotion agency, in spite of Government efforts in this direction. The creation of new and separate agencies to administer export zones and former military bases can be interpreted at least partly as a reflection of this failure. As a by-product, the decentralised nature of the regulatory and promotion regime for foreign investment in the Philippines has only added to potential investor uncertainty;

- *Continuing restrictions on FDI.* The Philippine constitution restricts foreign ownership of land and foreign firms may not generally acquire more than 40 per cent of the shares of local company. The Negative List of closed sectors is long by the standards of OECD countries, and there remain local content requirements in the automotive sector;

- *Inappropriate industrial targeting.* The sectors selected under the Investment Priorities Plan offer little scope for linkages with local firms owing to the lack of local capabilities in those activities. In spite of the clear success of the Philippines in creating an export-oriented electronics industry through the promotion of largely foreign investment, there is a risk of recreating the same structural weaknesses as were found in other ASEAN countries before the crisis. According to a recent study by the World Bank, 84 per cent of export value growth between 1991 and 1997 came from electronics.[1] This over-dependence on one sector creates a risk of disruption in the future should the existing advantages of the Philippines vis-à-vis other locations diminish;

- *Lack of policy consistency.* Investors often complain about policy inconsistencies. Sometimes one foreign investor will receive an incentive which was not offered to other investors. More often, local interests fight a rearguard action to frustrate attempts by foreign firms to enter the market, in spite of reforms intended to increase such access. Several examples have arisen during the privatisation process, such as the reclaimed land controversy over real estate investments in the Manila Bay. Apparent favouritism towards local companies in bidding for projects to be privatised is a major source of difficulty for foreign investors. Moreover, uncertainties remain even after a contract has been awarded

160

because of the possibility for the decision to be overruled in the courts.

– *Setbacks in the reform process.* In spite of the remarkable progress towards greater openness in a relatively short period of time, there remain occasional setbacks which may make some investors hesitate before committing substantial resources to the Philippines. These include the initial failure of oil deregulation and the increase in tariffs in certain sectors as a result of the crisis. Given the legacy of inward-looking policies and the relatively recent Philippine conversion to economic reform, these setbacks might have a stronger deterrent effect on FDI than they might otherwise.

I.   Direct investment trends

Historical trends

Considerable foreign direct investment occurred in the Philippines during the 1950s in response to the policy of import-substituting industrialisation. These investments were geared to replace imports of consumer goods which had already found acceptance in the local market. Many wholly-owned foreign subsidiaries were thus established to produce light manufactures in such sectors as textiles, pharmaceuticals, household appliances, car assembly, tyres and food products.

By the 1960s and early 1970s, however, new inflows of foreign investment, from the United States in particular, were reduced as the market became saturated, economic policies became more nationalistic and the preferential access for US firms in the Philippines expired.[2] Cumulative inflows during period were negative, indicating net disinvestment from the Philippines.[3] Except for a brief spurt after 1974, this pattern continued until the mid-1980s. Since 1985, inflows have reached record levels, but annual flows have been volatile, partly because of the relatively low level of inflows which implies that a large investment can have a significant impact on annual inflows.

In spite of relatively higher levels of inward investment in the Philippines in the past five years, total inflows since 1993 remain well below those into many other ASEAN countries, and the Philippines does not rank today among the top FDI recipients worldwide. In terms of cumulative FDI inflows between 1990 and 1997, the Philippines is only the fortieth most important host country worldwide, or eighteenth among non-OECD countries. The Philippines has only begun to attract significant amounts of FDI in the past decade.

The crisis has not yet had a major impact on FDI inflows. Total approved foreign investments in the first quarter of 1998 were significantly higher than in the same period of 1997, in contrast to the sharp drop in approved domestic investment projects. This growth is especially significant when one considers that total approvals by the Board of Investment (BOI) were already at record levels in 1997. The growth in approvals will take time to translate into greater realised investments, and some approved projects will not be carried through. Actual inflows as shown in Figure 1 fell as a percentage of GDP in 1997, as they had in the previous two years. Quarterly inflows have remained at roughly $200 million since early 1997. The different sources of FDI data in the Philippines are explained in an annex.

Figure 1. **FDI inflows as a percentage of GDP, 1963-97**

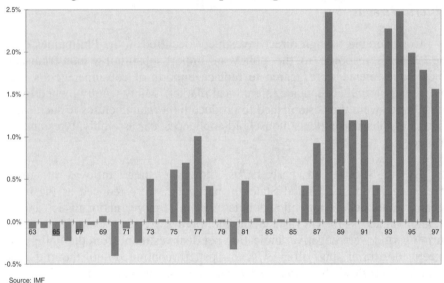

Source: IMF

The recent boom in FDI inflows has gone increasingly into special economic zones (Figure 2). Investments in these zones (referred to as ecozones) have taken off since 1994, following the passage of legislation expanding their scope. They offer numerous advantages for investors, subject to certain requirements related *i.a.* to exports. Investments have also grown quickly in the former military bases of Subic Bay and Clark, which are under yet another administrative system. These export zones have played the leading role in promoting Philippine exports of electronics which are now a significant part of total Philippine exports and which suffered less than those from other

ASEAN countries during the 1996 slump in the electronics sector. They have continued to grow at 30 per cent annually in spite of the crisis and slowdown in export markets.

Figure 2. **FDI through the BOI and PEZA, 1986 – June, 1998** (billion pesos)

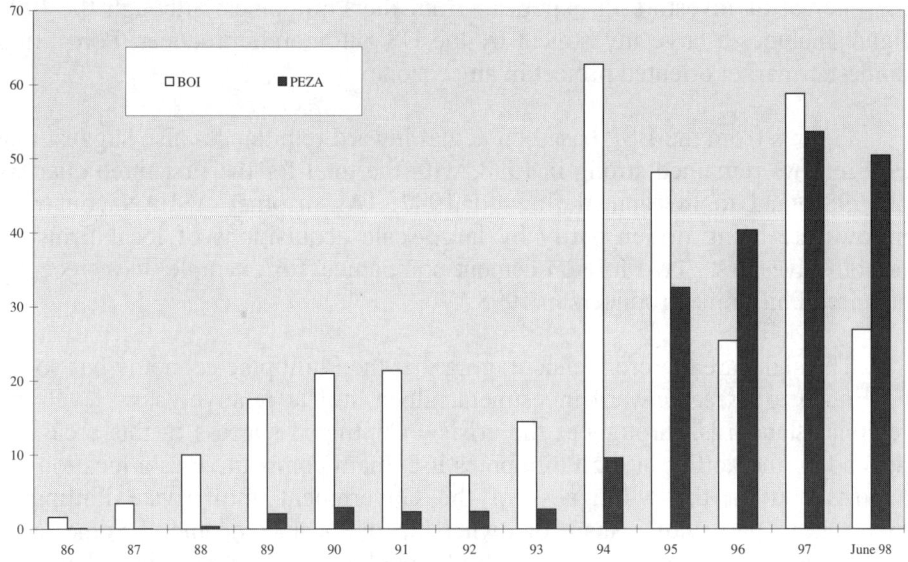

BOI: foreign equity share of approved foreign investments
PEZA: ecozone investments, excluding the establishment of ecozones
Source: BOI, PEZA

The BOI remains the principal investment authority in the Philippines, but with the rise of the ecozones, the BOI has become more focused on infrastructure investments. For BOI approvals in 1996, 90 per cent was accounted for by 20 projects for power plants, cement factories and railway or toll highway projects.

FDI flows since the beginning of the crisis

The Philippine government compiles its data on FDI from several sources, reflecting the relatively decentralised screening and promotion system in the country. To assess of the response of foreign investors to the crisis requires looking at each source separately. According to the BOI, total project costs of approved foreign investments grew by 50 per cent in 1996 and 150 per cent

163

in 1997 but fell by 35 per cent in 1998. The foreign equity in approved projects fell in 1998 and again in the first quarter of 1999 when the total foreign equity value was 60 per cent lower than a year earlier.

BOI approvals are just one form of inward investment project, as seen in Figure 2. In contrast to falling values of foreign investment in BOI projects, actual investments in ecozones have remained strong, with investments in the first half of 1998 equal to those during all of 1997. This growth partly reflects the interest of investors in exporting from the Philippines, although the 1998 figure includes a large investment by the US automobile producer, Ford , in a domestic-market oriented project in an ecozone.

Figures from the BSP based on actual inward remittances also suggest that FDI inflows remained strong in 1998, with the total for the first three quarters of 1998 equal to the annual flow for 1997. As in other ASEAN countries, inflows are being driven partly by large-scale acquisitions of local firms by foreign investors. Two foreign cement companies, for example, have recently acquired Philippine producers in 1998.[4]

The signs are therefore encouraging that the Philippine economy has so far continued to attract inward investment, albeit still at relatively low levels by regional standards, throughout the crisis. Continued success in this area will depend on the ability of the Philippines to remain competitive as a location for exports and on the willingness of the Government and private Philippine investors to part with a share of ownership of local companies. Some large Philippine conglomerates have instead opted to offer non-voting shares to foreign investors.[5]

Changing sources of FDI[6]

American firms are the largest investors in the Philippines (Table 1), but their share of the total stock has almost halved in the 1990s (Figure 3). Until 1988, investment by American firms typically represented over one half of inflows in any given year. American involvement has been overtaken by Japanese investments since the early 1990s in terms of annual inflows, in spite of a large US presence in infrastructure projects. Japanese firms have been the biggest investors in the 1990s by a wide margin. Despite a recent come-back over the past two years, American firms have seen their share of total FDI stock in the Philippines decrease substantially since the beginning of the present decade. Investment has also been growing from the NIEs, and, to a lesser extent, from Malaysia and Thailand.

164

European investment has been driven partly by major investments in the oil sector, with Royal Dutch Shell the largest foreign investor in the Philippines. UK companies were significant investors in 1993, partly because Shell increased its stake in its oil refining and marketing subsidiary. The importance of Swiss firms can be attributed partly to Nestlé which ranks among the five largest MNEs present in the Philippines.

Table 1. Registered foreign equity investments by country
(cumulative inflows 1973 - July, 1998, $ million)

United States	2 500	28.0%
Japan	2 135	23.9%
Netherlands	929	10.4%
Hong Kong, China	716	8.0%
United Kingdom	463	5.2%
Singapore	317	3.6%
Germany	215	2.4%
Chinese Taipei	166	1.9%
Korea	132	1.5%
Switzerland	129	1.4%
Australia	115	1.3%
France	74	0.8%
Malaysia	71	0.8%
Canada	59	0.7%
Sweden	48	0.5%
Offshore financial centres	486	5.4%
Others	340	4.1%
Total	**8 926**	

Source: Bangko Sentral Ng Pilipinas

While investments used to be driven by the need for access to the protected domestic market or attracted by ample natural resources, more recent investment – outside of infrastructure projects and privatisation – has been oriented more toward export markets. Investors have taken advantage of fiscal and other advantages in the ecozones and of the growing attractiveness of the Philippines compared to other countries in the region whose appeal is being undermined by rising labour costs.

Figure 3. Registrations of foreign equity investments by country of origin
(percentage of total inflows)

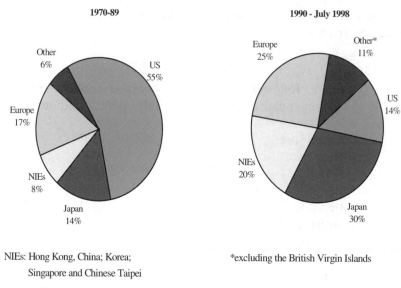

1970-89

1990 - July 1998

NIEs: Hong Kong, China; Korea;
Singapore and Chinese Taipei

Source: BSP

*excluding the British Virgin Islands

A survey of investment from Chinese Taipei in the Philippines sheds light on the motives for investing in the Philippines from a neighbouring country.[7] Firms from Chinese Taipei have been particularly interested in the Philippines as an export platform for markets elsewhere. The bulk of this investment from Chinese Taipei has come from small and medium-sized firms, representing investments of under $1.1 million in each case, particularly in the electronics sector and in textiles. The most commonly cited motive for this investment is the high level of education combined with the availability of low cost labour, followed by the favourable status of export-oriented firms in the Philippines. Two thirds of these firms export all of their output, mostly to third countries other than the home market. Over one half face local content restrictions which require a minimum of 30 per cent local content. Chinese Taipei investors make frequent use of the local Chinese community, particularly when it comes to providing information about market and labour conditions and to developing a better relationship with the local Government.

Because of the gap in development levels between the Philippines and its neighbouring ASEAN partners, some ASEAN-domiciled firms have also started investing in the Philippines lately. The Malaysian conglomerate Sime Darby, for instance, has invested in rubber, palm oil and cocoa production in the Philippines where it can take advantage of its pioneering technology, experience and world market networks while escaping Malaysia's higher land costs and acute shortage of plantation labour. The firm is currently involved in diverse activities in Philippines such as managing rubber plantations, processing and marketing natural rubber and distributing and servicing agricultural machinery. The economic slump and liquidity problems in source countries may cause some of these projects to be curtailed.

Many foreign investors perceive the Asian crisis as an opportunity to gain an access to the Asian market. American firms, in particular, have rapidly expanded their presence in the Philippines. Some European firms are taking advantage of opportunities arising out of the crisis to acquire local companies or to establish in the market. Lafarge, the French building material group, for example, has recently acquired Continental and Seacem, the Filipino cement company, for $460 million. In recent years, multinationals in services industry began to show interests in the Filipino market. Allianz, a German insurance group, announced this year that it would form a joint venture with Pioneer, a leading local insurer. As a result of the acquisition of four domestic cement manufacturers, foreign firms now produce as much as 60 percent of cement in the country.

Sectoral Distribution[8]

Since the 1970s, the bulk of approved foreign investment projects has been in manufacturing (Table 2). This sector accounted for more than 60 per cent of total registered foreign equity investments at the end of the 1980s and for more than half over the period 1990-96. The share of services (in particular banking and public utilities) has been on the rise over the most recent period, while mining and quarrying account for 13 per cent.

Although foreign firms are not present equally in all sectors, they are nevertheless important in major industries within the Philippine economy and have sometimes played a leading role in the development of those industries. The chemicals, coal and petroleum sectors have the greatest foreign participation, with more than 60 per cent of the sales accounted for by foreign-owned firms in these sectors. The electrical products sector ranks third with around 40 per cent of assets and 60 per cent of sales in the hands of foreign investors (UNCTC 1992). The dominance of foreign firms is also noticeable in the food sector.

Table 2. **Registered foreign equity investment by sector** ($ million)

	1973 - July 1998	
Banks & other financial institutions	1615	
of which: Banks		857
Manufacturing	4138	
of which: Chemicals & chemical products		714
Food		434
Basic metal products		336
Textiles		141
Transport equipment		317
Petroleum and coal		830
Metal products, except machinery		74
Machinery, appliances		410
Non-metalic mineral products		103
Mining	991	
of which: Petroleum and gas		803
Commerce	607	
of which: Wholesale		311
Real estate		249
Services	417	
of which: Business		139
Public Utility	789	
of which: Communication		459
Electricity		68
Agriculture, fishery, & forestry	56	
Construction	365	
of which: Transport facilities		11
Infrastructure		86
General engineering		63
Others	26	
Total	**8926**	

Source : Bangko Sentral Ng Pilipinas

Within the manufacturing sector, although the chemicals and food sectors used to be the most popular with foreign investors until the 1980s[9], the transport equipment and machinery sectors have gradually replaced them in the most recent years. In 1995, foreign investment in the latter two sectors reached almost half of the total FDI flows into the manufacturing sector.

Outward Foreign Investment

Direct investment abroad by Philippine firms remains marginal, with 0.5 per cent of total FDI outward stock of all developing countries, compared to about 4 per cent for Malaysian MNEs. The country nevertheless boasts one of the largest MNEs based in developing countries, namely San Miguel, a large Philippine company in the food and beverages industry. San Miguel ranked 33 in 1996 among the top 50 MNEs based in developing countries according to UNCTAD.

With an 85 per cent share of the local beer market, and a commanding presence in other food sectors, overseas expansion is the best hope for future growth (particularly in countries where the market is growing quickly). About one fifth of its sales are abroad, mainly in Hong Kong, China. Prior to the crisis, San Miguel was expanding rapidly overseas with a $1.9 billion drive. Two plants were opened in China and another was expected to open soon. It also doubled its capacity in Indonesia. San Miguel operates breweries, packaging and ice cream plants in Indonesia, Vietnam, Chinese Taipei and Guam. Since the crisis, this overseas expansion has abated and San Miguel has even withdrawn from some markets.

II.   Philippines' industrial development

The Philippines maintained an inward looking development strategy much longer than many other countries in the region. Half-hearted attempts at greater outward orientation did not achieve the desired results because of restrictions on majority ownership for foreign investors, inadequate infrastructure, the dominant role of the State in the economy, the overvalued peso, political uncertainty, and high tariff protection for which incentives could not compensate. The failure of export promotion policies highlights the importance of a comprehensive reform package. The successful switch to outward orientation did not occur until the 1990s. Since then, the Philippines has significantly reformed its economy through trade and FDI reform and privatisation and has in some ways exceeded many of its fellow ASEAN members in its openness.

1950s and 1960s

Following independence from the United States in 1946, the Philippines initially followed policies of economic nationalism. Import substitution was initiated, based on a full array of interventionist measures and frequent use of tariffs to protect infant industries from foreign competition. Foreign participation was prohibited in Government-designated strategic areas. In general, policies geared to industrial development were extremely selective. The Basic Industries Act passed by the Philippine Congress in 1961 attempted to strengthen the New and Necessary Industries Act (Republic Act 35) by granting to favoured industries exemptions from tax and customs duties on their imports of equipment, parts and machinery. Full exemptions were granted for the first four years, gradually diminishing over time. The Basic Industries Law of 1964 expanded the number of sectors eligible for these exemptions. Reportedly, as a direct result of these policies, foreign participation in the manufacturing sector increased dramatically.[10]

Import substitution had a number of detrimental effects. First it created an industrial structure dominated by import-dependent industries. Protected behind high tariff walls, firms engaged in low value-added assembly activities with a high import content. As a result, Philippine industry was highly inefficient. At the same time, capital-intensive industries were strongly encouraged. The vulnerability of the economy to balance of payments difficulties increased with the loss of the exchange rate as an instrument of adjustment because a devaluation would have been a fatal blow to the economy by making all imported goods more expensive. As a result even more interventionist policies based on import controls and high tariffs were put in place. The complex tariff structure, which the Government is currently simplifying, was established at that time. By the mid-1960s the ill-effects of import substituting industrialisation had become clear, with many uncompetitive industries only surviving behind high tariff walls.

Mid-1960s to 1970s

Despite the perceived need to correct the policy biases impeding sustained economic growth, the pressures for change and reform were stilled, first by the declaration of the martial law in 1972, and eventually by the 1973 oil crisis allowing easy access to cheap credit. At that time, the Philippines followed Latin America in preferring international lending to other forms of capital inflows, resulting in a high level of indebtedness.

Policies to encourage exports and, to a lesser extent, foreign investments were put in place, before the imposition of martial law (Investment Incentive Act of 1967, Foreign Business Relations Act of 1968, Export Incentive Act of 1970). Under the Export Incentive Act, various incentives (tax exemptions and deductions) were granted to export producers both in pioneer (involving new products or processes) and non-pioneer areas of investment. These were the first laws aimed at streamlining and rationalising foreign investment policies.[11] The BOI was established in 1970 to draw up an investment priorities plan which led to an increase in Government intervention. The strong Government presence could be felt at that time in a number of sectors, ranging from electricity generation to petroleum, coconut and sugar industries. As was the case with earlier legislation, discrimination against foreign investors was inherent in the Export Incentives Act. Apart from pioneer firms, wholly-owned foreign firms were not entitled to incentives granted by the Act even if such firms were potential exporters.

A step in the direction of export promotion was the Presidential Decree 66 passed in 1972 which paved the way for the country's export processing zones (EPZs). The first EPZ was established in Mariveles at the tip of the Bataan Peninsula, primarily to absorb abundant labour. As a result of the poor infrastructure at the EPZ, its remote location and disadvantages of the Philippines compared to other Asian countries, few export-oriented foreign investments were attracted. EPZs only accounted for 12 per cent of manufactured exports in the Philippines in 1976.[12]

The early experience of the Philippines with export promotion is not generally considered to have been successful. Indeed, by providing preferential access to the Philippine capital market at below market rates and by offering Government guarantees for loans to foreign investors, the incentives provided proved to be extremely costly. The relatively few firms which were establishing export platforms in Asia at the time preferred to go elsewhere where underlying economic conditions were more favourable.

1980s to the present: increasing the reliance on market mechanisms

The early 1980s were a difficult period for the Philippines, during which a serious debt crisis coincided with political turmoil following the Aquino assassination in 1983. As a result, most of the structural reforms that were launched at the time were put on hold. A deep economic slump in the mid-1980s ushered in a phase of significant market-oriented policy reforms in a number of sectors. These reforms have continued and even accelerated under successive governments. Overall, over the past decade economic policy in the Philippines has been much more market-friendly.

Protectionist trade policies were significantly liberalised during the 1980s, partly on the advice of the World Bank, which made granting of structural adjustment loans conditional on the achievement of trade liberalisation.[13] At the same time, a number of measures were taken in order to correct for the traditional anti-foreign bias of existing investment laws that shielded local entrepreneurs from foreign competition (described in a later section).

Privatisation

Under the Marcos administration, the government took over several private corporations and set up its own firms with private funds. Together, they numbered over 1000 in 1990, including the national oil company, steel, shipping, hotels, airlines and banking.[14] Since the 1990s, however, few Asian countries have attempted privatisation on the scale of the Philippines in such a short period of time.

The Philippine privatisation programme was first launched in 1986 but did not become effective until six years later. As in other countries, the twin aims of privatisation have been to improve efficiency and to reduce the Government's budget deficit as of 1996. The Government had raised 174 billion pesos ($6.6 billion) from the sale of 445 Government assets and companies by 1996, with over two thirds of these revenues generated since 1992. These receipts made a substantial contribution to the Government's budget surplus.

Privatisation has been managed by the Asset Privatisation Trust (APT) and has involved the selling of shares on the stock market, bidding, negotiated sales and direct debt buy-outs. Privatisation efforts have been directed at State monopolies in power, transport, water utilities, banks, airlines, pulp and paper, hotels, shipping, telecommunications, mining, fertilisers and steel. Around 130 Government-owned and controlled corporations remained to be privatised as of 1996.[15]

Among the prominent public institutions to be privatised has been the oil company, Petron, although the Government retains a strategic stake in the company. The downstream oil industry was to be fully deregulated in February 1997, but the Supreme Court ruled parts of the deregulation law unconstitutional. A new law, which restored most of the deregulation provisions of the original law while correcting its constitutional deficiencies, was passed in February 1998.

Efforts to open up the telecommunications sector to competition have brought in a large number of telecom companies to establish international gateway facilities and cellular mobile telephone services. In 1994, the Government broke the monopoly of the Philippine Long Distance Telephone Co. (PLDT) by awarding 11 different franchises to eight different carriers. Deutsche Telekom took a 35 per cent stake in Islacom, a local telecom company for $266 million in 1996. Taking a step further at the end of 1998, the Government sold a controlling stake in PLDT to the Hong Kong based company, First Pacific. In 1967, the Government had forced foreign investors to divest their shares in PLDT in what was hailed as a triumph of Philippine nationalism.[16]

Privatisation efforts have recently focused on power and water utilities, the latter being almost untried in Asia. Privatisation plans for Manila's Metropolitan Waterworks and Sewerage System (MWSS) was completed in August 1998. MWSS awarded 25 year concessions to two international consortia to assume full operational and investment responsibility. The Government had earlier encountered some difficulties in this privatisation. Early in 1997, it temporarily deferred approval and a court order held up the $7 billion sale.

National Power Corp. (NPC) announced in 1998 that the concession to operate electricity utilities would be opened to the private sector. NPC will offer seven separate concessions which are expected to yield a combined turnover of $1.5 billion. The initial decision to award the contract to an Argentine firm was deferred as the Senate energy committee warned the NPC that it had not followed the Build-Operate-Transfer law strictly. In October 1998, the Government awarded a hydroelectric project to the same Argentine firm. On 31 October 1998, NPC announced that it would apply a "Filipino First Policy" for its privatisation programme.

The IMF and World Bank have recommended that the Government sell off its 46 per cent stake in the Philippine National Bank, the largest commercial bank in the country. It has pledged to do so by March 2000 if not before via a block sale to the highest bidder.

Despite progress, there are real concerns that unfair practices may deter foreign investors. Privatisation is plagued by a lack of transparency in the bidding process in favour of domestic bidders. The contract for a new container terminal at Subic Bay was twice awarded to a Hong Kong company but was later given by Presidential order to the same Philippine company which manages the Port of Manila. Other setbacks include the Manila Hotel which the Government auctioned in September 1995. A losing local bidder obtained a restraining order on the grounds that historic buildings should be offered to Philippine firms first (based on the Filipino First section of the Constitution). The sale was bogged down in courts and finally the Supreme court overruled the award of the contract to a foreign (Malay-US) consortium in favour of the local bidder. In other incidents, a contract awarded to a Thai-Philippine consortium to reclaim land in Manila Bay encountered difficulties and a US-British joint venture to provide a state-of-the-art radar system was cancelled. In both cases, members of the Senate alleged that the deals were overpriced.

In a statement of concern, six chambers of commerce, including those representing companies from the US, Japan, the European Union, Australia and New Zealand, criticised "excessive challenges to public bidding" and urged the then President Ramos: "Do not change the rules after the game is played and expect to attract players for future biddings...They will go elsewhere unless the rules are clear, consistent and do not change to suit the losing bidders or other aggrieved parties".[17]

Trade reform

Reversing a long tradition of import substitution, Philippine reform of trade policies has been as comprehensive as it has for inward investment. According to the World Bank, "the trade regime today is relatively unencumbered by quantitative restrictions, average tariffs have been sharply reduced, and a credible schedule for further tariff reductions and unification is in place."[18] In the initial phase of reform, the rates of duty on over 4,000 tariff lines were modified, reducing maximum tariffs from 50 per cent to 30 per cent and compressing tariff levels from seven to four tiers, creating a more uniform and simpler tariff structure.[19]

The trade reform was initiated in the early 1980s but was temporarily suspended in 1983 owing to the economic crisis. Tariff rates were gradually reduced while quantitative restrictions were relaxed on a number of goods. The average tariff rate was reduced from 43 per cent in 1980 to 28 per cent in 1985, while peak rates were drastically cut and very low tariff rates were raised so as to reduce the dispersion around the average. The list of items requiring import licensing approvals from the Central Bank was also cut down starting in 1981. On the whole, from 1981 to 1988, the share of items subject to restrictions dropped from 47 per cent to 10 per cent in terms of number and from 33 per cent to 14.5 per cent in terms of value.[20]

In 1991, Executive Order 470 provided for a gradual approach to further tariff reduction, with an anticipated range of rates varying from 3 per cent for raw materials and capital imports to 30 per cent for certain consumer goods by the year 2003. The average tariff rate was to decline from 28 to 20 per cent. These reductions will apply to 94.4 per cent of all tariff lines. Certain sectors were permitted to maintain higher tariffs during the transition. Tariffs on motor vehicles, for example, will remain at 40 per cent until 1999, falling to 30 per cent in the year 2000. A uniform tariff of 5 per cent on industrial and non-sensitive agricultural products will be in place by the year 2004.[21] As of January 1997, 82 per cent of tariff lines were clustered around the 3, 10 and 20 per cent levels.

As part of the ASEAN Free Trade Area (AFTA), member countries including the Philippines are aiming for a five per cent common tariff on many items in intra-ASEAN trade by 2004.[22] The Philippine government expressed the desire to extend this tariff on an MFN basis to all countries. Most recently, the Government has agreed to sign the WTO accord on information technology products. As a result of the crisis, Philippine businesses have lobbied for increased protection but so far have received significant tariff increases on a temporary basis in only one area: garments, yarns, fabrics and threads.[23]

III.   Philippine Policies towards FDI (excluding finance)

Overview

The Philippines did not offer a favourable environment for foreign investment until recently. Economic nationalism, social unrest, political instability and a languid economy all deterred investors. Policies towards foreign investment provided incentives but placed restrictions on the degree of foreign equity participation in preferred non-pioneer areas of investment and allowed for nationalisation in pioneer areas. The ambiguous stance of FDI policy helps to explain the large drop in investment inflows (and even large disinvestments) until the mid-1970s.

The foreign investment policies of the Philippines since the end of the martial law regime in 1982 and the newly ratified constitution of 1987 have been increasingly liberal and geared towards identifying the specific sectors in which foreign investment can fulfil development objectives. Box 1 compares the declaration of policy from two acts governing foreign investment at two points in time. The change in emphasis is immediately apparent. Gone are references to economic nationalism, planning and the notion that foreign investments should be chosen so as to increase national income at the least cost.

The Omnibus Investment Code of 1987 was enacted in an attempt to improve the attractiveness of the Philippines as a location for investment. The Code introduced incentives and established a One-Stop Action Centre. It represented the first measures designed to shift the BOI away from screening and towards investment promotion. The requirement that applications would have to be processed within 20 days was instrumental in forcing the BOI to streamline its approval process by reducing the scope for red tape.[24]

With the enactment of the Foreign Investment Act in 1991, the restrictions on foreign equity participation were greatly relaxed in an attempt to offer conditions widely comparable to those prevailing in neighbouring economies. As a result, full foreign equity ownership is now permitted in most industries.

Under a Negative List, a limited number of sectors, including mass media, small-scale mining and retail trade, remain completely closed to foreigners, while local equity requirements are imposed in some other industries, such as advertising, public utilities, natural resources or finance and education. The Negative List adds to transparency and reduces the scope for discretion.

Box 1. Declaration of policy of Acts pertaining to foreign investment*

Republic Act No 5186 (September 1967)

To accelerate the sound development of the national economy *in consonance with the principles and objectives of economic nationalism and in pursuance of a planned, economically feasible and practicable dispersal of industries,* under conditions which will encourage competition and discourage monopolies, it is hereby declared to be the policy of the state to encourage Filipino and foreign investments, hereinafter set out, in projects to develop agricultural mining and manufacturing industries which *increase national income most at the least cost,* increase exports, bring about greater economic stability, provide more opportunities for employment, raise the standards of living of the people and provide for an equitable distribution of wealth. It is further declared to be the policy of the state to welcome and encourage foreign capital to establish pioneer enterprises that are capital-intensive and would utilise a substantial amount of domestic raw materials, *in joint venture with substantial Filipino capital,* whenever available.

Republic Act No 7042, as amended by RA 8179 (March 1996)

It is the policy of the State to attract, promote and welcome productive investments from foreign individuals, partnerships, corporations, and governments, including their political subdivisions, in activities which significantly contribute to national industrialisation and socio-economic development to the extent that foreign investment is allowed in such activity by the Constitution and relevant laws. Foreign investments shall be encouraged in enterprises that significantly expand livelihood and employment opportunities for Filipinos; enhance economic value of farm products; promote the welfare of Filipino consumers; expand the scope, quality and volume of exports and their access to foreign markets; and/or transfer relevant technologies in agriculture, industry and support services. Foreign investments shall be welcome as a supplement to Filipino capital and technology in those enterprises serving mainly the domestic market.

* emphasis added.

The Constitution restricts land ownership to Filipinos or to companies 60 per cent owned by Filipinos. Foreign companies may lease the land they occupy for a period of 50 years, renewable once for another 25 years. Prior to the enactment of the Republic Act 7652 in mid-1993, foreign investors were limited only to 50 years, with no possibility of extension. Once the Condominium Law is passed, foreign companies can own their plant facilities and become stockholders of the company that owns the land they occupy in areas designated as industrial estates, thus assuring permanency of tenure.

Foreign firms registered with the BOI may employ foreign nationals in supervisory, technical or advisory positions for up to five years. This limit may be extended for limited periods at the discretion of the BOI. Majority-owned enterprises have recently been allowed to employ foreign nationals in the positions of president, treasurer or general manager beyond the period of five years. Foreign nationals may be employed as members of the Board of Directors by election. Foreign enterprises entering into Government contracts for coal operations and exploration, and development of oil and geothermal resources are allowed to employ foreign nationals in any position.

The election of foreigners to the board of directors or governing body of a corporation or association engaged in partially restricted activities is permitted roughly in proportion to the permissible foreign participation or share of capital in such entities. A ten-member board of directors of a company is required to have at least 60 per cent Filipino ownership may include up to three foreigners.

Exchange controls on current transactions were lifted in 1993, after 40 years. Foreign exchange may now be freely bought and sold outside of the banking system, and foreign exchange receipts, acquisitions or earnings may be sold for pesos to unauthorised agent banks or outside the banking system, retained or deposited in foreign currency accounts, whether in the Philippines or abroad, or may be used for any other purpose. Henceforth, therefore, the free flow of foreign exchange and gold into and out of the Philippines by both residents and overseas investors is allowed, and the requirement that foreign exchange earned abroad by Philippine-based commodity and service exporters should be sold to Manila banks has been removed. Foreign investors may remit profits freely, subject to prior registration of the enterprise with the Central Bank.

Incentives play an important role in Philippine FDI policy. They are biased in favour of capital-intensive and export-oriented investments and are provided in the form of tax exemptions. The BOI, which is attempting to transform itself from a screening mechanism for inward investment to an investment promotion agency, identifies investment priority areas deemed strategic to the country's economic development. A foreign firm investing in preferred areas of investment as they are defined by the BOI may enjoy certain benefits and incentives. Investors also receive favourable treatment in ecozones.

Prospects for further deregulation

Further reforms are under consideration in the following areas[25]:

- an amendment to the Condominium Law which would allow foreigners to own factories and residences in industrial estates;
- repeal of the Retail Trade Nationalisation Act which would initially allow foreign ownership up to 40 per cent and after three years up to 100 per cent;
- amendment of RA 7721, to allow more than the initial 10 banks to enter and operate in the country;
- an amendment to the Financing Company Act to allow 100 per cent foreign ownership of financing companies;
- the liberalisation of provisions on foreign equity participation in investment banks and equity houses; and
- amendment of the Investment Company Act which would allow membership of foreign investors in the BOI companies and allow foreign investors in the mutual fund industry.

Foreign Investments Act of 1991 (Republic Act No. 7042)

The Foreign Investment Act, as amended by RA 8179, governs the entry of foreign investments without incentives. Signed in June 1991, the FIA liberalised the entry of foreign investment into the country and simplified procedures and conditions under which foreign investors may transact business in the Philippines. The FIA applies to the following cases: all new foreign-owned enterprises seeking to do business in the Philippines and not requesting incentives; existing Filipino-owned enterprises which would like to accept foreign equity participation above 40 per cent; and existing foreign-owned enterprises which would like to increase the percentage of their foreign equity participation. The FIA repealed only Book II of the Omnibus Investments Code which concerns investments not requesting incentives. Applications for foreign ownership exceeding 40 per cent are covered by the remaining five Books of the Code.[26]

Under the old laws, enterprises seeking more than 40 per cent foreign equity had to secure approval from the BOI. Full foreign ownership was only permitted in export processing zones or in "pioneer" priority industries. The BOI would evaluate the merits of each application, particularly those producing for the domestic market. The FIA allows full foreign ownership of export enterprises and of those local firms in activities not part of the Negative List (Box 2), provided the investor is not seeking special incentives.[27] After an initial three-year period, investors exporting 60 per cent or more of their output (or equivalent to 60 per cent of imports for hotels) may, in certain conditions, be permitted full foreign ownership even if the activity is on the Negative List.

Foreign-owned firms catering mainly to the domestic market shall be encouraged to undertake measures that will gradually increase Filipino participation in their businesses by taking in Filipinos, generating more employment for the economy and enhancing skills of Filipino workers. In order to enhance the transfer of technology to domestic firms, a technology supplier may benefit from an extra incentive if the firm assists the technology recipient in the export of the licensed products.

The Foreign Investment Negative List was established through Executive Order 182 and took effect in October 1994. In addition to clarifying which sectors are partly or wholly closed to foreigners, EO 182 also included substantial liberalisation. It effectively allowed foreign investment in areas previously limited to 40 per cent foreign ownership, such as wholesale and import trading not integrated with production, convention and conference organisers, life and non-life insurance, and insurance brokers. Restrictions on foreign investment in telecommunications, shipping, air transport, banking and mining have also been removed. Companies already 60 per cent-owned by Filipinos can still petition for their industry to be included on the Negative List, however.

List C items in the Negative List remained for a three-year transition period following the implementation of the Act but have since been eliminated. List C covered those areas of investment in which existing enterprises already served adequately the needs of the economy and the consumer and hence did not require further foreign investments as determined by the NEDA. They concerned the following areas: those import and wholesale activities not integrated with the production and manufacture of goods; services requiring a licence or specific authorisation, such as insurance firms and travel agencies; enterprises majority-owned by a foreign licenser or affiliates for the assembly, processing or manufacture of goods for the domestic market which are produced by Philippine nationals as of the date of entry into force of the FIA, under a technology, know-how or brand name licence from such licenser during the time of the licence agreement, such as pharmaceutical firms and producers of appliances with existing licensing agreements.

Box 2. The Foreign Investment Negative List

List A. Limited by Constitution or Special Laws

No foreign equity:
- Mass media except recording
- Licensed professions: law, accounting, engineering, medical and allied professions, architecture, criminology, chemistry, customs brokering, environmental planning, interior design, landscape architecture, teaching, forestry, geology, marine deck or engine officer, master plumbing, sugar technology, social work, librarian services.
- Retail trade
- Co-operatives
- Private security agencies
- Small-scale mining
- Utilisation of marine resources (except deep sea fishing)
- Ownership, operation and management of cockpits
- Manufacture, repair, stockpiling or distribution of nuclear weapons
- Manufacture, repair, stockpiling or distribution of biological, chemical and radiological weapons
- Manufacture of firecrackers and other pyrotechnic devices

25 per cent foreign equity
- Recruitment agencies
- Locally funded public works projects

30 per cent foreign equity
- Advertising

40 per cent foreign equity
- Natural resource development and utilisation
- Land ownership
- Public utilities
- Educational institutions
- Rice and corn industry
- Contracts for the supply of materials, goods and commodities to government-owned or controlled corporation, company, agency or municipal corporation
- Contracts for the construction of defence-related structures
- Project proponent and facility operator of a BOT project requiring a public utilities franchise
- Operation of deep sea commercial fishing vessels
- Adjustment companies
- Ownership of condominiums

60 per cent foreign equity
- Financing companies regulated by the Securities and Exchange Commission (SEC)
- Investment houses regulated by the SEC

List B. *Limited for Reasons of Security, Defence, Health, Morals and Protection of Small-and Medium-Sized Enterprises*

40 per cent foreign equity

- Firearms, explosives, telescopic and sniper devices
- Guns, weapons, ammunition, armaments, missiles, military equipment
- Dangerous drugs
- Massage clinics
- Gambling
- Domestic market enterprises with capital less than $200 000
- Domestic market enterprises which involve advanced technology or employ at least fifty direct employees with capital less than $100 000

List C. *Limited by Capacity of Existing Enterprises*

None

As a result of the suppression of List C, foreigners can now fully own all types of local manufacturing establishments, as well as businesses of indent, import and wholesale trading, travel agencies, tourist inns, life and non life insurance agencies and insurance brokerage establishments. Despite laws limiting foreigners to minority stakes in retail companies, franchising has been the way into this restricted market.

In order to liberalise further the entry of foreign investments into the country, Republic Act (RA) 8179 amended the FIA by reducing the equity requirements for domestic and export-oriented foreign-owned firms. The Philippine Congress may further liberalise the FIA. House Bill No. 12281 seeks to lower from $500 000 to $150 000 the minimum paid-in capital of foreign companies serving the domestic market.

Investment incentives and Special Economic Zones

The Omnibus Investments Code of 1987 (Executive Order No. 226) provides the rules by which foreign investors in the Philippines may avail themselves of incentives. It consists of six books which clarify the kinds of investments an investor may engage in. Book II (foreign investments without incentives) has been replaced by the Foreign Investment Act of 1991. The Code offers benefits to local and foreign enterprises engaged in activities considered by the Government as a high priority for economic development that register before 31 December 1994. These benefits are in the form of fiscal and other incentives including tax holidays, a preferential customs duty of three per cent on imported capital equipment until 31 December 1997, tax credits on domestic capital equipment, double deduction of labour expenses, and employment of foreign nationals. Firms located outside of Metro Manila shall be entitled to the incentive until 31 December 1999. The Code also provides the registration procedures for enterprises seeking incentives.

The investment incentive system is biased in favour of capital-intensive and export-oriented investments. Priority areas are those indicated in the Investment Priorities Plan (IPP) drawn up each year by the BOI (Box 3). Through the IPP, the BOI supports the regional dispersal of industries and encourages small and medium-sized enterprises and intra-sectoral linkages. The IPP provides that foreign investors may invest in the Philippines in pioneer areas up to 100 per cent ownership or exports 70 per cent or more of total output, subject to Constitutional or statutory limitations.

Box 3 Activities listed in the 1998 Investment Priorities Plan

Priority Investment Areas (Countrywide)

Export-oriented industries exporting at least 50 per cent of output, including exports of goods and services, export trading, tourism, agro-export processing estates and activities supporting exporters.

Catalytic industries or those industries with the potential to be competitive in export markets.

Industries undergoing structural adjustments due to the opening up of the Philippine market.

Support activities including infrastructure and services, environmental support facilities, research and development projects and other projects deemed by the Government to be priority programmes and social services.

Mandatory inclusions due to provisions of laws granting eligibility of particular sectors to incentives under EO226, such as projects designated under BOT Law, mining, iron and steel industry and ASEAN Industrial co-operation Projects.

Additional Priority Investment Areas for the Autonomous Region of Muslim Mindanao

Export activities; agriculture, food and forestry-based industries; basic industries; consumer manufactures; infrastructure and services; engineering industries

---

Source: BOI

Depending on the current year's requirements, activities listed in the IPP may carry a status of pioneer or non-pioneer, each with its own set of incentives. Within a period of time determined by the BOI, usually 30 years, pioneer enterprises must have at least 60 per cent Filipino ownership. Exempted are enterprises whose production is 100 per cent geared for exports. In 1996, an amendment to the Omnibus Investments Code suspended the nationality requirements for BOI-registered projects of ASEAN investors or multilateral financial institutions such as the Asian Development Bank or the International Finance Corporation.

In April 1998, the Government radically streamlined the IPP by halving the number of sectors eligible for fiscal incentives or tariff exemptions. As a result, certain industries such as cement, textiles, processed foods, pulp and paper and packaging products have been excluded from the IPP. Priorities are to be in mining, downstream oil operations, tourism, chemicals and BOT projects.[28]

An enterprise may still be entitled to incentives even if the activity is not listed in the IPP so long as at least 50 per cent of production is exported in the case of enterprises in which foreigners hold more than 40 per cent the equity.

Incentives are now offered regardless of whether the firm is registered with the BOI, although they are no longer available for those projects which locate in Metro Manila. Many incentives are tied to the system of Special Economic Zones (see below). A registered entity which locates a new or expanded project in a rural area of the Philippines is given the same incentives as those for a pioneer enterprise: full deduction from taxable income of the cost of infrastructure construction and of labour costs.

Special economic zones

In 1993, Proclamation N°. 167 declared export development the key to sustainable and balanced agro-industrial economic growth. The Export Development Act of December 1994 offered exporters the following incentives in addition to those granted by the BOI: exemption from deposits of duties at the time of opening of the letter of credit covering imports; duty-free importation of machinery and equipment and accompanying spare parts for a period of three years until 1997; tax credit for imported inputs and raw materials for five years; and tax credit for increase in current year export revenue within thirty days from exportation.

The Special Economic Zone Act of 1995 (Republic Act No. 7916 approved on 24 February 1995) provides a legal framework and mechanisms for the creation, operation, administration and co-ordination of special economic zones, with corresponding incentives establishing operations within these areas. The Act brings together the various policies on export promotion under one roof and is administered by the newly-created Philippine Economic Zone Authority (PEZA).

Special Economic Zones (Ecozones) may contain any or all of the following: industrial estates, export processing zones, free trade zones and tourist/recreational centres. Industrial estates, which can be privately managed, provide basic infrastructure and utilities. Export processing zones are separate customs areas in which firms may import capital equipment and raw materials free from duties, taxes and other import restrictions. A free trade zone is an area adjacent to a port or airport where goods may be held for immediate transhipment or stored, repacked, sorted, mixed, or otherwise manipulated without being subject to import duties.

Qualifying enterprises in these Ecozones are exempt from restrictions on foreign ownership. They may also avail themselves of the following incentives:

- exemption from corporate income tax from for 4-8 years, after which investors shall pay a five per cent tax on gross earnings in lieu of national and local taxes;

- exemption from the extended value-added tax;

- exemption from duties and taxes on imported capital equipment, spare parts, materials and supplies;

- tax credits for exporters using local materials as inputs and on domestic capital equipment and domestic breeding stocks and genetic materials;

- exemption from wharfage dues, and any export tax, duty, impost or fee;

- additional deductions for training expenses and for labour expenses (50 per cent of wages subject to certain conditions;

- employment of foreign nationals (up to five per cent of the labour force), including permanent resident status for foreign investors and immediate members of their family; and

- exemption from SGS inspection and simplified export-import procedures.

To qualify for these incentives and other advantages, investors must satisfy various performance requirements, including local content and export ratios. In certain instances, and subject to the approval of PEZA, 30 per cent of production may be sold in the domestic market. Those industries which are on a negative list drawn up by PEZA will not be allowed to sell their products locally. The motive for this restriction is to protect the domestic industry in question.[29]

In addition to the Ecozones administered by PEZA, there are two economic zones which have been created in the former US military facilities, the Subic Bay Freeport Zone and the Clark Special Economic Zone, which reverted to Philippine control in 1992 and which are administered separately. Subic Bay, the larger and more important of the two, has a total territory of 60,000 hectares, which is larger than Singapore. It includes an airport, shipping berths, a well-maintained road network, an electric power plant, telecommunications, water and sewage systems. Investors receive similar incentives to those in the Ecozones.

The various Economic Zones have been popular with foreign investors. Foreign investment in the eight main special industrial zones rose tenfold between 1993 and the end of 1996 to reach $1.6 billion. Investors from Chinese Taipei have been active at Subic Bay: a consortium of 45 companies has invested $423 million, together with a $20 million loan from the Taipei government to develop a 300 hectare site. In another Zone, 58 South Korean companies produce a diverse range of manufactured goods, from toys, apparel and stationery to electronics and components. The success of the more recently established EPZs and other ecozones, in particular Subic Bay and Clark, are clear proof that a favourable environment, including adequate infrastructure, is a necessary condition for such a strategy to succeed.

IV.   Regulations on FDI in the Financial Sector

The Philippine financial system is still relatively underdeveloped. As in the rest of the economy, the financial sector has a legacy of control and limits on foreign entry. As a result of recent financial reform beginning in the second half of the 1980s, the Government has adopted a policy of reducing its direct participation in the banking system and of gradually opening to foreign investors. Liberalisation has also occurred in other financial sectors, notably insurance.

Banking

The 1948 prohibition on entry of new foreign banks under the Banking Act remained in effect until 1994. Until that date, no new foreign bank licences were granted in the Philippines; as a result only four foreign banks operated as commercial banks, two of which were American.[30] They were not allowed to accept demand deposits but could establish additional branches with Central Bank approval.

The liberalisation of the banking sector began in 1994 with the abolishment of the ban on foreign banks' entry and the relaxation of some of the constraints imposed on already operating foreign banks. Under Republic Act (RA) 7721, new foreign investors are allowed to operate deposit-taking branches or set up subsidiaries, while the requirements imposed on foreign-ownership in existing local banks have been relaxed. At the same time, prohibitions on the expansion of branch networks have been partially removed. Foreign banks have also been allowed to join shared automated teller machines (ATM) networks.

An important limitation in the legislation is that foreign banks are limited to overall control 30 per cent of total banking system assets. The remaining 70 per cent must be held by domestic banks majority-owned by Filipinos.

In the five years following the enactment of the new banking law, six new foreign banks could enter on a branch basis, with four more allowed at presidential discretion. New foreign bank entrants are required to provide capital of 210 million pesos for the first 3 branches and 35 million pesos for each additional branch, whose location is also determined by the Monetary Board of the BSP. Banks entering on a full service branch basis can establish a maximum of six service branches, with Central Bank approval for the location of the last three.

New banks are allowed to enter the market either as a branch or as a subsidiary if they are among the top 5 banks (measured by assets) in their home countries or among the top 150 world-wide. The details on these criteria are in the law's implementing guidelines. Foreign banks are also allowed to become universal banks, which was formerly limited to Philippine banks, and to engage in securities underwriting for the local market, provided they meet given capital requirements (1.5 billion pesos or $55 million). They may not operate investment banking or engage in the trust business though.

Of the country's 50 banks, 16 are now foreign-owned.[31] Although there is by now a roughly level playing field for foreign banks already operating in the country, new entry remains subject to a number of restrictions. The entry of new foreign competitors will force local banks to improve their efficiency. The Philippines has a low domestic savings rate of 18 per cent which is half the regional average. Greater competition should eventually narrow the spread between saving and lending rates and improve the quality of banking practice.

There is much greater interest on the part of foreign banks in banking licences than in acquiring local banks, suggesting that most foreign banks are mainly interested in wholesale business, including servicing large MNEs from their home countries operating in the Philippines, rather than retail banking. The foreign banks are expected to add depth to the local money and foreign exchange markets, partly because they are likely to focus largely on foreign exchange business and partly because they may decide to use the forward markets as a means of funding themselves in pesos.

After 1972, foreign equity participation was allowed in domestic banks, up to a limit of 30 per cent of the voting stock of any banking institution. On a case by case basis, foreign equity could go up to 40 per cent of the outstanding shares, provided that equity participation in excess of 30 per cent was placed in non-voting stocks. Since 1986, in order to help alleviate the country's foreign debt, foreign banks have been permitted to buy additional shares in domestic banks through a debt-equity conversion scheme. Moreover, the new law also raises the allowable foreign percentage ownership in new locally-incorporated subsidiaries of foreign banks as well as in an existing Philippine bank. As of 1994, limits on foreign ownership in new subsidiaries incorporated in the Philippines and in existing domestic banks were raised to 60 per cent, although foreign participation in Philippine-owned universal banks continues to be limited to 30 per cent.

Specific requirements are imposed on lending to small and medium-sized enterprises and agri-business (25 per cent of their lending must go to these businesses). Even though these restrictions apply to all banks, domestic and foreign alike, they are more difficult to comply with for foreign banks without a branch network. In addition, banks must place 15 per cent of their deposits with the Central Bank as a minimum reserve requirement. They are also subject to a 5 per cent tax on gross income. Reserve requirements have been cut over time, however, and branching restrictions have been liberalised.

Other finance

Securities broker or dealers incorporated under foreign laws are not allowed to operate as branches in the Philippines but may enter the securities markets either as a representative office or as a wholly-owned, locally-incorporated broker-dealer. In the case of investment houses, which are allowed a broader range of securities activities (i.e. underwriting), foreign participation is limited to minority ownership (less than 60 per cent) which was recently raised from 50 percent by the Investment House Act (October 1997) and the Financing Company Act (February 1998). Finance and Leasing companies also benefit from the change. Paid-up capital for investment houses is now 300 million pesos. Paid up capital for finance and leasing companies is now at least 10 million pesos for those located in Metro Manila and other first class cities, 5 million pesos for those situated in other classes of cities and 2.5 million pesos for municipalities. For firms engaged in trust activities and mutual fund management, the foreign ownership limitation was, until recently,

40 per cent. It has since been raised to 60 per cent in order to improve the sector's competitiveness.

Because foreign banks are allowed under the new banking law to operate as universal banks, they may participate as lead underwriters of new security issues and no longer have to underwrite local equity and bond issues through indirect, minority ownership of a Filipino investment house. Once entry is made, there are no further distinctions made between wholly or partially foreign-owned firms and domestic firms.

Despite a more liberal stance towards foreign investors, there is still scope for improvement in the working of the securities market. Planned revision of securities market legislation is perceived by foreign investors as a priority, to make the rules more transparent.

Insurance sector

In October 1996, the Government pledged to accelerate moves to open up the insurance sector to foreign competition by awarding several new licences before the end of that year. In addition, it has lifted the former 40 per cent limit on foreign ownership of a local insurance company. By doing so, the Government has reversed its decision to limit competition to ten foreign companies in the life and non-life sectors. There are no longer any limits on the number of foreign companies in these sectors. "Government regulators say the decision to lift the remaining limits on foreign participation were motivated by the need to overhaul the domestic market, which is considered under-capitalised and inefficient. More than 100 companies compete in the domestic non-life insurance market, and 27 compete in life assurance."[32]

Four foreign companies control 60 per cent of that market. All of them have been in the Philippines for over 50 years. Under the new guidelines, applicants must have a local capitalisation of 300 million pesos ($11.4 million) and be publicly listed in their country of origin. The company must also be among the top 200 in the world in terms of market capitalisation. Not unexpectedly, local insurance companies, struggling to remain solvent, have criticised the liberalisation measures.

V.   The Experience with FDI in Specific Sectors

Although tremendous policy changes have been taking place since the beginning of the decade, the transformation of the Philippine economy remains limited so far. Industry's share of GDP remained unchanged between 1986 and 1995 at just over one third. Of the industry total, manufacturing represents around 25 per cent of GDP, a share much the same as in 1975. Indeed, the manufacturing share in the economy has actually fallen since the early 1980s, while deregulation has prompted a boom in the construction and property sector.

In spite of this poor performance in shifting towards manufacturing, exports of manufactured goods have increased rapidly as a result of recent inflows of FDI, reaching 80 per cent of total exports in 1995 (compared to less than 50 per cent a decade earlier). Much of this growth in exports comes from a few sectors such as electrical equipment/parts and telecommunications, with a declining share for garments.

Infrastructure development

In the Philippines, economic growth has often been hampered by infrastructural constraints. The recovery of 1987-90, for instance, was cut short by severe power shortages. Because infrastructure development is perceived as a high priority, the Government has been at the forefront in Asia in terms of creating a legislative framework to facilitate private investment in infrastructure through its Build-Operate-Transfer (BOT) programme. The BOT programme was initially a way to overcome fiscal constraints which impeded further public investment in infrastructure. In the initial stages of the programme when the need for investment was most critical, private companies invested in the necessary infrastructure in return for a Government guarantee to pay an adequate return to the investor after a fixed period of time. In this way, the Government was responsible for collection of payments for the services of the investor (electricity, water, etc.). Such contingent liabilities will be incorporated in the budget in the future.

The first BOT law was passed in 1990 and later amended (RA 7188) to make it more flexible. As a result, more than 25 BOT projects in power generation alone had attracted over $5 billion in investment before the crisis. Including Government funding and projects currently in the pipeline, the NEDA estimates that total project costs for BOT projects in all sectors have amounted to $35 billion. The brown-outs which paralysed the economy in the early 1990s have rapidly been brought to an end through the fast-track granting of licences to foreign power companies. In spite of these recent investments, a legacy of under-investment in infrastructure still constrains growth. The Asian Development Bank estimated in 1996 that the capital requirements of the infrastructure sectors such as power, transport, water supply, and telecommunications are an estimated $5 billion annually or about 6.5 per cent of GDP.

The latest BOT law expands the scope for private investment in infrastructure and provides both incentives and guarantees. The new law covers a wider scope of contractual arrangements that go beyond building, owning, operating and transferring. Nine different schemes are explicitly authorised. The list of eligible projects is expanded to cover a wide range of projects, including waste management, information technology networks and database infrastructure, education and health facilities and tourism projects. Investors may also lease, contract, add, rehabilitate or develop areas adjacent to existing BOT projects. Foreign firms are welcome to participate in BOT projects, and many have done so, but joint ventures with a local firm reportedly reduce significantly the degree of screening before approval is granted.

The Government offers cost sharing up to 50 per cent of the project cost, fiscal incentives, and various credit enhancement measures such as take-or-pay arrangements, *force majeure* risk cover and guaranteed foreign exchange convertibility. Generous guarantees were initially provided in order to end the power crisis, but the Government is now trying to minimise its project support. Subsidies are granted on a case-by-case basis, particularly in cases where the project is not financially viable in itself. Companies may submit unsolicited proposals for infrastructure development, but financial incentives are usually not available and investors are expected to bring in new technologies in such cases. Investors should bring additionality to the financing of BOTs. As with privatisation, there have been numerous delays and problems in particular cases because of legal obstacles created by losing local bidders.

The importance of the BOT programme is only poorly reflected in the balance of payments. One reason is that machinery brought in as part of a BOT project is counted as imports rather than as foreign capital investment. In addition, the Central Bank classifies the exposure of foreign companies in such projects as "advances" until the project is completed.[33] It is estimated that around one third of $14 billion in commercial loans in the balance of payments between 1992 and 1996 was for BOT projects. In certain activities, BOT proposals are graduated into FDI, i.e they are corporatised and privatised. This approach is more similar to a Build-Own-Operate project.

Oil, gas and petrochemicals

After a quarter of a century of State-control of the Philippine oil sector, deregulation was recently launched but encountered severe difficulties when the Oil Deregulation Act was struck down by the Supreme Court. The process of deregulation was to have culminated in the Government's withdrawal from oil pricing. The Government's thrust to deregulate the downstream oil sector has already spurred interest from both local and foreign investors. New competitors have entered aggressively, in addition to the Big three oil groups which had traditionally been operating in the Philippines (Petron, Shell and Caltex).[34] They have been focusing particularly on LPG, oil trading, and petrol retailing, the most accessible activities within the sector.[35] Between 1991 and 1995, the BOI approved 17 petrochemical-related projects.

By the same token, the Philippines has opened up the gas sector to foreign investors. Development of this sector could not have occurred without foreign participation. Two deals were signed early in July 1997, which may represent the birth of the Philippine natural gas industry. To encourage new exploration, the Department of Energy also plans to grant one 25-year service contract a year until 2025 with foreign equity participation up to 100 per cent. Foreign companies such as Arco and Murphy Oil of the US, Stirling of Australia as well as British Gas are already looking at other oil and gas exploration prospects.[36]

A build-own-operate (BOO) contract with the Government a joint-venture between Shell Philippines Exploration, a subsidiary of Royal Dutch Shell and Occidental Philippines Inc, will drill for gas in the Malampaya field. The project is the most significant infrastructure investment to date.

Mining

Liberalisation of the mining industry allows for 100 per cent foreign ownership in certain cases and lowers the excise tax on minerals to 2 per cent. The recently signed Mining Act institutionalised four modes of exploring and developing mineral resources (fixed management contracts to operate Government mines; BOT agreements; lease-purchase facilities; and a securitisation facility that allows the two parties to experiment with various equity arrangements). Three allow for 40 per cent foreign ownership: mineral production-sharing agreements, joint ventures with the Government to manage State-owned mines and co-production. For financial and technical assistance agreements, 100 per cent foreign ownership is permitted. The new law also removes the minimum investment requirement of $50 million under these assistance agreements.

A Presidential directive, following on the Mining Act of 1995, offers foreign investors five new ways of investing, in addition to purchases of Government mines. Until now, foreigners could only bid for mining companies which were being privatised. Foreign companies can repatriate 100 per cent of profits. The Government has also slashed excise taxes on gold, copper and other metals.

Foreign companies have complained about a Government scheme to levy an extra 15 per cent tax on their income, in addition to the taxes and fees which make up the current fiscal regime. Local companies do not have to pay this tax. The Government has retorted that foreign companies are already offered a tax exemption for up to five years from start of exploration.

Overseas interest surged following the liberalisation. However, hostility towards foreign investors has arisen because of an incident in which several tons of mining waste from a company 40 per cent foreign-owned spilled into a river. Foreign companies hope they can continue operating under Financial or Technical Assistance Agreements which allow them to skirt a Constitutional ban on mining by foreign-controlled companies. Since the FTAAs were created in 1995, the environment department has received over 70 applications, but the processing came to a halt following the incident.

Electronics

The electronics sector has probably benefited most from opening up the economy to foreign investors. In the past five years twenty major foreign chip-assembly companies have built or expanded their facilities throughout the country. The Korean company Amkor Anam has its biggest operation in the world in Laguna Technopark.[37] The American computer-chip maker Intel invested $350 million in flash memory production and in the expansion of a Pentium chip testing plant, one of its biggest in the world. Similarly, Texas Instruments will invest $100 million to expand facilities in order to test chips for various uses. Motorola and Phillips Semiconductors have also started implementing expansion plans. As a result of these developments, there are now over 300 electronics firms in the Philippines.

Electronics exports grew in parallel with other manufactured exports until 1993, but since then they have greatly exceeded the latter and now account for two thirds of total manufactured exports or 59 per cent of total exports (Figure 4). This growth coincides with the rapid growth in FDI in ecozones. Of the ASEAN member countries, the Philippines was the least badly hit by the cyclical downturn in the growth of world demand for electronic products in 1996. Electronics exports have grown over 30 per cent each year since 1996 and have largely driven the continued growth in total exports (19 per cent growth in 1998).

Electronics exports are now concentrated in computer chips and wireless phones, as well as audio and video equipment. Computer chips account for 60 per cent of electronic and electrical products exports and about 49 per cent of total exports (compared to 28 per cent in 1992). At the same time, the share of garments has declined from 22 per cent in 1992 to eight per cent in 1998. While the Philippine textile industry no longer appears competitive compared to countries such as China or Sri Lanka because of rising local wage rates for unskilled labour, the electronic industry is in exactly the opposite situation with the Philippines becoming increasingly competitive compared to Chinese Taipei, Korea and even Malaysia.

Figure 4. **Philippine manufactured exports, 1985-98**
($ billion)

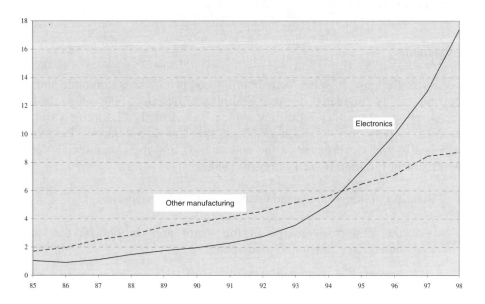

As in other neighbouring countries, the high import-content of exports is a major source of concern in the electronic sector, in particular in the computer chip industry.[38] Roughly 80 per cent of components are imported, with local value-added amounting to 15-30 per cent. Yet there is already sign of higher domestic value-added, as fewer electronic components are being imported per unit of exports.

In addition to the computer chip industry, consumer electronics has also gained ground. As industrial leaders such as Japan, Korea and Chinese Taipei move up to more technology-intensive production, the Philippines can provide its services as a manufacturer of lower-end electronic products such as radios, TV sets, and audio equipment. Three to five year tax holidays and duty free imports of equipment, make assembly operations in the sector lucrative. Also private companies have been allowed to set up industrial estates with the type of incentives that are available in Government-owned EPZs.

The Philippines was less affected than neighbouring economies by the cyclical downturn in the growth of world demand for electronic products, partly because it was just beginning to reap the benefits of a surge of foreign investment in this sector.

Automobiles

As is the case in other neighbouring countries, the automobile industry remains highly regulated in the Philippines despite some steps towards liberalisation. Assembly industries, which had virtually disappeared in 1986, resumed activity in 1988 as a result of the Car Development Programme launched by the Government at the end of 1987 and the Commercial Vehicle Development Program (CVDP) in early 1988.

These programmes are based on the following provisions:

–   the BOI is in charge of the sector and decides on the list of enterprises allowed to participate;

–   imports of completely built-up (CBU) vehicles were banned until 1995; imports are free for some commercial vehicles; imports of slightly knocked down vehicles (SKD) are moreover possible for some commercial vehicles;

–   firms allowed to participate may assemble a maximum of four types of vehicles, with a maximum of two versions per model for passenger cars and three versions for commercial vehicles;

–   passenger cars are classified in three categories, with category I corresponding to the "popular car" programme[39], while commercial vehicles are classified in five categories;

–   minimum local content requirements vary by category.

The automobile industry is among those industries deemed to be strategic; as a result, firms are required to increase their use of locally-manufactured parts.[40] The participants selected for the country's Car Development Programme are required to subcontract the manufacture of car parts to local firms. Forty per cent local content is required for passenger car production and 13 to 55 per cent for commercial vehicles (Table 3). For car makers participating in the 'popular car programme', the local content requirement is 51 per cent. Moreover, the price of the cars in the latter case should not exceed a given threshold imposed by the BOI. Assemblers must also produce themselves at least 9 per cent of the parts they need or have them produced locally.

Special benefits are furthermore granted to the producers exceeding local content requirements, those producing high technology components, such as engines or transmissions, and those importing parts from other ASEAN countries. All local content requirements were expected to be dropped by the BOI in 1998 in an attempt to liberalise the sector. In addition to local regulations, ASEAN membership also encouraged the emergence of a local parts and equipment industry.

The Government began to ease restrictions concerning participation in local production. The BOI has broadened the sectors where foreign enterprise are allowed to participate and has included the integrated manufacture of parts and the assembly of cars into the list. In early 1998, Ford was given an approval to set up a plant which will cater for the domestic market rather than for export. This is the first time that the incentives were provided for such a domestic market oriented investment.

The Philippine Government also regulates foreign exchange. As a result, foreign auto makers must secure the foreign currency to purchase their parts imports through their own exports. Under the CDP, 75 per cent of the cost of parts imports (compared to 25 per cent under the CVDP) must be purchased with foreign currency and that figure will go up to 100 per cent in 1998. To meet these currency requirements, foreign car makers in the Philippines tend to assemble and export higher value products, such as transmissions, to other ASEAN countries[41]

Prices are regulated so that the price of locally assembled cars remains below that of imported ones. The tariff on cars is 40 per cent, in addition to taxes, but by assembling locally, tariffs are under 10 per cent of the value of the car. In 1995, the BOI agreed to reduce tariffs to no more than 30 per cent by 1998 (compared to 40 to 55 per cent previously) and are expected to drop to 5 per cent in 2004. The average rate of import duty on completely knock down parts has been cut from 20 per cent to 3 per cent in the recent years .

Until recently, only three car-makers were allowed to participate in the CDP (Mitsubishi, Nissan and Toyota). Over the past few years, there has been a flood of new foreign car-assemblers, and more than 15 are now active on the Philippine market[42] through joint ventures, including most recently Ford, setting up a production operation targeting the domestic market. GM and Chrysler are also in discussions with the Government. Some companies are already bringing their suppliers with them. Honda is surrounded by at least 11 of its suppliers at its greenfield site outside of Manila.

Table 3. **Local Content Rates and Import Tariffs in the ASEAN Automotive Industry, 1995** (percentages)

	Malaysia	Indonesia	Philippines
Local content rates			
Passenger cars	40 - 55	20 - 60	40
Commercial vehicles	40	20 - 40	14 - 55
Import tariffs on CKD parts			
Passenger cars	5 - 42	0 - 100	20
Commercial vehicles	0	0 - 40	10 - 20
Import tariffs on CBU			
Passenger cars	140 - 200	0 -125	40
Commercial vehicles	35	0 - 75	55 - 65

Note: Imports are in principle banned in Malaysia and Philippines. All countries also impose value-added taxes, excise duty and luxury taxes.
Source: Fujita and Child Hill (1997)

Ford returned to Philippines in May 1998 after an absence of 15 years. The firm has started the operation of an assembly plant and components production. A larger factory is still in the process of construction, which is planned to start manufacturing both passenger and commercial vehicles by mid-1999. Supplier firms are following Ford to the Philippines: ten will begin the operation in 1999, followed by a further 30 by 2004.

Despite the protests of established automobile assemblers in the Philippines, the automobile assembling industry has been listed in the Investment Priority Plans 1998 for the first time. Ford became the only beneficiary of the investment incentives so far among the competitors in the Philippine market.

NOTES

1.   World Bank (1999).

2.   Tolentino (1993).

3.   Figure 1 is based on IMF data and includes reinvestment earnings (since 1978) and other long-term and short-term capital registered with the Central Bank.

4.   Lafarge (France) acquired two Philippine cement companies in late 1998 for $460 million, and Cemex (Mexico) bought a local producer for $400 million in early 1999.

5.   Such moves are partly driven by the need to remain within the 40 per cent limit of foreign ownership in local companies laid down in the legislation.

6.   The attribution of inward investment to individual source countries is becoming increasingly difficult because of the growing number of investments passing through countries such as the British Virgin Islands.

7.   Chung-Hua (1995).

8.   This section relies on BSP data which are the most comprehensive in terms of coverage and details.

9.   This is in sharp contrast to most other Asian developing countries. There is generally limited scope for foreign investment in the food industry, first because the technology in this industry is usually so simple that foreign firms possess limited firm-specific advantage and secondly because consumer preferences and income levels are such that it is difficult to promote brand name products, with a few exceptions such as beverages and tobacco.

10.   Tolentino (1993).

11.   Antonio (1997).

12.   Tolentino (1993).

13.   Antonio (1997).

14   Estanislao (1997), p. 193.

15.   Estanislao (1996).

16.   "Sale of Philippine phone stake marks 'sad' end to 31-year saga", *International Herald Tribune*, 26 November 1998.

17.   "Foreign Investors warn Philippines over privatisation", Financial Times, 6 February 1997.

18.   World Bank (1996), p. 19.

19.   Executive Order 413

20.   Antonio (1997).

21.   Gochoco-Bautista (1997).

22.   By January 2009, tariffs on all manufactured goods will be between 0 and 5 per cent.

23.   "Manila limits tariff increases", *Financial Times*, 19 January 1999.

24.   Wells and Wint (1991), p. 15.

25.   Based on Gochoco-Bautista (1997).

26.   The five remaining books of the OIC are as follows: Book I - Investments with incentives; Book III - Incentives to MNEs establishing regional or area headquarters in the Philippines; Book IV - Incentives to MNEs establishing regional warehouses to supply spare parts or manufactured components and raw materials to the Asia-Pacific region or other foreign markets; Book V - Special investors resident visa (SIRV); and Book VI - Incentives of export processing zone enterprises.

27.   Concerning the FIA, "stockbrokers say they are unclear as to how the law applies to listed companies -- shares are divided into A and B shares, and only the B shares, making a maximum of 40 per cent of the company can be bought by foreigners" *Financial Times*, 17 February 1992.

28.   "Manila cuts protection for domestic industry", *Financial Times*, 8 April 1998.

29.   Section 26 of the Special Economic Zone Act of 1995.

30.   Citibank, Bank of America, Hong Kong and Shanghai Banking Corp and Standard Chartered Bank.

31.   Including 2 Japanese, 2 European, 2 ASEAN, 2 other Asian banks and 2 each from United States and Australia.

32.   "Philippines insurance market opened wider", *Financial Times,* 4 October 1996

33.   "Philippines: Trade and Investment", *Far Eastern Economic Review*, 19 June 1997.

34.   In 1995, the oil and petrochemicals sector was divided between Petron, the privatised Philippine oil company [44 per cent of market], Caltex [24 per cent] and Shell [32 per cent].

35.   *Financial Times*, 15 April 1997.

36.   *Financial Times* 2 July 1997.

37.   "Chips with everything", *Far Eastern Economic Review*, 19 June 1997.

38.   High import content was already identified as a major characteristic of non-traditional manufactured exports (electronics and garments) from the Philippines in the mid to late 1980s (Ali 1988).

39.   Daihatsu, Fiat, Honda and Kia participate in this programme, despite highly uncertain profitability.

40.   Mandatory increases in purchases from local enterprises have been a constant policy in the Philippines and can also to be found in the Philippines' Progressive Car Manufacturing Programme in the 1970s (Germidis 1977).

41.   Fujita and Child Hill (1997)

42.   BMW, Daewoo, Daihatsu, Fiat, Hino, Honda, Hyundai, Isuzu, Kia, Mazda, Mercedez-Benz, Mitsubishi, Nissan, Suzuki, Toyota, Proton, Volvo.

REFERENCES

Ali, Ifzal, "Manufactured Exports from the Philippines: A Sector Profile and an Agenda for Reform", ADB Economic Staff Paper, n° 42, September 1988.

Antonio, Emilio T. Jr, "Industrial Policies in the **Philippines**: Growing Reliance on Market Mechanisms", in Masuyama, Seiichi, Donna Vandenbrink and Chia Siow Yue (eds.), Industrial Policies in East Asia, ISEAS and NRI, Singapore, 1997.

Asian Development Bank, Asian Development Outlook 1996 and 1997, Asian Development Bank, Manila, 1996

Baldwin, Robert E., Foreign Trade Regimes and Economic Development: the Philippines, Columbia University Press, New York, 1975.

Chung-Hua Institution for Economic Research, Taiwan's Small and Medium-Sized Firms' Direct Investment in Southeast Asia, Chung-Hua Institution for Economic Research, Taipei, October 1995.

Comité des Constructeurs Français d'Automobiles, Répertoire mondial de activités de production et d'assemblage de véhicules automobiles, Paris, December 1995.

Dobson, Wendy and Pierre Jacquet, High Stakes: The Global Financial Services Talks, Institute for International Economics, Washington, D.C., forthcoming.

Eby Konan, Denise, "The Need for Common Investment Measures within ASEAN", ASEAN Economic Bulletin, vol. 12, n°3, March 1996.

Estanislao, Jesus, "The institutional environment for investment in China and ASEAN: current situation and trends", in Oman, Charles, P., Douglas H. Brooks, and Calm Foy, Investing in Asia, OECD Development Centre, Paris, 1997.

Fujita, Kuniko and Richard Child Hill, "Auto Industrialization in Southeast Asia : National Strategies and Local Development", ASEAN Economic Bulletin, vol. 13, n°3, March 1997.

Germidis, Dimitri (ed.), Transfer of Technology by Multinational Corporations, OECD Development Center Studies, Paris, 1977.

Gochoco-Bautista, Socorro "Domestic Adjustments and Globalization: the Case of the Philippines", mimeo, paper presented to the Asia Pacific Agenda Project held in Bali on January 10-12, 1997, January 1997.

Harrold, Peter, Malathi Jayawickrama and Deepak Bhattasali, "Practical Lessons for Africa from East Asia in Industrial and Trade Policies", World Bank Discussion Paper, n°310, 1996.

Healey, Derek, Les exportations japonaises de capitaux et le développement économique de l'Asie, OECD, Paris, 1991.

Hill, Hal and Brian Johns, "The Role of Direct Foreign Investment in Developing East Asian Countries", Weltwirtschaftliches Archiv, vol. 120, 1985, pp. 355-81.

Lamberte, Mario B. and Gilberto M. Llanto, " A Study of Financial Sector Policies : the Philippine Case", in Zahid, Shahid N., Financial Sector Development in Asia - Country Studies, Asian Development Bank, Manila, 1995.

Lee, Chung H., "Korea's Direct Foreign Investment in Southeast Asia", ASEAN Economic Bulletin, vol. 10, n°3, March 1994.

Okamoto, Yumiko, "FDI, Employment and Production Efficiency in the Philippines: Does APEC Liberalisation Matter?", mimeo, March 1997.

Oman, Charles, Douglas H. Brooks and Colm Foy (eds.), Investing in Asia, OECD Development Centre, Paris, 1997.

Tolentino, Paz Estrella E., Technological Innovation and Third World Multinationals, Routledge, London, 1993.

UNCTAD, World Investment Report 1997 - Transnational Corporations, Market Structure and Competition Policy, United Nations, Geneva, 1997.

UNCTC, World Investment Directory 1992, United Nations, New York, 1992.

Villegas, Bernardo, "Multinational Corporations and Transfer of Technology: the Philippine Case", in Germidis, Dimitri (ed.), Transfer of Technology by Multinational Corporations, OECD Development Center Studies, Paris, 1977.

Wells, Louis and Alvin Wint, Facilitating Foreign Investment: Government Institutions to Screen, Monitor, and Service Investment from Abroad, Foreign Investment Advisory Service, Occasional Paper 2, 1991.

World Bank, "Philippines: Strengthening Economic Resiliency", report, n°15985, November 8, 1996.

World Bank, "Philippines: From Crisis to Opportunity", Operations Evaluation Studies, 10 March 1999.

Annex

SOURCES AND METHODOLOGIES OF FDI
STATISTICS IN THE PHILIPPINES

Data on FDI in the Philippines are compiled by various agencies based on different sources and methodologies. In order to address the problems, the National Statistical Co-ordination Board (NSCB) was instructed to study the current situation and to implement a new foreign investment information system (FIIS). The FIIS does not cover outward FDI to the same extent.

Actual FDI flow data

Actual FDI in the Philippines covers 1) capital or equity contributions/remittances from abroad, 2) reinvested earnings, 3) technical fees, 4) royalties converted to equity, 5) bonds and other debt converted to equity, 6) imports converted to equity. The figure is obtained from the balance of payments compiled monthly by BSP based on forms submitted to domestic banks and forms submitted by enterprises to the bank. For this type of data, both inward and outward FDI figures are available.

While aggregate statistics are obtained by measuring individual balance of payments cash transactions, country and industry breakdowns are estimates. Estimates apply the combined ownership structure of some registered foreign direct enterprises to total actual foreign investment which is recorded in the balance of payments data. Samples of registered foreign enterprises are taken from the information gathered by SEC and BTRCP. Registration with SEC and BTRCP does not translate into actual flows as captured by the BSP. SEC and BTRCP define foreign investments as the foreign equity (paid-up) capital and exclude reinvested earnings.

Approval base data

Approved FDI shows commitments which may come in the near future. It represents the amount of proposed contribution or share of foreigners to various projects in the country. These investments consists of cash, investment "in kind" (such as machinery, equipment, raw materials and other supplies), reinvested earnings and technical fees converted into equity.

Investment promotion agencies (BOI, PEZA, SBMA, and CDC) generate data on their investment registrations or approvals. Total reported project costs are summed in order to arrive at total approved investments, including both foreign and Filipino investments. The data are compiled monthly.

Inter-Agency Committee on Foreign Direct Investment Statistics

Based on the recommendation of the study, the NSCB set up the Inter-Agency Committee on Foreign Direct Investment Statistics. The Committee brought together various agencies which are involved in FDI data compilation. All the member agencies will jointly implement FIIS in order to rationalise the process of data collection, processing and dissemination. With the guidance of the committee, NSCB co-ordinates agencies, prepares an integrated FDI statistics and report it quarterly. Table A-1 summarises the members of the committee and their assigned responsibilities.

Definition

The Philippine FIIS follows the conceptual definition of FDI set out in the *IMF Balance of Payment Manual* Fifth Edition and the *OECD Benchmark Definition of Foreign Direct Investment* in which FDI is defined as an investment to acquire a lasting interest by a resident entity in one economy in an enterprise resident in another economy. As the manual and the benchmark definition suggest, a direct investment enterprise is defined as an incorporated or unincorporated enterprise in which a direct investor who is resident in another economy owns ten percent or more of the ordinary shares or voting power to the equivalent.

Under the BOI definition, a firm is considered foreign if more than 40 per cent of its capital stock outstanding is held by foreign nationals.

Table A-1: **Type of Data Submitted by Each Agency**

Agency	Responsibility	Type of the data provided
National Statistical Co-ordination Board (NSCB)	co-ordination body	
Board of Investments (BOI)	investment promotion[a] and approval for incentives	cost of approved projects by the agency
Philippine Economic Zone Authority (PEZA)	investment promotion[a]	cost of approved projects by the agency
Clark Development Corporation (CDC)	investment promotion[a]	cost of approved projects by the agency
Subic Bay Metropolitan Authority (SBMA)	investment promotion[a]	cost of approved projects by the agency
Central Bank of the Philippines (BSP)	monitoring remittances of foreign investment, profits, royalties and licensing fees	Balance of Payments data
Securities and Exchange Commission (SEC)	registration, licensing, regulation and supervision of foreign corporations or partnerships[b]	country and industry breakdown data on foreign corporations' or partnerships' investment[c]
Bureau of Trade Regulation and Consumer Protection (BTRCP)	registration and supervision of foreign sole proprietorship within the metropolitan area[b]	country and industry breakdown data on foreign sole proprietor-ship investment
National Statistics Office (NSO)		
National Economic and Development Authority (NEDA)	issues the rules and regulations to implement Foreign Investment Act	

[a] Any enterprise seeking incentives must register with one of these agencies.

[b] The definition of investment used here differs from the BSP definition. It does not include re-invested earnings.

[c] Single proprietorships in the provinces should register with the provincial offices of the Department of Trade and Industry.

Source: NSCB 1996, The Central Bank of the Philippines 1996, IMF/OECD Survey of Implementation of Methodological Standards for Direct Investment 1998

Chapter 4

THAILAND

Introduction and summary

Until the summer 1997 Thailand was one of the world's fastest growing economies and, since the 1960s, it has been one of the most successful developing countries. Impressively high real growth rates of 8-9 per cent were maintained for almost 30 years. Before the crisis, the economy had reached a size almost four times as large as in 1970. In spite of occasionally high world interest rates, oil shocks, cyclical declines in demand for Thai exports and terms of trade shocks, Thailand had not, until 1997, experienced a single year of negative growth in the past three decades.

Exports have been the main engine of economic growth, particularly since the mid-1980s. Historically one of the world's leading rice exporters, Thailand has become a major exporter of manufactured goods, rising from only one third of total exports in 1980 to over 80 per cent by 1997. This shift in exports is mirrored in the structural transformation of the Thai economy, away from agriculture and into industry. While agriculture's contribution to GDP was three times that of manufacturing in 1960, by the early 1990s it was less than half as important as manufacturing.

Foreign direct investment (FDI) has played a key role in this process. Electronic products, particularly computer parts and integrated circuits, make up almost one third of the country's total exports. These sectors are dominated by foreign multinational enterprises (MNEs). Through inward investment, Thailand has become the ninth largest exporter of computers during the 1990s, with computer exports growing fourfold in the past five years. Thailand is also a major producer of automobiles, mostly by Japanese companies. As a result of extensive foreign investment in these sectors, Thailand is now a major destination for FDI inflows in the developing world, ranking eighth in terms of inflows in the 1990s, or twenty-second worldwide.

Trends in FDI in Thailand

Much of this investment has come since the mid-1980s. Until then, Thailand received far less FDI than its smaller neighbour, Malaysia. Although the Government generally welcomed foreign investors interested in greenfield sites, attracting FDI was not a priority, and in the early stages of its development the Thai economy was dominated by local capital. Foreign investors tended to focus on those sectors where the Government promoted import substitution and, as a result, much of this production was intended for the local market.

The situation changed in the second half of the 1980s. As with Malaysia, Thailand benefited from a massive relocation of production away from Japan, Chinese Taipei and other economies in the region as a result of currency appreciation in these economies at the time, as well as the loss of preferential access to major export markets and rising costs of production (especially labour costs) at home. Although Thailand was clearly in the right place at the right time, it also had in place the right policy environment to encourage and to accommodate these massive inflows.[1] This environment included sound macroeconomic stabilisation policies and a growing emphasis on outward looking policies.

Recent trends since the crisis indicate a continued strong interest on the part of foreign investors in the Thai economy. Information from the Bank of Thailand, based on actual FDI inflows across all sectors, shows that inflows doubled in baht terms in 1997 and grew by another 64 per cent in 1998. Growth rates in dollar terms are more modest because of the sharp depreciation of the baht, but even so, FDI inflows in 1998 of around $4.7 billion exceeded inflows in 1997 by almost $1 billion.[2] Inflows declined in the second half of the year, however.

Furthermore, direct investment has held up in the face of a sharp decline in domestic investment and net outflows of other forms of international capital. In 1997, for example, international bank lending to Thailand represented a capital outflow of $22 billion, compared with FDI in Thailand of $3.8 billion. Similarly, while applications to the Board of Investment (BOI) for investment projects were evenly divided between foreign and domestic investors in 1996, in the first seven months of 1998, applications by foreign investors were 162, compared with only 15 for domestic investors. These trends indicate the resiliency of FDI for both balance of payments financing and investment in the local economy.

Some large, capital-intensive projects have been postponed and foreign investors oriented towards the domestic market are suffering from the sharp drop in demand, but new opportunities for investment have opened up elsewhere in the economy. Some foreign investors have raised their stakes in their affiliates, while others have taken advantage of liberalisation in sectors such as banking.

Thai policies towards FDI

Foreign investment policies in Thailand have traditionally reflected the broader development strategies in place at the time. Early foreign MNEs were enticed by high tariff barriers to locate assembly production in Thailand to supply the domestic market. The second wave of FDI came in the late 1980s in order to take advantage of favourable unit labour costs and exchange rates, as well as export promotion policies, to establish export platforms for markets elsewhere. Although import substitution and export promotion policies have tended to converge over time, foreign investment in Thailand still tends to be divided sharply between local market oriented and export-oriented production.

This dichotomy is reflected in policies towards FDI in Thailand. Firms wishing to export most of their output have traditionally faced few restrictions. They can locate anywhere and hold all of the shares in the affiliate, as well as the land on which the factory is built. They also receive tax holidays and, more importantly, exemptions on duties for imported inputs. In contrast, firms wishing to sell mostly in the local market are either prohibited or restricted in a number of ways depending on the sector. They often have to settle for minority ownership and can only lease land for a fixed period. In some cases, they require an authorisation through a lengthy and not always transparent process. In the automobile sector, foreign investors have also faced cumbersome local content requirements.

Unlike policy initiatives in other areas, this dualistic policy towards foreign investors was changing only slowly before the crisis. There have been proposals to amend the Alien Business Law in the past, but as with earlier efforts to amend the ABL, this one is meeting opposition in Parliament.[3] The reforms proposed as a result of the crisis represent a significant step towards a more open and unified approach to FDI policy. Nevertheless, the fact that reforms have been enacted during an economic crisis and that some, such as in banking or concerning majority foreign ownership of joint ventures, appear to be temporary might suggest to potential investors that they are not based on a fundamental reappraisal of development strategies and hence will not survive the return of economic growth.

The ongoing financial crisis in Thailand and the structural problems which it has brought to light present an opportune moment to reassess whether existing policies towards FDI in Thailand, as part of more general growth strategies, have best served the interests of economic development. Export promotion policies based on foreign investment had proved highly successful at generating massive exports in sectors in which Thai firms had no experience. But at the same time, the years before the crisis were characterised by growing concerns over shortages of skilled labour and rising wages not matched by productivity. As a result, Thai low-technology exports were declining in the face of stiff competition from China, Bangladesh and Vietnam, and this shortfall was not being offset by sustained growth in medium- to high-technology exports.

Experience in both OECD and non-OECD countries suggests that too great an emphasis on export promotion does not always yield the expected benefits. Not only has the resulting export growth often proved unsustainable, but such exports are also often highly dependent on imported components because of the need for high quality inputs in order to compete effectively in export markets. This dependency reduces both the potential benefit to the balance of payments and the responsiveness of the economy to exchange rate changes. In addition, because highly export-oriented firms are less likely to source locally, such investment limits potential technology transfers between foreign affiliates and local suppliers.

In contrast, local market oriented firms are more likely to source locally and hence offer greater potential scope for technology transfers. Furthermore, because they often offer goods and services of higher quality and lower prices, they make it easier for Thai firms which make use of these goods and services to compete in world markets, thus assisting in the development of indigenous exporting capabilities. Recent reforms in FDI policies in Thailand have reduced this strong bias in favour of export-oriented investment projects and could open the way for more FDI by firms wishing to supply the Thai market. If these reforms prove to be durable, the Thai economy may be poised in the medium term for a period of more sustainable growth, with local firms contributing more to export growth.

I. Direct investment trends

Overall trends in FDI

Although Thailand has become a major destination for FDI inflows in the developing world, ranking eighth in terms of inflows in the 1990s, foreign investors have not traditionally played a dominant role in the Thai economy, except in certain sectors. Until the mid-1980s, Thailand received far less FDI than its smaller neighbour, Malaysia. The Thai government generally welcomed foreign investors, but attracting FDI was not a priority. In the early stages of its development, the Thai economy was dominated by local capital. Foreign investors tended to focus on those sectors where the Government promoted import substitution and, as a result, much of this production was intended for the local market.

The situation changed in the second half of the 1980s. As with Malaysia, Thailand benefited from a massive relocation of production away from Japan and the Newly Industrialising Economies (NIEs). As shown in Figure 1, FDI inflows took off dramatically after 1987 from previously very modest levels and peaked in 1990 at a level that was ten times as high as in 1986.[4] The share of FDI flows in gross fixed capital formation rose from four per cent over 1970-85 to 10 per cent on average over the period 1985-90 but dropped again in the most recent period to reach about 3.5 per cent on average in 1991-95. Following the 1990 peak, investments fell precipitously until 1994. Concerns of the Government about ensuring a steady inflow of foreign capital prompted a round of liberalisation beginning in 1993.

Figure 1. **FDI inflows as a percentage of GDP, 1970-98**

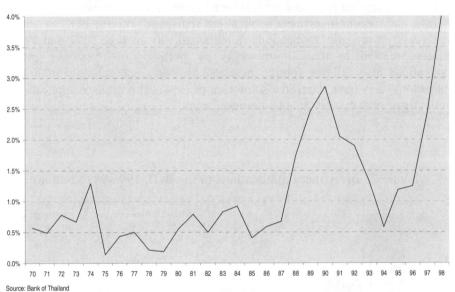

Source: Bank of Thailand

The trend reversal observed after 1990 may be attributed to both internal and external factors. In February 1991 a bloodless military coup ushered in a phase of political unrest in Thailand, including pro-democracy demonstrations in May 1992 which may have frightened investors away. Economic factors compounded domestic political problems. Concern about Thailand's overloaded transport networks (including the clearing system at ports), a shortage of skilled workers and other problems also played a role. The drop in 1994 was mainly due to a sharp slowdown in Japanese investments, partly as a result of economic difficulties at home.[5]

FDI since the crisis

The crisis has not yet discouraged foreign investors from establishing or expanding in Thailand. Indeed, inflows have reached record levels, partly because of the window of opportunity to gain control of domestic firms in a number of sectors which were previously restricted or where owners were not willing to cede control. In baht terms, FDI inflows doubled in 1997 and grew by 64 per cent in 1998. Even in dollar terms growth rates have been impressive: 65 per cent in 1997 and 25 per cent in 1998.[6]

Another source of data comes from applications to the Board of Investment.[7] Foreign investment, like domestic investment, is cyclical and is affected by the performance of the overall economy, but BOI figures reveal that it has held up much better than domestic investment since the onset of the crisis. Figure 2 shows domestic and foreign investment applications registered with the BOI over the past three years. Domestic applications fell dramatically in both 1997 and 1998, as investors reacted to the current crisis by putting off investment projects. Applications also fell for foreign investors in 1997, but unlike with domestic applications, they have recovered somewhat in 1998. The value of applications by foreign firms now exceeds that by domestic ones.

Figure 2. **Investment applications to the BOI, 1996-98** ($ billion)

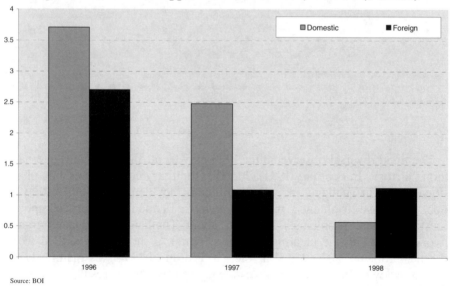

Source: BOI

Some approved projects have subsequently been cancelled owing to the continuing economic slump, including 63 major projects worth 364 billion baht, which received privileges from 1995 to July 1997.[8] Most of these projects were in the chemicals, paper, plastics and steel sectors, heavily reliant on imported raw materials.

Foreign firms have continued to invest in Thailand in the face of a major contraction of demand by taking advantage of export opportunities. Data on the number of foreign and domestic applications which intended to export over 80 per cent of their output show an increase from 59 per cent of total projects in 1996 to 80 per cent in 1998.

Some large investors have had to inject capital into their affiliates or into suppliers, and sometimes this has involved the acquisition of all of the shares not already in the parent company's hands. A temporary revision in the regulation has made such acquisitions possible, if agreed to by the local shareholders. Honda, for example, has recently taken a 97 per cent stake in its Thai subsidiary, formerly restricted to 49 per cent. Although this purchase was subject to BOI approval, it was expected to go ahead since Honda had indicated a willingness to sell back a majority stake to local shareholders once the economy picked up.[9] It has been estimated by the BOI that 123 Thai-controlled joint ventures with foreign firms have ceded control to the foreign partner since the inception of the new law at the end of 1997, representing a capital inflow of around 16 billion baht.

FDI versus other forms of capital inflows

Foreign direct investment became increasingly important as a means of bridging the savings-investment gap in Thailand in the late 1980s and early 1990s, but this trend had been reversed before the crisis. The share of FDI in total net private capital inflows rose from 10 per cent in 1980 to 50 per cent in 1990 and dropped again to reach 23 per cent in 1995. Inflows of FDI were being superceded by rising short-term debt which was one of the factors leading to the financial crisis in July 1997. Financial deregulation and the opening of the Bangkok International Banking Facilities (BIBF) in 1993 made loan funds more easily available.[10]

Figure 3 shows quarterly inflows of capital into Thailand immediately before and after the crisis. The reversal in bank lending in the second quarter of 1997 is immediately apparent and dwarfs any changes in FDI and portfolio flows. Significantly, quarterly inflows of direct investment rose in the aftermath of the crisis, even when expressed in dollar terms. Only in the third quarter of 1998 did they fall back somewhat but still remain well above pre-crisis levels.

213

Figure 3. **Quarterly capital inflow into Thailand, 1995-97** ($ million)

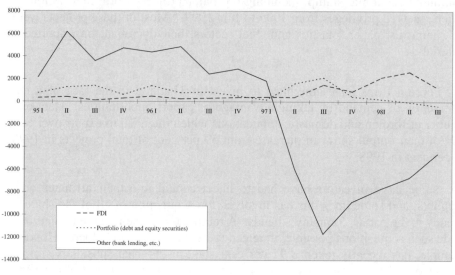

Source: IMF

Sectoral distribution

Manufacturing represents the largest sector for inward investment in Thailand but less than all other sectors taken together (Table 1). Over one quarter of manufacturing investment is in the electrical equipment sector. Outside of manufacturing, foreign firms have invested most in distribution and trade in order to tap into the growing discretionary spending of Thai consumers. Direct investment in the property sector, particularly hotels, has always been volatile, rising tenfold and then falling back by an equal amount in the past five years. At its peak in 1995, investment in the property sector represented 42 per cent of total inflows, partly reflecting the construction boom at the time. Volatility of FDI in petroleum products results partly from the lumpiness of such investments.

The electronics industry has the highest FDI penetration ratio, with foreign investments constituting about 95 per cent of total investment. Foreign investors are also particularly active in the automotive and metal-working industries where they account for roughly 80 per cent of total BOI-promoted projects. In agri-industries, in contrast, wholly Thai-owned projects are on a par with foreign projects.

214

Table 1. **FDI inflows into Thailand, 1980-98** (million baht; per cent)

	96	97	98	1980-98	
Industry	17 942	58 337	81 034	**324 935**	**42.9%**
Food, beverages, tobacco	1 143	6 971	2 775	**23 329**	3.1%
Textiles, leather, clothing	1 247	1 493	3 944	**16 451**	2.2%
Metal and non metallic products	2 851	6 610	12 801	**41 003**	5.4%
Electrical equipment	6 095	18 446	9 884	**90 902**	12.0%
Machinery and transport equipment	2 749	12 873	26 428	**55 976**	7.4%
Chemicals	4 631	6 054	8 342	**44 537**	5.9%
Petroleum products, coal	-6 332	452	12 737	**10 442**	1.4%
Construction materials	88	- 395	- 75	**1 139**	0.2%
Other manufacturing	5 470	5 833	4 208	**41 158**	5.4%
Financial institutions	1 823	3 725	26 586	**61 482**	8.1%
Trade	13 798	33 947	37 711	**158 534**	20.9%
Construction	1 782	5 786	6 466	**56 309**	7.4%
Mining, quarrying, petroleum	490	653	2 332	**25 001**	3.3%
Agriculture	51	37	19	**3 506**	0.5%
Real Estate	19 054	3 467	8 629	**87 843**	11.6%
Services and other	2 532	11 737	30 268	**72 272**	9.5%
TOTAL	**57 472**	**117 689**	**160 058**	**756 895**	

Source : Bank of Thailand

The significant increases in inflows in 1997-98 were not confined to any specific sectors (Figure 4). The fastest growth in 1998 occurred in the financial sector, as the crisis created opportunities for foreign investors to acquire or increase their stakes in Thai financial companies. Growth has also been dramatic in the past two years in industry and distribution. Among the major sectors, only property investments recorded a significant decline, as the crisis hit property values. Among manufacturing sectors, metals, machinery and transport equipment have all increased significantly since 1997.

Sources of FDI

Firms from the United States took an early lead in investing in Thailand, encouraged in part by the US-Thai Treaty of Amity of 1966 which accorded national treatment to US investors. Much of this investment involved fully foreign-owned affiliates in areas such as petroleum and chemicals. The US role in Thailand was gradually eclipsed by that of Japan, beginning slowly in the early 1970s and then decisively in the late 1980s. Early Japanese investments were designed either to avoid tariffs by establishing assembly operations, particularly for consumer goods, or as export platforms back to Japan and to third countries. Japanese investors were followed in the 1990s by firms from Singapore, Chinese Taipei and Hong Kong, China. The NIEs were by far the largest investors in Thailand between 1990 and 1996, though Japan has regained its position since 1997. Thailand has benefited from a diversification of sources of FDI over time, much as it has across sectors.

Figure 4. **Net flows of FDI into Thailand by sector, 1980-98** (billion baht)

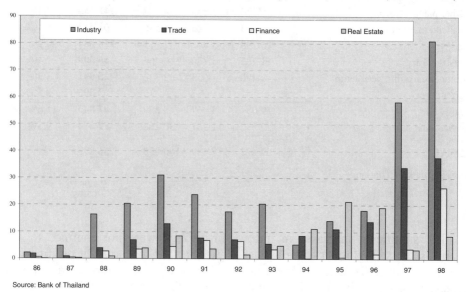

Source: Bank of Thailand

In terms of cumulative FDI inflows, Japanese and US firms account for almost one half of the total, with NIEs representing another 29 per cent and the top five European investors only 12 per cent (Table 3). In 1998, Japanese and US firms maintained their shares of total inflows, while the cumulative stock of investments by Singapore firms grew by almost 40 per cent, suggesting that firms from Singapore are capitalising on their relatively stronger financial position during the crisis to expand within the region. One such purchase involved the acquisition of a Thai bank.

Table 2. **Share of FDI in Thailand by principal investors** (period averages)

	70-79	80-84	85-89	90-96	97-98
Japan	30%	25%	42%	26%	34%
United States	35%	26%	23%	15%	19%
NIEs	5%	19%	19%	35%	27%
Other	29%	29%	16%	24%	20%

Source: Bank of Thailand

Table 3. **Cumulative FDI flows by country, 1980-98 (billion baht)**

	1970-95	96	97	98	70-98	
Japan	131.3	13.3	44.1	61.0	**249.6**	30.9%
United States	70.3	10.9	23.0	34.3	**138.5**	17.1%
Hong Kong, China	68.5	5.4	15.7	17.8	**107.4**	13.3%
Singapore	36.5	7.0	8.3	26.0	**77.7**	9.6%
Chinese Taipei	27.2	3.5	6.1	4.4	**41.2**	5.1%
UK	15.7	1.4	3.7	7.0	**27.9**	3.4%
Netherlands	8.7	-1.0	4.4	12.7	**24.8**	3.1%
France	9.8	0.8	0.0	7.5	**18.0**	2.2%
Germany	8.4	1.1	2.1	3.2	**14.9**	1.8%
Switzerland	7.7	1.3	3.4	2.3	**14.7**	1.8%
Australia	4.0	0.9	3.8	1.9	**10.5**	1.3%
Korea	2.7	0.6	0.9	3.7	**8.0**	1.0%
Others	47.5	12.4	2.2	11.6	**73.7**	9.1%
Total	439.6	57.5	117.7	193.3	**808.1**	

Bank of Thailand

Japanese investments, mostly involving joint ventures[11], are concentrated in chemicals, electrical machinery and transport equipment. Japanese investors also dominate the automobile industry with about 90 per cent of projects involving foreign equity, although US firms were beginning to make inroads in this sector before the crisis. Japanese firms also account for 65 per cent of foreign investments in the electronic industry and 59 per cent in the metal working industry. While in the past Japanese investors were mainly large multinationals, many new Japanese entrants are small and medium-sized firms supplying parts and components to large Japanese joint-venture manufacturers already based in

Thailand.[12]   Unlike in the 1960s and 1970s, when Japanese investment concentrated in assembly of consumer goods, newer Japanese investment has diversified into intermediate goods and export industries.

Investors from Hong Kong and Singapore tend to focus on non-industrial sectors, particularly finance.   One French company is quite active in oil exploration.   British firms invest primarily in chemical and petroleum products while French companies are active in the area of construction materials, such as cement and plaster, and services and utilities such as electricity.   Direct investment from Chinese Taipei has been concentrated in manufacturing, notably electronic appliances, textiles and chemicals, followed by the trade and property sectors.

Thai direct investment abroad

While negligible before 1987, Thai direct investment abroad increased rapidly from 1990 as a result of the wider provision of information for investors, foreign exchange liberalisation and the advent of offshore banking. The Thai government has encouraged such investment as a way to find new sources of raw materials and technology as well as to diversify markets.   This is also in line with Thailand's objective to play a pivotal role in Indochina.   Such investment has fallen since the crisis.

Thailand does not have any major business group belonging to the top 50 largest multinationals based in developing countries.[13]   Despite this modest presence at the global level, however, Thai firms are important actors in neighbouring countries, such as Indochina (Cambodia, Laos, Myanmar, and Vietnam), Indonesia, and China.   The main sectors are forestry, property, telecommunications, finance and assorted manufacturing.   The CP (Charoen Pokpand) Group is the largest foreign investor in China, with interests in agro-industry, telecommunications, petrochemicals, retailing, manufacturing and property.   In an unusual example of outward Thai investment, the Thai affiliate of a Danish company acquired its Danish parent in 1992.

The recent crisis may cause some large Thai conglomerates to shed certain overseas assets.   The CP Group, for example, was reportedly considering selling its 50 per cent stake in a Chinese motorcycle company which dates from 1985.[14]

Methodological issues

Data on FDI in Thailand are available from both the Bank of Thailand or the Board of Investments.   The BOI reports all FDI applications, approvals and start-ups which have requested BOI promotion.   Certain important sectors which fall

—

outside of the ambit of the BOI are excluded, notably finance, insurance, real estate, and retail and wholesale trade. The BOI also excludes acquisitions of Thai companies. The Bank of Thailand figures include actual net flows of FDI, although they do not include retained earnings. The absence of retained earnings from both the BOI and the Bank of Thailand data could lead to a serious understatement of actual foreign investment in Thailand, especially as the stock of such investment grows — although other methodological differences may work in the opposite direction. While the BOI does not have information on retained earnings, their FDI data on expansion of existing companies may capture some of this reinvestment.

As a comparison, the United States reports total investments in Thailand at the end of 1997 of $3.5 billion, compared with Bank of Thailand estimates of $4.1 billion (at an exchange rate of 25 baht to the dollar). Japanese figures from the Ministry of Finance show a cumulative stock of investment in Thailand of $14.5 billion, compared to Bank of Thailand reported investments from Japan of $7 billion at the end of 1997. Home and host countries rarely record similar levels of investment, but the discrepancy in the case of Japan is significant. Partly this may result from the choice of exchange rate to convert to dollars, because of the recent volatility. It is also possible, however, that the Japanese presence is much greater than that indicated by the Bank of Thailand.

II. Thailand's development strategy

In spite of frequent changes of government[15], Thai macroeconomic policy has varied little over time. Like other countries in the region, Thailand has experienced a long-term structural shift as agriculture has been overtaken by industry. The shift from import substitution to greater emphasis on export promotion was key in the rapid growth of manufactured production and exports. Yet export success came relatively late, with favourable exchange rate policies and an investor-friendly legal framework. The World Bank (1993) suggests that Thai development is best seen as having three distinct stages, mirroring similar developments in other Southeast countries, although the timing is different in each country.

Agriculture-based growth (1960 - early 1970s)

As in many developing countries, Thailand historically produced and exported primary and agricultural products derived from its rich natural resources (rice, teak, tin and rubber contributed 80 to 90 per cent of Thailand's total exports from the 1920s to the 1950s). Until the early 1970s, growth was mainly based on exports of agricultural goods, with manufactured goods such as textiles and garments playing a minor role. High rates of growth, averaging eight per cent annually, were achieved.

During this first phase, the Government focused on developing the necessary economic infrastructure such as roads, dams and reservoirs, and on diversifying agricultural production. Trade was heavily controlled: in particular, rice exports were under the control of a State marketing monopoly and were discouraged by significant export taxes. Export production was also hampered by a multiple exchange rate system. The Government intervened heavily in a number of other sectors. Firms were generally oriented towards the small domestic market, resulting in a high degree of concentration. Growth was driven by the improved exploitation of the country's primary resources but foreign (in particular American) aid provided an additional stimulus. Although industrialisation occurred during this period, mainly with the help of US capital, the share of industry was still less than 16 per cent by 1969.

Import-substitution strategies maintained (1971-80)

In the early 1970s, the Thai authorities adopted the import-substituting strategies favoured by many developing economies at the time. The main objectives were to reduce Thailand's dependence on imports of foreign goods, thus saving foreign exchange and increasing domestic value added, and to diversify away from agriculture[16]. Industrial policies favoured large-scale producers in capital-intensive, import-substituting industries, mainly textiles, automobiles and pharmaceuticals. Overall levels of effective protection were modest by developing country standards, although by the end of 1978, nine import categories, including automobiles, had tariff rates above 90 per cent. Nominal tariff rates ranged from 30 to 55 per cent for consumer goods. In the late 1970s import substitution extended to capital and intermediate goods. To that end, the Eastern Seaboard Scheme was launched to build new port facilities and to develop a chemical industry complex fueled by natural gas from the Gulf of Thailand.

During the 1970s voices were raised pressing for a change in economic orientation. Leading banks and businessmen were supported by technocrats within the Government. The future of import substitution was publicly questioned by the National Economic and Social Development Board (NESDB) as early as 1967 and in 1971 the preamble to the third 5-year plan recognised the need for export promotion, yet little was done to promote exports during the 1970s[17]. The Ministry of Finance, the military and protected firms formed a powerful lobby against any dramatic policy shift. Import tariffs supplied 30 per cent of total tax revenue in 1971, and as a result, tariffs kept increasing between 1974 and 1981 on 35 categories of goods and reduced only in 19 in an attempt to sustain the growth of import substitution. From 1977 the BOI was allowed to impose surcharges to provide extra protection to promoted firms.

Thailand could maintain its policy of import substitution longer than some other countries within the region for several reasons. First, the relatively large size of its market, combined with rapid economic growth, meant that market saturation did not occur as quickly as elsewhere. In addition, a rise in world agricultural prices and continued inflows of foreign capital allowed Thailand to weather the first oil shock. Military aid from the US government (which started in 1957) also benefited the Thai economy by easing balance of payments position, stimulating domestic demand and inflating government revenues as a large part of military expenditures were financed from abroad.

Import substitution pushed the share of industrial value added in GDP from 16 per cent in 1970 to 22 per cent in 1980, but the preference for capital-intensive projects meant that industry's share in the labour force increased only from 5 to 9 per cent over the same period. The consumer goods portion of total imports dropped from 19 per cent in 1970 to 10 per cent in 1980, while the share of capital goods also shrank from 35 per cent to 24 per cent.[18]

A number of problems arose in the 1970s which led to the need to move away from the import-substitution strategy. First, as a result of a serious decline in the international terms of trade for primary products[19], the rate of agricultural expansion slackened thus putting growing pressure on the balance of payments. Second, the second oil shock, together with the discontinuation of US military aid, led to a rising public sector deficit. External foreign debt rose from almost nothing in 1973 to 21 per cent in 1980 and 38 per cent in 1986. The service of the debt on the private and public foreign loans since 1975 soared.

The ratio of exports to GDP stagnated during this period. At the same time, the national savings rate fell from 22 per cent in 1975 to 18 per cent in the mid-1980s, largely as a result of a decline in public sector savings.[20] The consolidated public sector deficit reached 7 per cent of GDP by 1980-81. The overvaluation of the baht as a result of the dollar peg, together with the need to finance the public sector investment-savings gap, led to rising real interest rates and thus to a sharp growth slowdown. Growth nevertheless remained positive in the first half of the 1980s, partly because self-sufficiency in food and basic wage goods helped to ease potential balance of payments problems.

The widening savings-investment gap exacerbated the current account deficit, leading to a series of baht devaluations in the 1980s: 14 per cent against the dollar in 1984, followed by a further depreciation of the baht vis-à-vis its other major trading partners (Japan and the EU) as a result of the Plaza Agreement which took the dollar down, and the baht along with it, in 1985. Overall the Thai currency depreciated by 30 per cent in trade-weighted terms and by 100 per cent vis-à-vis the Japanese yen between 1986 and 1989. The depreciation helped to make Thailand an attractive destination for export-oriented foreign investment and, along with the recovery of world trade after 1985, contributed to a sharp improvement of Thailand's export performance (Figure 5).

Figure 5. **Exports of goods and services as a percentage of GDP**

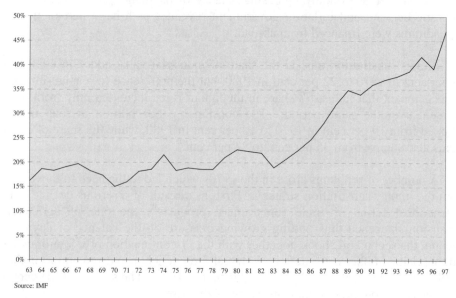

Source: IMF

Reform and export-based growth (1980 - 1996)

In parallel with the baht devaluations, the Government moved towards export promotion and away from import substitution. Overall levels of protection were reduced by lowering tariffs and relaxing other protective measures including price controls. Exports were promoted more vigorously through exemptions from import duties on machinery and raw materials used for export production. Investment incentives were changed, both in form and in implementation, in order to favour export-oriented projects. Several export taxes were also abolished at that time and the Bank of Thailand established special credit facilities for exporters. Most of the macroeconomic policies implemented were market-oriented, such as flexible exchange rates and fewer constraints on interest rates. The role of the State was scaled back after 1987 as outlined in the Sixth five-year plan.

The widening of the trade and current account deficits, together with the quadrupling of the debt service burden, also induced a relaxation in the implementation of FDI restrictions for export-oriented foreign firms. Both direct and portfolio foreign investment soared after 1986. With a large supply of low wage workers possessing good basic education and skill, Thailand was in an ideal position to take advantage of the changes in comparative advantage between Japan and the NIEs which allowed it to push into the export market for technologically and skill-intensive products such as cars and electronic consumer products.[21]

The structure of the economy was deeply affected by these changes and by other favourable conditions, such as a drop in oil prices and a sharp rise in the value of the yen: the share of agriculture in GDP fell from more than 25 per cent in 1980 to 12 per cent in 1993, while the share of industry rose from 16 per cent in 1980 to 30 per cent in 1996. The rapid decline in the share of agriculture was partly a result of faltering world trade and falling prices; from 1980 to 1985 world rice prices dropped by about 50 per cent. Despite industrialisation, four out of five workers were employed in agriculture in 1970, and almost two thirds still in 1990.

Encouraged by the policy change, manufacturing exports started to surge in the early 1980s, with traditional light manufacturing industries such as garments and leather products increasing their share of manufacturing value-added from 20 to 23 per cent and heavy industry decreasing its share from 43 to 37 per cent. The export boom of 1984-88 was triggered by the exchange rate devaluation and sustained by the availability of capital from Japan and Chinese Taipei for developing export industries. In 1985, manufactured exports exceeded agricultural exports for the first time.

This trend in the structure of exports has continued, with manufactured exports accounting for more than 80 per cent of total exports in 1997, compared to 35 per cent in 1980. The boom in manufactured exports has been driven by labour-intensive industries such as integrated circuits and electronics assembly, footwear and toy-making. Since 1990, the fastest growth has been observed in higher technology goods, such as computer accessories and motor parts, making Thailand the ninth largest computer exporter in the world.

Although the industrial sector is now broadly-based, agriculture is still important, and Thailand remains a major agricultural exporter, despite the rise in exports of manufactured goods and services. Agricultural exports account for about 14 per cent of total exports. Moreover some of the most important manufacturing activities continue to involve the processing of agricultural products. The food industry is still the second largest sub-sector (with about 15 per cent of manufactured output) but should be soon overtaken by textiles and electronics.

These trends have not occurred evenly throughout the country. Regional inequalities are a major feature of Thailand's industrial development, as manufacturing industry has concentrated in Bangkok and the surrounding areas. In 1994, 28 per cent of Thailand's factories were located in Bangkok and the four contiguous provinces. As a result of these imbalances, industrial decentralisation has become a major objective of Thailand's industrial policy since 1987.

The 1997 currency crisis

Thailand managed to maintain strong economic growth (8 per cent on average) over the period 1990-96, but the Thai economy was seriously affected by the 1996 export slowdown. Although many countries in the region were affected by sluggish world demand for electronic goods, structural weaknesses exacerbated the slowdown in Thailand as the economy suffered from a loss of competitiveness due to rising wages not matched by productivity increases.

The 1996 slowdown in exports of low-technology, labour-intensive products was not matched by an increase in the export growth of medium to high-technology products. This has been attributed to inadequate human resources.[22] Thailand has higher costs of production relative to other nations producing similar products and has had difficulty altering the structure of production towards more skill-intensive activities. Goods, such as electronics and cars, classified as medium to high-technology products do not require a highly-skilled labour force for that part of their production actually taking place in Thailand. As a result, these exports are likely to come under increasing pressure from the low-wage and unskilled labour economies.

Several other factors contributed to the currency crisis which erupted in July 1997. The credit boom of the early 1990s gave rise to a financial and a real estate bubble, making the Thai economy vulnerable to a shift in expectations. This was exacerbated by the weakness in prudential supervision in the banking sector and the ease with which funds could be borrowed from abroad, particularly through the BIBF. The shift in expectations materialised as a result of the export slowdown and the attempt by the Thai authorities to defend the exchange rate through very high interest rates. The rigidity of exchange rate policy (the baht was pegged to the dollar, thus encouraging unhedged foreign borrowing) played a key role in the build up to the crisis.

III. Policies towards FDI

Historical overview

Policies towards FDI have formed part of both the import-substitution and the export-promotion strategies of successive Thai governments. Although every development plan since the early 1960s has targeted promotion of FDI, policies towards inward investment in Thailand have never been either particularly restrictive or unusually welcoming compared with other countries in the region. Export earnings from agriculture and a relatively dynamic local business sector made promoting FDI less of a priority. In spite of occasional backlashes against the rapidly growing foreign presence in Thailand, policies towards FDI have been relatively stable over time. Investment promotion began in earnest once the economy began to encounter balance of payments difficulties. Liberalisation of restricted sectors has been gradual but has accelerated as a result of the crisis. US firms are granted preferential treatment under the US-Thai Treaty of Amity.

There has been very little sectoral targeting, although import substitution policies which varied tariff rates greatly across sectors implicitly encouraged foreign investors in some sectors more than others. Significant tariff reforms over time have dampened but not completely eliminated this sectoral bias.

Investment policies in Thailand are implemented by the Board of Investments which was established in 1954 to stimulate both foreign and domestic investment, all behind a high level of protection. The Office of the Board of Investment which serves as secretariat for the Board was established in 1965. At first its powers were limited: it had to comply with laws dictating which industrial activities to promote, but since 1962 it has been permitted to issue promotion certificates and to add to the list of eligible activities. Since 1960, the BOI has granted investors fiscal incentives (such as tax and import duty reductions)[23] and non-fiscal concessions (eased restrictions on foreign investment and employment of foreigners) on the basis of various criteria. In the early years of operation, the BOI's promotional privileges tended to skew development towards large concerns, giving little incentive to small firms or to technical innovation.[24]

The Investment Promotion Act of 1960 provided tax and tariff concessions for both local and foreign investors. The Government allowed foreign firms to repatriate profits, gave specific guarantees against nationalisation, modified the land code to make it easier for foreign firms to occupy land and abolished labour unions and outlawed strikes.[25] In 1972, the military government introduced a new labour law which legalised labour associations within strict limits.

In line with the import substitution strategy followed at the time, the gap between high tariff rates imposed on imports of consumer goods and lower rates on capital goods and inputs was made even wider for promoted firms. In 1968, restrictions were imposed on FDI in export-oriented industries, in heavy industries as well as in processing industries using domestic resources. In 1977, the BOI was allowed to impose tariff surcharges to provide additional protection to promoted firms. As a result of import substitution, most FDI in the 1960s and early 1970s was concentrated in production geared to the protected domestic market. Because of the domestic market orientation, foreign capital often chose to ally with domestic capital to get access to local knowledge and local marketing networks.

Today the BOI is officially governed by the 1977 Investment Promotion Act (IPA), as amended by the Investment Promotion Act of 1991. Since the enactment of the IPA, one of the criteria on joint ventures is that a firm should export at least 80 percent of the output if foreigners hold a majority share (or all output for fully foreign-owned firms). Large tax and tariff exemptions are given to export-oriented firms. The mandatory export rate for those industries was eventually decreased. In 1982, NMB Thai Co. Ltd (Japan) received the first promotion certificate.

In recent years, the importance of investment incentives provided by the BOI has tended to decline as the tax structure improved and the incentive structure became more generalised. Industrial decentralisation has been particularly emphasised so as to correct the imbalances between urban and rural areas. The BOI issues a regularly updated list of activities eligible for investment promotion.

The recent financial crisis has brought forward another round of liberalisation, although much of this still awaits the approval of the Parliament. Recent proposals open more sectors to greater foreign participation, including finance. The new Foreign Investment Law, if it is approved, will provide greater scope for foreign participation in the Thai economy, but the fundamental impediments relating to land ownership and participation in Thai companies will remain, albeit in a more investor-friendly form.

A.   *Restrictions on inward investment*

Policies towards foreign direct investment in Thailand are governed by the Alien Business Law (ABL), the Land Code and supplemental sectoral restrictions. Although all of these are currently under review, the description which follows is based on existing legislation. Foreign majority or wholly foreign ownership is allowed in all activities except those in List A, B and C (as described in Box 2) and those restricted by specific laws and regulations in certain areas such as the banking sector. The Alien Business Law generally limits foreign shareholding to a maximum of 49 per cent.[26] Other laws impose even lower limits in particular sectors. The Commercial Banking Act limits foreign shareholding in a Thai commercial bank to 25 per cent. The Finance, Securities and Credit Foncier

Business Act limits foreign shareholdings in a Thai finance company to 25 per cent. In addition, foreign ownership limits may be imposed by any Thai company in its articles of association, and most listed companies have such limits. US investors receive special treatment under the US-Thai Treaty of Amity (see below).

Majority ownership is nevertheless possible in non-restricted sectors and for greenfield investments in sectors promoted by the Board of Investments, subject to certain conditions relating to i.a. the location of the investment and its export propensity. Of the more than one hundred foreign investment projects approved by the BOI in the first half of 1998, roughly one third involved full foreign ownership.

The Land Code limits foreign shareholding in a Thai company owning land to 49 per cent. Under the 1977 IPA, promoted foreign companies are entitled to own land used for factories. Foreigners may also own a limited number of housing apartment units. Petroleum concessionaires may own land necessary to perform their activities. In other cases, foreign investors may sign long term leases. In early 1997, Thailand's cabinet approved a proposal to let foreigners own small pieces of land, but restricted eligibility to individuals and companies which invest at least 25 million baht in the country. The cabinet also increased the limit on foreign ownership of condominiums to 49 per cent of any one complex, up from 40 per cent. Under recent regulations, BOI-promoted companies are now entitled to own land for residential and business purposes. The same applies to investments in Industrial Estates. Foreign companies will also be allowed to purchase a specified number of existing buildings, within a given time frame.

The Government screens all projects seeking BOI promotion. The BOI is the principal Government agency responsible for providing incentives to enhance investment in Thailand. Any entity wishing to do business in Thailand must register with the Department of Commercial Registration in the Ministry of Commerce. Firms engaging in productive activities need to register with the Ministries of Industry and Labour.

To encourage decentralisation, in 1994 the BOI allowed promoted manufacturing projects located in Zone 3 (see below) to have foreign majority ownership even if the production is mainly for the domestic market. Since the financial crisis began, the Government has proposed several reforms of its FDI legislation. Foreign investors are allowed to take full control of their Thai subsidiaries. Majority foreign ownership of existing promoted companies located in Zones 1 or 2 is now permitted if agreed to by Thai shareholders. BOI approval will be granted on a case by case basis, and the new regulations will only remain in force for as long as the liquidity crisis lasts.[27] Foreigners are now permitted 100 percent ownership in commercial buildings and condominiums. Similarly foreigners are allowed to obtain permanent residence permits by investing at least 10 million baht in new investment projects, Government bonds, State enterprise bonds or condominiums.

Amendments to the Alien Business Law, as well as to other associated laws, have been submitted to the Parliament with the aim of liberalising foreign investment limits in selected sectors, such as securities and brokerage services, condominiums and land-leasing arrangements. The proposed Foreign Investment Law (FIL) continues to restrict foreign participation in 38 categories to either 25 or 40 per cent, as well as maintaining preferential treatment for US investors under the US-Thai Amity Treaty. The FIL was expected to be approved by Parliament by the end of October 1998 but has encountered opposition.

Box 1 provides a description of Thai liberalisation commitments in the area of foreign direct investment, as stated in the Fifth Letter of Intent with the IMF. These reforms are described in more detail in the sections which follow. Not all reforms were enacted within scheduled timeframe.

Alien Business Law

The Alien Business Law[28] of 1972 serves to define and narrow the scope of foreign participation in Thai business activities. Its objective is stated in the Preamble:

> "Whereas the National Executive Council considers that, at present the number of aliens engaging in business within the Kingdom is great and is steadily increasing and the Thai people are increasingly capable, both in technology and finance, to engage in business in various fields, and that it is expedient to prescribe business regulations for aliens, in order to maintain the balance of trade and economy of the country and in order that the business of aliens should benefit the country as a whole..."

The law is applied to natural or juridical persons with at least one half of their capital owned by aliens or where at least half of shareholders or partners are aliens. Clause 9 prohibits aliens from owning local businesses unless permission is granted by the Director-General who may prescribe any conditions whatsoever. In addition, Clause 4 sets out three categories of business activities where foreign legal entities are (A) prohibited, (B) permitted only when promoted by the BOI and (C) permitted by the Ministry of Commerce or when promoted by the BOI (Box 2). While businesses in Category C remain open, the authorities grant permits to foreigners for work in these categories only when they are convinced that such new businesses could not be competently conducted by an organisation in which the majority ownership is Thai. The decision is the responsibility of the Director General of the Ministry of Commerce.

Box 1. **Market opening policies in the Fifth Letter of Intent with the IMF**

Measure	Date
I. Foreign Ownership of Business Activities (Alien Business Law)	
Amend the ABL to enhance competitiveness, increase transparency of criteria, contribute to increased liquidity in key sectors, and be consistent with international obligations, with the following principal features:	Cabinet approval: 18 August 1998
• Establish the principle of freedom of business activities by foreigners, except in those cases specifically restricted under the two existing lists.	Parliamentary approval expected: October 31, 1998
• Reserve for Thai nationals (but open to foreign investment if approved by the Cabinet/Minister of Commerce) activities relating to: (i) national safety and security, culture, tradition, folk handicraft, as well as natural resources and environment; and (ii) activities restricted because of specified and well justified strategic reasons.	
• Further liberalise a number of activities, including: brokerage services, wholesale and retail trade, construction, non-silk textile, garment, footwear, hotel, beverage production, auction business, etc.	
• Classification of activities will be reviewed on an ongoing basis by an advisory committee, comprised of both public and private sector representatives, and eminent persons.	
II. Foreign Ownership of Real Property (Land Code and Condominiums Act)	
Liberalise existing restrictions on foreign ownership of property:	Cabinet approval: August 18, 1998
• Amend the Land Code to (1) allow individual foreign investors investing specified amounts in activities of productive interest for Thailand to own up to one rai (0.4 acre) of residential land; and (2) allow Thai citizens married to foreigners to own land.	Parliamentary approval expected: October 31, 1998
• Amend the Condominiums Act to allow foreigners to purchase during the next five years 100 percent of condominium building of 5 rai (2 acres) or less.	
• Amend the lease provisions of the Civil and Commercial Code to extend the period of least of selected real estate property of 50 years (from the existing 30-year limit), renewable for an additional 50 years. The exact modalities will be defined in the law.	

Source : IMF

Box 2. **Alien Business Law**

Category A - Closed to aliens

Agriculture: rice farming, salt farming (incl. manufacture but excluding rock salt mining)
Commerce: wholesale trade in local agricultural products; real estate
Services: accounting, law, architecture, advertising, brokerage or agency, auctioning, hairdressing
Others: building construction

Category B - Closed to aliens unless promoted by the Board of Investment

Agriculture: cultivation, orchard farming , animal husbandry (including silk worm raising), timbering, fishing

Industry, handicrafts: manufacture of flour, sugar, beverages, matches, ice, and drugs; products from gold, silver or bronze; alms bowls and lacquerware; Buddha images (including casting); products from silk, silk thread and silk cocoons; garments or footwear, except for export; plywood, wood veneer, chipboard or hardboard; and lime, cement, or cement by-products.
wood processing and wood carvings
cold storage
rice milling
silk combing, silk weaving, or printing of pattern on silk
newspaper publication and printing press operation
dynamiting or quarrying rocks

Commerce: retailing (excluding items in category C)
trading in ore (excluding items in category C)
selling of food and beverages (excluding items in category C)
trading antiques, heirlooms or other fine art objects

Services: tour agencies; hotel construction; photographic processing; laundering; tailoring and dressmaking

Others: domestic land, water and air transport

Category C - Open to aliens in most cases

Commerce: wholesale trade except in items listed in Category A
exporting
retailing machinery, equipment and tools
sale of food and beverage for the promotion of tourism

Industry, handicrafts: mining
textile manufacturing , dyeing and pattern printing
manufacture of glassware and light bulbs; crockery; writing and printing paper; animal feeds
extraction of vegetable oil

Services: all appropriate items not listed in Categories A or B

Others   construction not specified in Category A.

A proposed revision of the Alien Business Law reduces the number of categories closed to foreign investment to 34 from 63 and raises the ceiling on foreign shareholdings in restricted areas to as much as 75 per cent. Among the sectors where further liberalisation has been proposed are brokerage services, wholesale and retail trade, construction, non-silk textiles, garments, footwear, hotels, beverage production and auction businesses.[29]

Under the new law there will be two lists of protected businesses, the first dealing with national security or exploiting natural resources, the second including those sectors where Thai firms are not considered to be sufficiently competitive. In the first list, it is not always clear what the exact relationship is between some of these sectors and national security. Such sectors include advertising, pharmaceuticals of all types, newspapers, printing and broadcasting, transport, mining and quarrying, as well as many sectors which the Government wishes to reserve for Thai nationals such as Buddha image production.

Exemptions can be sought in certain cases from the Ministry of Commerce and the Cabinet, especially where they involve the transfer of technology, employment creation and other benefits to the nation. The new draft law requires a minimum Thai holding of between 25 and 40 per cent in 11 activities. The 25 per cent limit applies to restricted businesses, while businesses related to national security will need a minimum Thai holding of 40 per cent and two fifths of the seats on the board.

US-Thai Treaty of Amity

The Treaty of Amity and Economic Relations between the Kingdom of Thailand and the United States was originally signed in 1966 and was limited to ten years, subject to renewal. It has been in force since then and was recently renewed for another ten years. Under the Treaty, US investors are accorded both fair and equitable and national treatment with respect to establishing or acquiring interests in business activities in Thailand. In practice, however, the Thai authorities require that a firm apply to the Department of Business Registration to get permission to enjoy the national treatment benefit. The Treaty exempts US investor from many of the restrictions of the Alien Business Law but not from the Alien Occupation Law. Thus, while US investors may acquire Thai law firms, for example, US lawyers may not practice in Thailand. The Treaty restricts US investment only in the following areas: communications, transport, fiduciary functions, banking, land and natural resources, and domestic trade in agricultural products.

Thailand has lodged an MFN exemption for the Treaty in the WTO which will remain in place until the year 2005. The Treaty replaced an earlier

Friendship, Commerce and Navigation Treaty and it currently resembles, in many respects, a bilateral investment treaty, although Thailand has signed no exactly similar treaty with another investor country. In a recent review of Thai trade policies by the WTO, Thailand was urged to extend the same benefits enjoyed by US firms under the Treaty to all WTO members.

Board of Investment approvals

The BOI oversees foreign and domestic investment projects in agriculture, animal husbandry, fisheries, mineral exploration and mining, manufacturing and some service sectors. Several sectors fall outside of the purview of the BOI, including finance, insurance, real estate, and retail and wholesale trade. Projects may be approved if the BOI determines that the products, commodities or services are a) are either unavailable or insufficiently available in Thailand or are produced by an outdated process; b) are important and beneficial to the country's economic and social development, and to national security; or, c) are economically and technologically appropriate, and have adequate preventive measures against damage to the environment.

The following criteria are used in determining the economic and technological suitability of a project for which promotion is requested. These criteria apply for both domestic and foreign investors.

i)   For a project with investment capital not exceeding 200 million baht ($8 million):

- The value-added is not less than 20 per cent of sales revenue, except projects which export at least 80 per cent of total sales, or use domestic agriculture products as raw materials, or involve conserving, restoring or developing natural resources and the environment.

- Registered capital of a newly-established project amounts to at least 20 per cent of total investment;

- Modern machinery and production processes and new equipment are used.

- Adequate environmental protection systems are installed.

ii)   For a project with investment capital in excess of 200 million baht, the following additional considerations apply:

- The impact of the project on its own industry and related industries;

- The impact of the project on Government revenue and any additional burden on the Government;

- The effect on consumers;

- The contribution to technological development.

The BOI has been criticised in the past by both foreign and domestic investors for delays in approving projects, together with excessive red tape and poor co-ordination with other Government agencies. These complaints led to an overhaul of the approval process in 1995 as part of broader efforts to transform the BOI from an approval authority to a promotion agency. Project applications with investment less than or equal to 500 million baht (excluding land costs and working capital) will be considered by the BOI within 60 working days, and 90 days for projects larger than 500 million baht.

Foreign equity restrictions

As a general rule, foreign equity participation in approved projects is restricted according to the Alien Business Law. Thai investors must therefore hold 51 per cent of the registered capital in investment projects in agriculture, animal husbandry, fishery, mineral exploration and mining or in the service sector, and also for manufacturing projects, if the production is mainly for the domestic market (previously 60 per cent for Thai investors). The BOI may, however, grant the following exceptions based on the size, location, export propensity and sector of the project:

- For investment projects over 1000 million baht in agriculture, animal husbandry, fishery, mineral exploration and mining or in the service sector, foreign investors may initially hold a majority stake, but Thai nationals must hold at least 51 per cent within five years of staring operations;

- For manufacturing projects located in Zone 3 (see below), foreigners are permitted to own up to 100 per cent and there is no export requirement.

- In Zones 1 and 2, where at least 50 per cent of total sales is for export, foreign investors may hold a majority of the shares. Where at least 80 per cent of total sales is exported, foreign investors may hold all shares.

The BOI has taken a more progressive stance towards industrial decentralisation since 1993 when, for the first time, certain industries were no longer promoted if they located in the Bangkok Metropolitan Area or close to it (Zone 1), even if they were primarily exporters.[30]

Starting from 1997, the BOI has allowed foreign companies to own land for residential and business (e.g. office building) purposes.

B.   *Investment promotion*

BOI incentives

The BOI does not generally tend to target specific sectors for promotion but rather gives special consideration to priority areas based on the following broad guidelines:

- locate operations in regional areas;
- establish or develop industries that form the base for further stages of industrial development;
- develop public utilities and basic infrastructure;
- conserve natural resources and reduce environmental problems;
- conserve energy or replace imported energy supplies;
- contribute to technological development, and
- significantly strengthen the balance of payments.

The BOI is empowered to grant a wide range of incentives and guarantees to investment projects meeting these objectives. Incentives are offered to local and foreign investors on a non-discriminatory basis. Until 1990, the BOI relied almost exclusively on tax-based incentives. In September 1990, the Government lowered tariff rates on machinery from 20 to 5 per cent and approved a plan to cut tariff rates on raw materials, thus reducing the importance of the BOI's tax incentive package. The present incentive scheme is geared towards encouraging industrial decentralisation, and hence the level of incentives depends on the location of an investment project.   Remote areas are granted more tax incentives to lure companies to locate outside the Bangkok Metropolitan Region. No tax incentives are offered at a sub-national level. The BOI also offers comprehensive business-related services to investors and potential investors, ranging from working with investors to help them obtain required licenses and permits to the identification of promising investment projects and joint-venture partners.

The BOI offers both tax-based incentives (tax holidays or tariff exemptions) and non-tax privileges (guarantees, tariff protection, permits and services).   The latter are available to all BOI-promoted projects (regardless of location, industry or condition), while tax-based incentives are linked to location, export production, or industries identified as priority activities.

Non-tax privileges:

- Guarantees (against nationalisation, competition from new State enterprises, State monopolisation of the sale of products similar to those produced by the promoted project, price controls, export restrictions and duty-free imports by Government agencies or State enterprises).

- Protection (imposition of a surcharge on imports at a rate not exceeding 50 per cent of the c.i.f. value for a period not more than one year at a time, import ban on competing products, etc.)

- Permits to bring in foreign nationals, including technicians and experts, to undertake feasibility studies and to work on promoted projects, etc.

Tax incentives:

- Incentives available to all projects are as follows: exemption or reduction of import duties on imported machinery, raw materials and components; exemption of corporate income taxes for three to eight years with permission to carry forward losses and deduct them as expenses for up to five years, exclusion of dividends derived from promoted enterprises from taxable income during the corporate income tax holiday.

- Additional incentives for enterprises in the *Special Investment Promotion Zones*. Under the current regime, export-oriented firms located in Zones 1 and all firms located in Zone 2 are granted 50 per cent reduction on import tariffs for machinery, while firms located in Zone 3 get full exemption. These firms may also get corporate income tax exemptions for three to eight years, as well as exemptions of import tariffs for raw materials and necessary materials.

- Incentives granted to projects in *priority activities* (basic transport systems, public utilities, environmental protection or restoration, direct involvement in technological development, basic industries): corporate income tax exemption for eight years regardless of location, 50 per cent import duty reduction on machinery which is not included in the tariff reduction of the Ministry of Finance and which is subject to import duties greater

235

than or equal to 10 per cent for projects located in Zone 1 or Zone 2, import duty exemptions on machinery for projects located in Zone 3.

- Additional incentives for *Export Enterprises* (those exporting not less than 80 per cent of total sales): exemption of import duties on imported raw materials and components as well as on re-exported items; exemption of export duties; allowance to deduct from taxable corporate income an amount equivalent to 5 per cent of an increase in income derived from exports over the previous year, excluding the cost of insurance and transport.

Promoting Regional Industrialisation

The Thai government has long promoted regional industrialisation. BOI promotion differs depending on which zone a firm is located in, although the definition of the zones has changed over time. In order to encourage industrial development in regional areas, the BOI also grants incentives to existing activities which may or may not have been promoted, if they relocate to the regions.

Regional industrialisation was added to the more general goal of industrial promotion as included in the National Economic and Social Development Plan of 1972. At the start of the Plan, a policy of industrial decentralisation was initiated to counter the concentration of industry in and around Bangkok. The decentralisation plan involved tax incentives, financial support and infrastructure development. In line with this policy the BOI designated seventy-two districts in twenty-one provinces as investment promotion zones (IPZs) in 1973.

At the end of the plan, 57 per cent of the country's manufacturing GDP was still generated by industries in Bangkok and its vicinity (BOI 1996). Because of the difficulties in promoting such a large area with limited resources, the locational scheme was altered in 1978 to four zones each centred on a regional urban centre; in addition firms located in industrial estates could receive BOI benefits. In 1983, locational incentives were expanded under the Fifth plan: firms located outside of Bangkok and the surrounding five provinces were granted a one year extension on corporate income tax exemptions. The establishment of industrial estates in the regions was given high priority in an attempt to offset the lack of regional infrastructure and other weaknesses. The Eastern Seaboard Development Programme was initiated at that time. The proposed industrial development zone included the construction of two deep-sea ports, one for export industries and the other for heavy industries.

In October 1987, the BOI reorganised the country into three zones for incentive purposes: Zone 1 included Bangkok and Samut Prakarn, Zone 2 included the inner ring provinces and Zone 3 comprised all remaining provinces. With this change, firms in Zone 1 received no corporate income tax holidays unless they met export or employment targets. The IPZs were revised in 1989 when Zone 1 was expanded to include Bangkok and the inner ring provinces, and Zone 2 was changed to 10 provinces surrounding Zone 1 or the outer ring.

The BOI announced new Policies and Criteria for Investment Promotion in April 1993 that divided the whole country into 3 areas. Zone 3 and the Laem Chabang Industrial Estate are now designated as Investment Promotion Zones and as such may receive additional incentives, including further tax and duty reduction. There was an attempt to create a fourth zone comprising 12 remote north-eastern provinces in which special tax incentives were to be given to firms willing to relocate, but this initiative was finally dropped in 1997 because of doubts over the inadequate level of infrastructure in some targeted provinces.

Regional policies and FDI inflows

Over the past couple of years, FDI flows have been mainly concentrated in Zone 3 in terms of both the number of projects and the amount. While this suggests some success for the regionalisation policies of the BOI, much of this investment has gone to the Eastern Seabord. In addition to the deep-sea ports and an excellent road and communications infrastructure, the region also offers convenient proximity to Bangkok. More remote areas have been much less successful at attracting investment away from the Bangkok area.

The Eastern Seaboard is Southeast Asia's most concentrated area of heavy industry and is popular with foreign investors. The Eastern Seaboard Development Programme was initially launched in the late 1970s in an attempt to extend the import-substituting industrialisation strategy into capital and intermediate goods, but the Programme did not really take off until the late 1980s. It includes deep-sea ports facilities, a natural-gas-based petrochemical complex, a soda-ash project, a fertiliser plant and an integrated steel complex. Since 1992, the Eastern Seaboard's four provinces have attracted $56.6 billion in new investment, creating 356 838 jobs according to the Thai authorities, compared with $11.7 billion and 267 357 employees in the four provinces that make up greater Bangkok. The logic of agglomeration economies is fully at work in this area. The development of this industrial area is now forging ahead on the basis of natural gas supplies from the Gulf of Thailand feeding a growing petrochemical industry. Foreign investors involved comprise Exxon, Dow Chemicals, and Chevron of the US, as well as Tuntex of Chinese Taipei. Refineries built by Shell and Caltex since 1996 are also located in the Eastern Seaboard.

As a result of the financial crisis, the BOI has developed a series of measures to encourage both expansion by existing investors and greenfield investments. BOI-promoted projects in three sectors (textiles, footwear, and food processing) are now eligible for exemption from import duty on replacement machinery utilising higher technology. Agribusiness ventures exporting at least 80 per cent of their output are now exempt from duties on imported machinery, regardless of which zone they are located in. The duration of the corporate income tax holiday is still determined by the existing zoning guidelines.

To promote further export industries, the BOI added 61 activities to the list of those eligible to import machinery duty-free in Zones 1 or 2. In addition, existing BOI promoted companies in Zones 1 and 2 can apply for promotion of expansion projects. To qualify they must "contribute greatly to the Thai economy" through job creation or by generating foreign exchange earnings. Approved expansion projects will receive corporate income tax exemptions based on existing zoning guidelines. An income tax waiver for 3 years will be provided if the project is located in Zone 1 and up to 5 years for projects in Zone 2 (located outside Industrial Estates or Industrial Zones).

In order to promote import substitution and curb foreign exchange expenditures, some specific sectors have been classified as priority activities. The new categories include machine production, measuring devices and equipment, ABS brake systems, electronic fuel-injection systems, and components for catalytic converters. Investment projects will be granted an 8-year corporate income tax exemption and exemption of import duties on machinery, regardless of location, and foreigners may hold all or the majority of shares in these projects.

BOI-promoted projects, whose benefits from exemption of import duties on raw and essential materials used for export manufacturing have expired, may now apply again for this incentive. BOI-promoted projects may apply to increase production capacity beyond the level stipulated on their investment promotion certificates by increasing the number of working hours.

The 30 per cent export requirement for exemption of import duties on raw materials used in the manufacture of exports has been eliminated. Companies exporting less than 30 per cent of total output are thus also eligible for import duty exemptions on raw materials.

The conditions governing location for activities eligible for promotion are relaxed: promoted export projects may now be located in any zone, with incentives following the existing criteria for each zone.

C.   Restrictions on FDI in the financial sector

Banking sector

Until recently, foreign banks were severely constrained in their ability to compete with local banks. Foreign entry into the market was prevented by a number of means. First, there was a prohibition on new bank licences in effect since 1978, applying to both foreign and domestic investors. Second, foreign investors were limited to an aggregate 25 per cent of a local bank's shares and an individual limit of five per cent. Although this limit applied to all individual investors, it did not include shares held by the Government. Furthermore, major private shareholders have not had to divest their shares in excess of this limit, thus perpetuating the high degree of concentration in the sector. The top three Thai banks accounted for one half of banking assets compared to only six per cent for all 14 existing foreign banks as of the end of 1993.

In addition to entry barriers, established foreign banks have not generally been accorded national treatment. Although foreign banks are generally permitted to engage in the same activities as domestic banks, the 1964 prohibition against the expansion of foreign banks meant that each foreign bank (with one exception) was only allowed to operate one branch, so the foreign banks together had 15 branches, compared with 2700 branches of Thai banks in 1993. Since ATMs are considered as branches, foreign banks were also prevented from having any external ATMs, thus making them far less attractive to the public than their local competitors. They are now permitted in principle to join local ATM networks subject to the approval of ATM pool members. In practice, it has proved difficult to negotiate satisfactory agreements with local banks.[31]

In prudential regulations, foreign banks have also been treated differently from their domestic counterparts. They face a reserve requirement of 125 million baht, which must be invested in low-yielding Government securities. They are also restricted in the number of expatriate management personnel, which is a problem because of the lack of qualified Thai nationals. On the other hand, foreign banks are not subject to the same directed credit requirements that apply to domestic banks.

This situation in the banking sector remained largely unchanged throughout the 1980s and early 1990s. Since then, there have been a number of changes, and this liberalisation has accelerated during the crisis. In January 1994, Thailand's cabinet approved a financial liberalisation package allowing foreign banks with offshore banking licences to open branches outside Bangkok, relaxing foreign exchange controls, and encouraging Thai finance and securities companies to separate the two sides of their business. Foreign banks with offshore licences under the BIBF (Bangkok International Banking Facilities) will be allowed to establish two branches outside Bangkok, and each branch will be able to lend up to one billion Thai baht as well as granting foreign currency loans. In 1993, there were 47 commercial banks granted BIBF's licences: 15 domestic commercial banks, 12 branches of foreign banks already established in Thailand, and 20 new foreign banks with no branches in Thailand. Initially 32 foreign banks were granted licences.

In late 1996 the government agreed to allow foreign banks with branch status to open new branches for the first time. In 1996 seven foreign banks were upgraded to full branch status (the first time in more than a decade). This is in line with making Bangkok a large financial centre, a process begun with the establishment of the BIBF.

Rapid changes are expected as a result of the 1997 crisis. Liberalisation of foreign equity investment in the financial sector is a crucial part of Thailand's IMF economic programme. Foreign ownership limits on financial institutions (banks and finance firms) were raised to 49 per cent, up from 25 per cent in 1997 in order to encourage mergers. As part of its plan for restructuring the financial system, the Thai government has granted foreigners the right to own Thai banks. They are allowed to own up to 100 per cent of banks and finance houses for up to 10 years, after which capital increases will be restricted to Thais, and new investment will be restricted to 49 per cent ownership.[32] This is in line with Thailand's WTO offer which includes the provision that foreign equity ownership will be capped at 49 per cent after 10 years, but existing investments will be permanently grandfathered. As an incentive, the Government is to waive the 10-year foreign share holding limit for the four nationalised banks (Bangkok Metropolitan Bank, First Bangkok City Bank, Bangkok Bank of Commerce and Siam City Bank). The Government reserves the right to screen potential foreign investors.

As a result of the change in the regulations, the banking sector has been deeply restructured. A number of banks have already found foreign partners, including a 54 per cent stake of Thai Sri Danu Bank which was bought up by the Development Bank of Singapore, and a 75 per cent stake in the Bank of Asia by ABN Amro. In addition, the Laem Thong Bank has agreed to transfer 65 per cent to Middle Eastern and Hong Kong Chinese investors and Thai Farmers Bank up to 40 per cent.[33] Citibank had been interested in a majority stake in First Bangkok Bank, but the Thai bank was ultimately taken over by the Government.[34] In April 1999, Standard Chartered Bank (UK) took a 68 per cent stake and management control in the Nakornthon Bank, with an agreement to increase the stake to above 75 per cent after five years.[35]

In insurance joint ventures, foreign ownership is restricted to 25 per cent of total shares. The 1992 revision of the Insurance Act allowed the Minister of Commerce to grant licences to foreign companies without obtaining cabinet approval, but until 1995 it was not the Government's policy to do so. No new insurance licences were granted between 1982 and 1995, when the Government agreed to allow new licences, partly as a result of pressure from the WTO. Thailand's WTO offer does not actually increase access for foreign insurance providers. Thailand bound the 25 per cent equity ownership limit for foreign insurance firms in the life and non-life sectors. Subsidiaries in auxiliary insurance services can be 49 per cent foreign-owned.

Higher foreign ownership is envisaged in insurance (first to 49 per cent then to 70 per cent), as has occurred in banking. For the time being, most insurance companies are local. In 1994, there were 11 local and 1 foreign life insurers, and 77 local and 5 foreign non-life insurers in Thailand.

Based on legislation from 1979, foreigners are not allowed to act as brokers and are limited to minority stakes in brokerage and securities firms. An attempt by some directors of the Stock Exchange of Thailand (SET) to reduce foreign shares to 25 per cent was rejected by the SET in 1995. In practice, foreigners are reportedly granted management control, even with a minority stake.[36] Foreign brokerages have significantly increased their share of the industry in Thailand as a result of the crisis. It is estimated that of the top ten brokers by volume in early 1998, seven had significant foreign stakes. These top ten account for one half of all turnover on the exchange.[37]

The 1979 legislation also limits foreign involvement in finance and credit firms to 25 per cent for acquisitions after 1979 and 40 per cent for those prior to the new legislation. Although they face no ownership restrictions when purchasing onshore mutual funds, foreigners cannot exercise voting rights. Foreign investment in the stock exchange increased rapidly however in the 1980s. The share of foreign trading turnover rose from 2 per cent in 1982 to 18 per cent in 1993 and is now estimated at almost one half of all trades.

IV. Privatisation

Thailand has traditionally had neither a large public sector nor an ambitious privatisation programme. Between 1961 and 1986, only 31 out of a total of 100 State enterprises were liquidated, mostly involving relatively small commercial entities. Since 1980, 13 State enterprises have been fully privatised, but this represents only one per cent of the total combined assets of the public sector.[38] In many cases, privatisation has consisted of listing a minority stake in a State-owned enterprise on the stock market.[39] Until the crisis, recent privatisations had taken several forms, including the following: one State enterprise had been liquidated, two sold and one leased to private investors, and in four important cases, some shares were sold to private investors through the Stock Exchange. In addition, concessions and BOT projects were awarded. The State-owned Telephone Organisation of Thailand was partially privatised in the early 1990s. Resistance to privatisation from State enterprise employees has caused many privatisations to be delayed or postponed.[40] Public sector workers enjoy significantly higher wages on average than those in the private sector.

The Government has no specific policy either to restrict or promote FDI in privatised enterprises, but the restrictions in the Alien Business Law apply equally to newly-privatised enterprises. The decision to admit foreign investors has been made on a case-by-case basis. For example, the Government initially allowed foreigners to hold seven per cent of shares in Thai Airways, and there is a proposal to raise this limit to up to 30 per cent by mid-1999. Several foreign carriers are said to be interested. Foreigners already hold 40 per cent of the shares in PTT Exploration and Production. Legal limits on foreign participation in Thai companies have impeded a foreign role in privatisations because amendments to existing legislation have been required before the privatisation could go ahead.

A more active programme was adopted in April 1997, before the crisis erupted, and has since gained momentum. It has been supplemented by a State Enterprise Reform Master Plan in September 1998. Box 3 provides details of the privatisation strategy as outlined in the Fifth Letter of Intent with the International Monetary Fund. Some of the targets were not met by the anticipated deadlines. Planned privatisations are in telecommunications, water, energy, transport. State enterprises have been grouped according to their past performance to determine their schedules for privatisation, with the energy, telecommunications and transport sectors on a fast track. In some cases, the State may trim its shareholdings in existing enterprises (as with Thai Airways International) or in other cases it may offer concessions to private enterprises, including foreign ones.

The Parliament gave final approval in March 1999 to a bill designed to facilitate future privatisations. As a first step, State enterprises may now be converted into limited liability companies, with a portion of shares subsequently sold off to private investors. The privatisation process is also now in the hands of the Prime Minister, rather than the Finance Ministry. The bill also stipulates that representatives of both the supervising ministry and the State enterprise employees must sit on the committee designing the privatisation of each enterprise.[41]

According to the Seventh Letter of Intent with the IMF, privatisation is being prepared for the Airport Authority, and private sector participation will be permitted in the Metropolitan and Provincial Water Authorities and Wastewater Management Authority. The divestiture of the State share in Esso Thailand will take place as soon as market conditions are favourable.

Box 3. **Privatisation plan for selected enterprises**

Energy	
• Sale of EGAT's stake in Electricity Generating Co. Ltd.	Done
• Sale of a significant stake in PTT Exploration and Production.	Done
• Issue bidding documentation for the sale of Government share in Esso Thailand.	Fourth quarter 1998
• Bangchak Petroleum Company:	
- Complete due diligence progress and recapitalisation plans;	Fourth quarter 1998
- Issue bidding prospectus for the sale of Government's stake.	First quarter 1999
• Privatisation of Ratchaburi Power Plant.	
• Corporatisation and conversion of EGAT, preparatory to privatisation.	Fourth quarter 1999 Under study
Telecommunications	
• Telephone Organisation of Thailand (TOT) and Communication Authority of Thailand (CAT):	
- Corporatise and begin reorganisation;	Second quarter 1999
- Issue bidding prospectus for the sale of a significant Government stake.	Second quarter 1999
Transport	
	Fourth quarter 1998
• Thai Airways:	First quarter 1999
- Select financial advisor;	
- Issue bidding prospectus for the sale of Government's stake.	
	Fourth quarter 1998
• Commence financial and restructuring plans of State Railways.	First quarter 1999
• Corporatise and reorganise Airport Authority of Thailand.	Third quarter 1999
• Begin privatisation process for the Regional Airport Company	
Water	
• Government approval of detailed modalities for private sector participation in Metropolitan Water Authority and Provincial water Authority.	Second half of 1999
Other	Done
• Cabinet resolution to sell/liquidate Textile Organization, Batter Organisation, Preserved Food Organisation, and the Cold Storage Organisation.	First quarter 1999
• Complete study outlining strategic options for Tobacco Monopoly.	

Source: IMF Letter of Intent with the Government of Thailand, August 1998.

V. The Role of FDI in Thailand's Economic Development

Case Studies

Electronics

Foreign investment in the Thai electronics industry began in the early 1960s, but Thailand was slower than some neighbouring countries in developing a large-scale export orientation in this sector.[42] As in the automobile sector, initial investments were for final assembly of consumer electronics for the local market. Although total FDI in Thailand was relatively unimportant by any standard, investment in this sector was nevertheless a large share of overall inflows in manufacturing.

The emphasis shifted gradually away from consumer electronics into the production of computer components and parts[43]. As the latter is more export-oriented, the Thai electronic industry has recently become the driving force behind industrial development and rapidly growing exports, largely as a result of investment by firms from Japan, Korea, Chinese Taipei, Singapore and the United States. The electronics sector has taken over from textiles as a major engine of export growth. Most major operators in Thailand are subsidiaries of leading multinationals like Seagate of the United States and Minibea, Sony and Sanyo from Japan. The majority of semiconductor component manufacturers in Thailand are joint ventures between foreign and Thai companies. Only a few, such as Hana Microindustry, are independent domestic firms not associated with multinationals. Altogether, only 10 per cent of electronic firms are locally-owned.

Seagate Technology, the world's largest independent producer of hard disc drives, is Thailand's largest employer with nearly 40 000 workers. Its exports have helped make computer parts Thailand's fastest growing export category. The HDD industry, which began to develop in the 1980s with Seagate, soon followed by Fujitsu, is largely export-oriented and dominated by foreign-owned firms from the United States or Japan.

Electronic products, particularly computer parts and integrated circuits, make up about 30 per cent of the country's total exports in value terms, but value added is limited. A number of operations in the electronics industry are still largely labour-intensive assembly. Foreigners typically provide technology, research and development (R&D), procurement and marketing. There is reportedly no R&D in electronic components in Thailand, and the industry is still largely seen as an export enclave with very few local firms acting as suppliers. In computer production, there are few technologically-sophisticated or globally competitive indigenous firms. Moreover, exports originate from a limited number of major firms such as Seagate and Minibea. Seagate exports of hard disk drives account for four per cent of the total value of Thai exports.

The BOI has promoted the electronics industry but, unlike Malaysia, Thailand has never specifically targeted electronics, nor has it formulated a development strategy based on the sector. Under-investment in human resources is a major obstacle to upgrading production in Thailand. The electronics industry is currently asking for State incentives to help it become more than an assembly operation. So far the industry has been excessively reliant on costly imported materials. The Government's tax structure is said to impede the development of the industry as imported parts are taxed at 1 per cent while materials are taxed at 20 per cent. This makes it dearer to manufacture components in Thailand than it does to import them[44].

The electronic industry is affected by the recent economic crisis because of the aggregate demand slump in Asian export markets, but a number of parts and products are also exported to the United States. In the case of consumer electronics, the crisis may have a positive impact in the short and medium-term to the extent that the depreciation of the baht helps the industry regain some competitiveness, thus giving it some breathing space and time to upgrade. At the same time, however, the devaluation may ease the pressure for change until the situation repeats itself in the future.

Rising wages were a major problem in the Thai electronic industry before the crisis: Hana Microindustry had to shift its board-assembly testing plant from Thailand to China because wages were deemed too high in Thailand.

Textiles

Foreign investors are not as prominent in the textile industry as they are in the electronics sector, though they are active through subcontracting which has many of the characteristics of FDI but is not recorded as such. Among foreign investors, Japanese firms have been the major players in the Thai textile industry since the early 1960s, usually through joint ventures with Thai investors in which the local firm is dependent on foreign technology. Following the yen rise in 1985 existing Japanese textile joint ventures in Thailand increased their capacity in order to reduce costs as well as to find a way around the GSP. In the course of the 1980s, some garment firms from Chinese Taipei followed suit.

Textile exports were the top foreign exchange earner for Thailand from 1986 to 1990, growing on average more than 30 per cent annually, but exports slowed down in the 1990s, with a sharper contraction in 1996. Although the sector is not ostensibly FDI driven to the same extent as automobiles and electronics, it has suffered from similar weaknesses, in particular rising wage costs that were not matched by rising productivity. The industry has failed to upgrade, and as a result it is still mainly producing for the low end of the market where competition from low-wage countries such as China, India or Vietnam is getting fiercer. The slowdown of the Thai textile export production is due to the failure to modernise and adjust to falling competitiveness. Heavy import content even in traditional production such as garments plays a key role in this respect.

Automobiles

Thailand is a major automobile producer and the most important vehicle market within ASEAN. As in many other countries in the region, successive governments have attempted to develop a local industry through import substitution policies which combined barriers to imports with inducements for foreign investors. Once established, foreign investors began to face local content requirements and some assemblers left as a result. They have since been induced to return owing to the growth and size of the Thai automobile market, as well as prospects in the ASEAN region. The Asian financial crisis has caused a sharp contraction in this sector, but this has so far only led to a postponement of the start-up dates for these firms.

Foreign producers began to locate assembly operations in Thailand in the 1960s as a result of high tariffs on completely built-up (CBU) cars and the 1962 Industrial Investment Promotion Act which offered foreign assemblers temporary reductions on import duties and exemptions from corporate income, and permission to remit foreign exchange and to bring in foreign experts and technicians. Many assemblers, particular Japanese, established operations in Thailand at the time.

To promote localisation, the Government imposed local content requirements in the 1970s. The small size of the market at the time made it difficult for many assemblers to comply with these requirements, and US producers withdrew from Thailand. In 1978, to promote economies of scale, the Government prohibited the establishment of new assembly plants or the introduction of new models and banned imports of CBU passenger cars.

Rapid industrial development in Thailand created a strong demand for domestically procured parts and components. Large auto makers found it most profitable to have their subcontractors set up supply lines in Thailand, taking advantage of more cost effective labour, shorter delivery time, and closer access to suppliers. There was at that time a second investment boom as many Japanese component manufacturers rushed to invest in Thailand.

The 1990s have seen the diminishing importance of protection and an increasing emphasis on incentives to promote the local industry. In April 1991, the Government lifted the remaining import bans on small passenger cars and in 1996 pledged to abolish all local content requirements imposed on passenger cars as of July 1, 1998, one and half years ahead of the transition arrangement schedule allowed under the WTO TRIMs agreement. This acceleration of liberalisation commitments was ostensibly used to lure General Motors to establish in Thailand rather than the Philippines.[45] This deadline has been delayed until 1999, as GM has not yet progressed with its investment plans as a result of the crisis. Local content requirements for pickup trucks and commercial vehicles will remain in place until 2000.

At the same time, the total import tax burden on passenger cars was reduced by two thirds for both large and small engine cars, and the import duty rate on completely knocked-down (CKD) kits was also reduced by even more.[46] Thailand has the lowest tariffs on CKD passenger cars in the region. In 1992 the import duties on CBU for passenger cars were further reduced, but a temporary increase in import duty of CBU cars was decided in October 1997 and is supposed to prevail until the end of 1999.[47]

The BOI has also designed incentive packages to attract foreign auto makers and strengthen the industry's competitiveness. Although most activities within the sector are promoted, the BOI also offers generous tax incentives in 14 priority supporting industries.

The Thai automobile industry owes its development to foreign firms investing in response to these policies. Japanese companies have dominated the market for almost three decades and currently command over 90 per cent of the overall market, with two firms sharing one half of the market. Since the sharp appreciation of the yen beginning in 1985, Japanese producers have actively persuaded their supplier sub-contractors to invest in Thailand. The establishment of such plants has also been encouraged by the Brand to Brand Complementation (BBC) scheme.[48] As a result, Japanese manufacturers also dominate the components sector through direct investments, joint ventures and technical licensing agreements. Since 1994, Japanese car manufacturers established in Thailand have exchanged parts in order to benefit from greater economies of scale.

US automobile firms have begun to challenge this Japanese domination through recent plans to establish operations in Thailand. At the moment, only Chrysler produces vehicles in Thailand, although General Motors won BOI promotional privileges in 1996 for an 18.75 billion baht project to manufacture passenger cars for the domestic and export markets and the Ford Motor Company received BOI approval for its 8.6 billion baht plant to produce pickup trucks. Ford left Thailand in 1976. These two projects were supposed to begin producing by mid-1999 but will probably have to be scaled back in the short term, at least for the domestic market.

BMW has announced plans to establish a wholly-owned plant in order to benefit from changes in the tariff regime and the expected termination of local content rules. The tariff burden will be shifted from CKDs to parts. At the same time, Mazda of Japan has decided to close its existing plant.

Assessment

An assessment of the success of Thai policies in this sector in promoting development depends on assumptions about what alternative policies might have been. And, any success in creating a viable foreign-owned automobile industry must be weighed against the cost of several decades of protection. Nevertheless, some general conclusions can be drawn.

To some extent, Thailand is emerging as a regional hub for MNE production, but the degree of integration within ASEAN is not yet at a stage where Thailand could fully perform this role. Exports in this sector have grown quickly (13 per cent in dollar terms in 1997 and 85 per cent in baht terms in the first half of 1998) but remain at very low levels, representing only 2.5 per cent of total production in 1996. Nevertheless, the attraction of Thailand for foreign automobile producers has been reaffirmed strongly by the decision of all three major US producers to locate in Thailand, in spite of aggressive promotional bids from other countries, notably the Philippines. General Motors, for example, plans eventually to export 80 per cent of its Thai output, mainly to Japan and Australia.

To what does Thailand owe this success in attracting foreign investors, and what has been the effect of such investment on Thai development? Part of the appeal of Thailand is that it is the largest market for vehicles in Southeast Asia.[49] Because national market size remains a strong determinant of FDI patterns, host countries can sometimes create a virtuous circle, whereby initial success in attracting investments creates an agglomeration benefit for subsequent investors. Although early investors were attracted by the prospects of producing behind high tariffs, the most recent interest on the part of foreign investors is likely to stem from the 1991 tariff reforms which provided a strong impetus to demand.

Another consideration relates to the policies followed in other ASEAN countries. Unlike Indonesia and Malaysia, Thailand has never developed a national car project, relying instead on foreign producers to satisfy local demand. National car projects make it very difficult for foreign firms to compete effectively against the national producer, even when foreigners are allowed to invest. Thailand has also not forced firms to merge or shut down in order to alleviate the problems of excess capacity, as Malaysia has done. Rather, it has gradually reduced tariffs in order to put greater pressure on firms to rationalise.

A more important question than how much FDI has Thailand received is what effect this investment has had on the Thai economy. Although there are some local parts suppliers, the industry is still largely foreign-owned or heavily dependent on foreign technology.[50] Nevertheless, because of the long history of the automobile industry in Thailand, there are more advanced indigenous parts producers than in other ASEAN countries. The growth of parts production has been stunted, however, because tariffs on CKD kits are lower than those on individual parts.[51] Furthermore, the parts industry is still highly dependent upon the local market and the original equipment market is dominated by joint ventures relying on foreign technology while the replacement market involves mostly small Thai companies with low technological capability. The role of parts suppliers located in Thailand has gradually increased. They supplied 17-24 per cent of parts used by auto assemblers in 1988 and 50 per cent in 1996.[52]

Another problem is that exports are still suffering from a lack of competitiveness, in addition to barriers abroad. The Government has attempted to remedy this by reducing import barriers in order to create a more dynamic market, but numerous obstacles to free competition still remain — not least a tariff of 80 per cent on imported cars and a ban on imports of second-hand vehicles. A recent study nevertheless found that the competitiveness of the parts industry is improving rapidly.[53]

An overview of FDI in Thailand's development

Linkages with global and regional production networks obtained through FDI have been crucial to the change in Thailand's industrial structure, shifting the economy away from agriculture towards manufacturing and, within manufacturing, away from textiles into electronic goods. This move away from the most labour-intensive activities should not disguise the fact that value-added in Thailand, even in more technological-intensive sectors, originates in relatively labour-intensive operations.

Foreign firms are major contributors to industrial employment and played an important role in the expansion of manufacturing employment by one million in the 1980s. The expansion of largely export-oriented FDI led to a surge in investment as a result of the export boom. The large inflow of FDI beginning in the mid-1980s was matched by an unprecedentedly high rate of Thai domestic investment, suggesting that foreign and domestic investment were largely complementary during this period. This boom was made possible because large local firms such as Siam Cement or CP Group were favoured as partners in joint ventures with foreign investors. Moreover, smaller Thai firms engaging in trade, services or manufacturing were able to take advantage of the greater integration of the Thai economy with the outside world to expand the scope of their activities and to move into exports. Local investment was also stimulated by the capital market which developed institutions to mobilise new sources of capital.

While FDI may not have crowded out domestic capital, the rapid expansion of employment in certain export sectors may have served to deprive other firms of skilled labour at affordable wage rates. Over time, the supply of human capital will expand in the economy to meet the need, but in the short term, there may have been some crowding out of firms which did not export.

FDI and export performance

Foreign direct investment has played a key role in the industrial transformation of the Thai economy. FDI inflows concentrated in industry in the 1980s and helped develop and diversify the industrial structure, including into textiles, automobiles and more recently electronics. Foreign firms played a major role in the export boom in electrical and chemical products and also, indirectly, in textiles. The development of manufactured exports began with the textile industry which was dominated by foreign firms, as they relocated from Japan, Chinese Taipei and Hong Kong, China beginning in the 1970s. Following the yen appreciation in the mid-1980s, existing Japanese textile joint ventures in Thailand increased their capacity.

In electronics, FDI contributed much later to Thailand's export performance because it was at first primarily domestic market-oriented. Electrical and electronic products now represent almost one third of total Thai exports, and these come primarily from foreign-owned firms. In 1997, the 125 most prominent BOI-promoted electronics companies, which are mostly 100 percent foreign-owned or Thai-foreign joint ventures, accounted for 90 per cent of total exports of electronic and electrical products.

Foreign affiliates in Thailand have become more export-oriented over time, in response to both export promotion policies and to favourable exchange rates after 1985. The average export propensity of foreign firms rose from 10 per cent in 1971 to 33 per cent in 1984 and to more than 50 per cent in 1988. Between 1985 and 1990, export-oriented firms accounted for 60 to 80 per cent of total BOI-promoted FDI projects.[54] Over 80 per cent of Thailand's total exports are now in manufacturing, including electrical appliances, machinery, transport equipment parts, and chemicals, mostly produced by foreign investors or joint-ventures.

The potential impact of MNE activities on the Thai balance of payments goes beyond their contribution to exports. Foreign affiliates also import goods and services, as well as bringing in capital and repatriating interest, income and royalties.[55] FDI is frequently accompanied by an increase in imports of capital goods as the project comes on line, but many affiliates also import a large share of their inputs from abroad. This is particularly the case for export-oriented investment where investors must find competitively priced and high quality inputs in order to be able to compete effectively in global markets.

Heavy reliance on imported inputs is a constant for FDI in Thailand. It was estimated in the 1980s that, for foreign investment projects which received promotional privileges from the BOI, 90 per cent of all machinery and equipment was imported and over 50 per cent of raw materials.[56] According to UNCTAD data, the ratio of imports of parts to exports of finished goods is 60 per cent for electronic products in Thailand (the highest ratio in the region). On average the import content of exports is estimated at 43 per cent in Thailand.

In terms of net exports, therefore, sectors dominated by FDI do not rank as highly as they do if one only looks at the export side. Computers and parts exports, for example, are roughly on a par with exports of agricultural and fishery products, but in terms of their contribution to net exports, the latter group figure much more prominently because of the high level of imports of components in the computer industry. The same could be said of other sectors dominated by MNEs.

In the wake of the crisis, the importance of FDI as a potential source of net capital inflows has been emphasised. It has clearly demonstrated its benefit in this regard, compared to other forms of capital flows. At the same time, however, it is useful to stress that, in the long term, FDI should be judged by its impact on the capacity of the Thai economy to respond to the opportunities offered by global economic integration. One measure of this is the impact of FDI on the export performance of the economy as a whole, rather than in specific sectors dominated by foreign MNEs. In this respect, FDI in sectors supplying goods and services to local firms at competitive prices may have a significant impact on Thai exports even if the affiliates themselves do not export.

Unfortunately, this effect is difficult to establish empirically. For one reason, capital inflows as a result of FDI may cause an appreciation of the real exchange rate which might reduce exports in other sectors. Attempts to measure the effect of FDI on aggregate Thai exports have tended to have mixed results. In one study, the relationship between exports and cumulated FDI inflows appears to be quite strong for the period 1986-91 but becomes much weaker during 1992-96.[57] Another finds only a weak causal effect of FDI on Thai exports in the manufacturing industry, although there is a clear impact of FDI in specific sectors.[58] The same study reveals that FDI appears to lag growth in exports, suggesting that foreign investors respond to the export opportunities offered by currency realignments, etc. often after a lag and that this response has been slower than that of domestic firms. This certainly appears to be the case in the mid-1980s, with the beginning of the export boom preceding the FDI surge.

Technology transfer and industrial upgrading

The overall export effect of inward investment is itself just a proxy for the technology transfer and industrial upgrading which are at the heart of FDI. Various studies have found that technology transfers from FDI in Thailand have been moderate.[59] One study finds some evidence of transfer through foreign firms' training of high level staff, while another finds little evidence of transfer through the training of local suppliers. These studies generally cover the period of the 1980s when FDI was relatively recent and when certain sectors were still heavily protected. A more recent analysis suggests that technology transfer has arisen to some extent through relations between foreign companies and local suppliers.[60]

The Director of Technology Transfer at the Thai Ministry of Science, Technology and Environment has characterised the technology transfer process in Thailand as slow and inefficient.[61] Significantly for investors, the BOI does not monitor aspects of promoted investment activities such as technology transfer, creation of supply linkages and skill training.[62] Nevertheless, requirements attached to certain investments are implicitly intended partly to promote such transfers: joint venture and local content requirements, limits on expatriate employment, etc.

As a result of the poor performance in technology transfer, the Government has developed several schemes to facilitate the process. The BOI Unit for Industrial Linkages Development (BUILD) has the objective of enhancing local sub-contracting through the provision of information and technical assistance. In addition, new national initiatives have been launched to promote technology transfer. The promotion of such transfers is one of the goals of the 8th National Economic and Social Development Plan (1997-2001). Support is granted to foreign investment in production requiring advanced technology, research and development. These efforts are nevertheless hampered by the weak absorptive capacity of local management.[63]

Estimating technology transfer is often more of an art than a science. Another way of capturing any potential beneficial effect of FDI is to look at whether inflows have been accompanied by industrial upgrading in the sectors in which FDI has occurred. Lim and Pang (1991) look specifically at the automobile and electronics sectors, two of the most important recipients of FDI. In the former, they find that foreign firms have "transferred technology and skills, and promoted backward linkages and the development of local supporting industries. Domestic value added in the industry has risen over recent years".[64] In the latter, "the influx of new foreign investments...has benefited the country in terms of industrial growth and deepening, including diversification, integration and technological upgrading of the local industry".[65]

Although from 1988 onwards the fastest export growth came in medium-technology products such as computer components, automobile components and electrical goods, and although this category accounted for one third of all exports in 1994, for most of these products Thailand was merely an assembly base. In Thailand, high-technology production is not associated with high value-added. Rather, the high-technology character of Thai exports is a reflection of high-technology imported inputs. As a result, the electronic industry is not yet a valuable earner of foreign exchange, nor a vehicle for industrial upgrading. Assembly activities may be seen as a stepping stone toward developing more advanced capabilities, but this has been a slow process given the lack of a sufficient human capital base.

Problems of upgrading in medium-technology sectors include the slow development of most capital goods industries, such as iron and steel, non-electrical machinery, metal products and transport equipment, as well as a heavy reliance on imports of both capital and intermediate goods, etc.[66] As Thailand's comparative advantage in labour-intensive productions declines, the need to shift to production involving more skills and more capital becomes pressing.

Conclusion

The evidence presented here suggests that foreign firms have played an important role in the structural transformation of the Thai economy and, consequently, in its exports. Through FDI, the Thai economy has been transformed far more rapidly than could have been achieved through internal resources alone. Furthermore, through this investment MNEs have transferred technology to their affiliates in Thailand. Such transfers have sometimes been disappointing, but nevertheless it is commonly agreed that they have arisen in sectors dominated by foreign firms. The question is whether Thailand could have been made more of the investment which it did receive.

To some extent, the failure to upgrade and the growing threat that factories would shift to China or Vietnam as wages in Thailand became uncompetitive were part of the structural problems faced by the Thai economy which ultimately made the high growth rates of the recent past unsustainable. In retrospect, the problems are easy to identify — inadequate human capital, infrastructure bottlenecks, overly-protected industries, too great an emphasis on export promotion — and, in fairness, the Government had taken steps to alleviate many of these problems even before the crisis erupted.

To expand the skill level of the population, the Government increased the number of years of compulsory education, encouraged private schools, provided scholarships for foreign study, etc. To relieve the pressures on infrastructure in the Bangkok area and to reduce the regional disparities in income levels, the BOI promoted a greater decentralisation of investment projects away from the Bangkok Metropolitan Area. Tariff levels were also coming down in protected industries before the crisis, such as in the automobile sector, and remaining local content requirements were being phased out as part of the TRIMs agreement. These latter policies were given a strong vote of confidence when three major US investors decided to establish a regional hub in Thailand for the export of cars and parts.

Nevertheless, in spite of these measures, the Thai policy towards inward investment — although relatively open by developing country standards — could still be characterised until recently as an appendage of more general import substitution and export promotion policies. Firms wishing to export most of their output faced few restrictions. They could locate anywhere, hold all of the shares in the affiliate, as well as the land on which the factory was built, etc. They also received tax holidays and, more importantly, exemptions on duties for imported inputs. In contrast, firms wishing to sell mostly in the local market were either prohibited or restricted in a number of ways depending on the sector.[67] They often had to settle for minority ownership and could only lease land for a fixed period (unless they received BOI promotion and the conditions attached). In some cases, they had to receive an authorisation through a lengthy and not always transparent process.

Unlike the policy initiatives in other areas, this dualistic policy towards foreign investors was changing only slowly before the crisis. There have been proposals to amend the Alien Business Law in the past, but it is only now that such an amendment is expected to pass through Parliament.[68] The reforms proposed as a result of the crisis represent a significant step towards a more open and unified approach to FDI policy. Nevertheless, the fact that reforms have been enacted during an economic crisis and that some, such as in banking or the majority foreign ownership of joint ventures, appear to be temporary might suggest to potential investors that they are not based on a fundamental reappraisal of development strategies and hence will not survive the return of economic growth.

The on-going financial crisis in Thailand and the structural problems which it has brought to light present an opportune moment to reassess whether existing policies towards FDI in Thailand, as part of more general growth strategies, have best served the interests of economic development. Export promotion policies based on foreign investment had proved highly successful at generating massive exports in sectors in which Thai firms had no experience. But at the same time, the years before the crisis were characterised by growing concerns over shortages of skilled labour and rising wages not matched by productivity. As a result, Thai low-technology exports were declining in the face of stiff competition from China, Bangladesh and Vietnam, and this shortfall was not being offset by sustained growth in medium- to high-technology exports.

Experience in both OECD and non-OECD countries suggests that too great an emphasis on export promotion does not always yield the expected benefits. Not only has the resulting export growth often proved unsustainable, but such exports are also often highly dependent on imported components because of the need for high quality inputs in order to compete effectively in export markets. This dependency reduces both the potential benefit to the balance of payments and the responsiveness of the economy to exchange rate changes. In addition, because highly export-oriented firms are less likely to source locally, such investment limits potential technology transfers between foreign affiliates and local suppliers.

In contrast, local market oriented firms are more likely to source locally and hence to transfer technology in many cases. Furthermore, because they often offer goods and services of higher quality and lower prices, they make it easier for Thai firms which make use of these goods and services to compete in world markets, thus assisting in the development of indigenous exporting capabilities. Recent reforms in FDI policies in Thailand have reduced this strong bias in favour of export-oriented investment projects and could open the way for more FDI by firms wishing to supply the Thai market. If these reforms prove to be durable, the Thai economy may be poised in the medium term for a period of more sustainable growth, with local firms contributing more to export growth.

NOTES

1. IMF 1996, p.29.

2. The appropriateness of expressing trends in dollars or baht depends on what is being stressed. If the interest is in the capital inflows represented by FDI, then figures in dollars are more appropriate. If the interest is in how much actual investment in the Thai economy is represented by foreigners, then baht data are more relevant.

3. Since 1992, three Thai governments have pledged to revise the Alien Business Law, but in each case, the Parliament was dissolved before legislation could be approved. ("Thailand quietly eases rules governing foreign ownership", *Financial Times*, 23 June 1998.

4. BOI data on FDI projects approvals point to the same direction. The maximum volume of FDI projects was reached in 1990 even if the maximum number of projects was registered in 1988.

5. This decline is apparently also due to the change in reporting as a result of companies' extensive shift to the Bangkok International Banking Facilities (BIBF) in lieu of foreign equity or investment loans.

6. The appropriateness of expressing trends in dollars or baht depends on what is being stressed. If the interest is in the capital inflows represented by FDI, then figures in dollars are more appropriate. If the interest is in how much actual investment in the Thai economy is represented by foreigners, then baht data are more relevant.

7. The BOI data do not cover all sectors and relates primarily to greenfield investments or their subsequent expansion.

8. The Bangkok Post, January 14, 1998.

9. "Honda to take 97 per cent of Thai unit", *Financial Times* 17 March 1998.

10. The BIBF is an offshore centre supposed to allow Thailand to compete with Singapore. Through this facility, banks may mobilise funds offshore and on-lend to

Thai residents (out-in transactions) or non-residents (out-out transactions). In the first two years of operation of this facility most transactions were out-in transactions and not out-out transactions.

11. The prevalence of joint ventures is partly the result of policy restrictions imposed by the Thai authorities, but it also thought to reflect the response of Japanese investors to anti-Japanese protests in the early 1970s (Phongpaichit and Baker 1995).

12. EIU, 1997.

13. Big Thai conglomerates which had emerged in the 1940s, expanded in the 1960s and consolidated in the 1980s. They were initially bank-based, locally-rooted, founded on commerce but then expanded into industry.

14. "CP Group unit eyes motocycle disposal", *Financial Times* 23 March 1998.

15. There have been more than 25 changes of government, coups or attempted coups since 1972.

16. Poapongsakorn and Fuller (1996).

17. The offical commitment to export-led growth emerged in the early 1970s, with the Third National Economic and Social Development Plan (1972-77) and the 1972 revision of the Investment Promotion Act, yet the trade regime remained essentially unchanged until the late 1970s.

18. Vichyanond (1995).

19. The overall terms of trade index declined from 100 in 1970 to 56 in 1982.

20. The public savings ratio dropped from 4.3 per cent in 1970-79 to 3.2 in 1980-86.

21. Jisutchon et al. 1993.

22. ADB 1998, p. 208.

23. The World Bank has questioned whether the complexity of the incentive system in Thailand has not discouraged some potential investors.

24. EIU 1997.

25. Phongpaichit & Baker (1995), p. 128.

26. WTO members complained in a recent Trade Policy Review of Thailand that the ABL was a serious constraint to services trade and investment.

27. "Thailand quietly eases rules governing foreign ownership", *Financial Times*, 23 June 1998.

28. National Executive Council Decree No. 281.

29. Letter of Intent by the Thai Government to the IMF, 25 August 1998.

30. Poapongsakorn and Fuller (1996).

31. US Treasury (1994), p. 481.

32. In earlier legislation as a result of the crisis, foreigners could have a majority interest only for five years, after which they would have to sell their stakes outright.

33. EIU(1998), p. 36.

34. "Citibank halts Thai bank buy", *Financial Times* 11 February 1998

35. "StanChart to lift Thai bank stake", *Financial Times* 29 April 1999.

36. "Thailand succumbs to overseas brokers", Financial Times 12 May 1998.

37. Ibid.

38. "Hurry up and wait", *Far Eastern Economic Review* 14 May 1998

39. "Thais asked to dig deep to save oil group from the clutches of foreigners", *Financial Times*, 12 June 1998.

40. Manimai (1996), p. 88.

41. "Path cleared for Thai privatisation programme", *Financial Times*, 11 March 1999.

42. Lim and Pang (1990), p. 120.

43. The recent crisis may attract renewed FDI in consumer electronics industry as the result of the widening production cost differential due to the sharp depreciation of the baht.

44. The rationale for such a policy is that the tax structure favours the majority of the industry because there are more local assemblers than manufacturers.

45. "Bumper to bumper", *The Economist*, 17 August 1996.

46. Tariffs were reduced from 300 per cent to 100 per cent for those engines over 2300 cc and from 180 per cent to 60 per cent for those with no more than 2300 cc. CKD car tariffs were reduced from 112 to 20 per cent.

47. From 60 per cent to 42 per cent for small engines and from 100 per cent to 68.5 per cent for engines over 2400 cc.

48. The BBC began in 1988 and allows automotive parts produced within the ASEAN region to be imported free of some duties.

49. Automobile sales rose by 23 per cent in 1987, 46 per cent in 1988, 22 per cent in 1989 and 38 per cent in 1990.

50. Most of the 225 medium and large companies in the original equipment market are either joint ventures depending on foreign technology or foreign subsidiaries (Poapongsakorn and Fuller 1998, p. 52).

51. Import tariffs on the majority of auto parts are around 60 per cent.

52. Poapongsakorn and Fuller (1998), p. 52.

53. TDRI (1998)

54. OECD (1993).

55. The balance in terms of capital inflows and repatriations could not be calculated owing to the difficulties in separating portfolio from direct investment income in the balance of payments data.

56. Pongpisanupichit et al. 1989, quoted in Jansen 1995.

57. BIS (1998)

58. TDRI (1994)

59. See TDRI (1994) for a survey.

60. TDRI (1994).

61. Suda (1997), p. 4.

62. Lim and Pang (1991), p. 48.

63. Poapongsakorn and Fuller 1998, p. 57.

64. Lim and Pang (1991), p. 159.

65.   Ibid p. 122.

66.   UNCTAD 1996, pp. 120-23.

67.   Although a firm could technically invest without BOI promotion and hence be free to sell where it chose, in practice, certain incentives such as tariff exemptions or land ownership were critical for these firms (FIAS 1995, p. 18).

68.   Since 1992, three Thai governments have pledged to revise the Alien Business Law, but in each case, the Parliament was dissolved before legislation could be approved. ("Thailand quietly eases rules governing foreign ownership", *Financial Times*, 23 June 1998.

REFERENCES

Board of Investment (BOI), *An Investor's Guide - Thailand's Regional Areas*, July 1996.

Board of Investment (BOI), *A Guide to the Board of Investment*, Office of the Board of Investment, Office of the Prime Minister, Royal Thai Government, August 1997.

Chung-Hua Institution for Economic Research, *Taiwan's Small- and Medium-Sized Firms' Direct Investment in Southeast Asia*, October 1995.

Dobson, Wendy and Pierre Jacquet, *Financial Services Liberalization in the WTO*, Institute for International Economics, Washington, D.C., 1998.

Economist Intelligence Unit (EIU), Country Report of Thailand, 1998.

Froot; Kenneth, "Japanese Foreign Direct Investment", NBER working paper, n°3737, June 1991.

Fujita, Kuniko and Richard Child Hill, "Auto Industrialization in Southeast Asia: National Strategies and Local Development", *ASEAN Economic Bulletin*, vol. 13, n°3, March 1997.

Harrold, Peter, Malathi Jayawickrama and Deepak Bhattasali, "Practical lessons for Africa from East Asia in Industrial and Trade Policies", World Bank Discussion Papers, n°310, 1996.

International Monetary Fund (IMF), *Thailand: The Road to Sustained Growth*, Washington, December 1996.

Jansen, Karel, "The Macroeconomic Effects of Direct Foreign Investment: The Case of Thailand", *World Development*, vol. 23, n°2, pp. 193-210, 1995.

Lian Choon Beng, Daniel, "Gradual Financial Reform in Action", *ASEAN Economic Bulletin*, vol. 10, n°3, March 1994.

Lim, Linda and Pang Eng Fong, *Foreign Direct Investment and Industrialisation in Malaysia, Singapore, Taiwan and Thailand*, OECD Development Centre, 1991.

MacIntyre, Andrew J., "Indonesia, Thailand and the Northeast Asian Connection", in Higgott, Richard, et al., *Pacific Economic Relations in the 1990s - Cooperation or Conflict?*, Lynne Rienner Publishers, Boulder, Colorado, 1993.

Manimai Vudthitornetiraks, "The Privatisation Experience in Thailand", in *Privatisation in Asia, Europe and Latin America*, OECD, Paris, 1996.

OECD, *Privatisation in Asia, Europe and Latin America*, Paris, 1996.

OECD, *Foreign Direct Investment - OECD Countries and Dynamic Asian and Latin American Economies*, Paris, 1993.

Phongpaichit, Pasuk and Chris Baker, *Thailand - Economy and Politics*, Oxford University Press, Oxford, 1997.

Poapongsakorn, Nipon, "Industrial Location Policy in Thailand - Industrial Decentralisation or Industrial Sprawl?", in Masuyama, Seiichi, Donna Vandenbrink and Chia Siow Yue (eds.), *Industrial Policies in East Asia*, ISEAS and NRI, Singapore 1997.

Poapongsakorn, Nipon and Belinda Fuller, "The role of foreign direct investment and production networks in the development of the Thai auto and electronics industries", in Institute of Developing Economies and JETRO (eds.), *Can Asia Recover its Vitality: Globalisation and the Roles of Japanese and US Corporations*, Tokyo 1998.

Pongpisanupichit, J. et al., "Direct foreign investment and capital flows", Background Paper no. 6, TDRI Year End Conference, Bangkok, TDRI, 1989.

Siamwalla, Ammar, "Can a Developing Democracy Manage its Macroeconomy ? The Case of Thailand", mimeo, J. Douglas Gibson Lecture delivered at School of Policy Studies, Queen's University, Kingston, Ontario, Canada, October 15, 1997.

Somchai Jisutchon and Chalngphob Sussangkarn, "Thailand", in Taylor, Lance (ed.), *The Rocky Road to Reform - Adjustment, Income Distribution and Growth in the Developing World*, MIT Press, Cambridge, 1993.

Suda Sirikulvadhana, "Promotion of Technology Flow in Thailand", paper presented at a Seminar on National Policies and Technological Capability Building in Developing Countries, 17-19 November 1997, New Delhi, India.

Thailand Development Research Institute (1998), "Forecast of the twenty most important Thai exported items in the world market". Paper prepared for the Department of Business Economics, Thai Ministry of Commerce.

United States Department of the Treasury, *National Treatment Study*, Washington, 1994.

Vichyanond, Pakorn, "Financial Sector Development in Thailand", in Zahid, Shahid (ed.), *Financial Sector Development in Asia*, ADB, Manila, 1995.

World Bank (1993), *East Asian Miracle*, Oxford University Press.

OECD PUBLICATIONS, 2, rue André-Pascal, 75775 PARIS CEDEX 16
PRINTED IN FRANCE
(14 1999 06 1 P) ISBN 92-64-17082-0 – No. 50727 1999